ABOUT OMEGA

Omega was founded in 1977 at a time when holistic health, psychological inquiry, world music and art, meditation, and new forms of spiritual practice were just budding in American culture. Omega was then just a small band of seekers searching for new answers to perennial questions about human health and happiness. The mission was as simple as it was large: to look everywhere for the most effective strategies and inspiring traditions that might help people bring more meaning and vitality into their lives.

Since then, Omega has become the nation's largest holistic learning center. Every year more than 25,000 people attend workshops, retreats, and conferences in health, psychology, the arts, and spirituality on its eighty-acre campus in the countryside of Rhinebeck, New York, and at other sites around the country. While Omega has grown in size, its mission remains the same. Omega is not aligned with any particular healing method or spiritual tradition. Its programs feature all of the world's wisdom traditions and are committed to offering people an opportunity to explore their own path to better health, personal growth, and inner peace.

The name Omega was inspired by the writings of Teilhard de Chardin, a twentieth-century mystic and philosopher who used the word to describe the point within each one of us where our inner spiritual nature meets our outer worldly nature. Teilhard believed that the synthesis of these two domains presented the greatest challenge—and the greatest hope—for human evolution. Of his belief in the balance between world and spirit, Teilhard wrote, "I am going to broadcast the seed and let the wind carry it where it will."

Omega has taken on the task of helping spread that seed so that a better world for all of us can continue to take root and grow.

An Omega Institute Mind, Body, Spirit Book

Vitality and Wellness

❖

Stephan Rechtschaffen, M.D.

and

Marc Cohen, M.A.

A DELL TRADE PAPERBACK

A DELL TRADE PAPERBACK

Published by
Dell Publishing
a division of
Random House, Inc.
1540 Broadway
New York, New York 10036

Written by: Caren Goldman
Series consulting editor: Robert Welsch
Series editor: Kathleen Jayes
Series manager: James Kullander
Literary Representative: Ling Lucas, Nine Muses and Apollo Inc.

Library of Congress Cataloging in Publication Data
Rechtschaffen, Stephan.
    Vitality and wellness / by Stephan Rechtschaffen and Marc Cohen.
        p.   cm.—(The Omega Institute mind, body, spirit series)
    Includes bibliographical references and index.
    ISBN 0-440-50868-1
    1. Health.   2. Vitality.   3. Physical fitness.   I. Cohen, Marc, M.A.
II. Title.   III. Series.
RA776.R346   1999
613.7—dc21   99-28317
                    CIP

Printed in the United States of America
Published simultaneously in Canada
September 1999

10 9 8 7 6 5 4 3 2 1

RRD

BOOK DESIGN BY JENNIFER ANN DADDIO

Permissions

Omega Institute sends out heartfelt
thanks and appreciation
to staff members and teachers
for their support and contribution
in the preparation and publishing
of this book.

Contents

Introduction

By Stephan Rechtschaffen, M.D.

Wellness. When we commit ourselves to attaining and keeping it, we come alive to all the pleasures the world has to offer. This book, which is rooted in a week-long exploration of the word *wellness* that I teach at the Omega Institute for Holistic Studies in Rhinebeck, New York, is about how each of us can raise our health up in a way that both celebrates it and enlivens us.

When I cofounded Omega in 1977, I envisioned it to be a nurturing, safe center where people from all walks of life could go to develop skills in many areas to help them become better equipped to take responsibility for their daily lives. Today we offer over three hundred courses in the form of workshops, professional trainings, conferences, and retreats that cover five major areas of learning—Self, Others, Expressions, World, and Spirit. Included is my core workshop, called "The Omega Wellness Program."

"One of my primary goals as a doctor is to help you discover how good and empowering it can be to go by yourself into positive health," I tell students at the start of each new session.

"What does that mean?" someone always asks.

For starters I explain that it means our health is *not* static, but ever changing. Therefore *we* and only *we* are responsible for whether or not our health moves in the

> You already have the precious mixture that will make you well. Use it.
>
> —RUMI

direction of wellness or disease. The longer we put off doing for ourselves what we either hope or expect others will do for us, the greater the risk that our body's natural ability to seek balance and wellness will falter.

Not too long ago a sign that read CHOOSE YOUR RUT CAREFULLY, YOU'LL BE IN IT FOR THE NEXT TEN MINUTES appeared on one of the roads near Omega during spring mud season. It reminded me how easily many of us fall into habitual ruts that affect our health. When such a rut appears in the guise of stress or mild depression, we may unconsciously adapt to it and accept that it's part of the terrain. And what happens when we fall into a habitual rut such as smoking or eating high-fat foods that can lead to serious illness? If, in the past, we've tried but failed to break out of such a rut, we may despair that we're destined to travel through life that way. At Omega, however, we believe otherwise. We believe that for each of us there is a way out. We also know how difficult it can be to put your desire to get back on a safer, smoother road into action. We hope this book will help pave the way by providing you with the guidance, tools, and resources that can empower you to choose healthful habits and avoid habitual ruts.

Annually over twenty thousand people come to Omega to attend hands-on programs and workshops to help them to remake their lives, reestablish a sense of balance between their inner and outer worlds, discover their creative potential, and increase their confidence in their own responsibility for their health. By the time they leave Omega, most of the participants in the Wellness Program have the knowledge they need to develop a health-conscious lifestyle and a sustainable health plan that includes:

+ eating wholesome foods and taking appropriate supplements
+ regular exercise

- stress-reduction techniques that include meditation and relaxed breathing

- adopting a slower, steadier rhythm using an innovative technique called "time-shifting"

- play and laughter

- taking retreats and vacations that nourish the body and soul

Throughout this book we will show you that wherever you are, whatever you are doing, you, too, are in exactly the right place to begin taking steps that will support and maximize your health awareness and innate capacity to feel well and whole. And while it often seems the effort to do that requires lots of hard work, occasionally a simple moment of clarity, an "aha," is all that's needed.

I remember such a life-changing "aha" well. I was looking out the window of my office one morning. I saw a man leading a meditation retreat in Omega's lush vegetable and flower garden. Of course, he was no ordinary man. He was Thich Nhat Hanh, a Vietnamese Buddhist monk who was nominated for the Nobel Prize by the Reverend Dr. Martin Luther King. He immediately drew my attention and I found myself staring at Thich Nhat Hanh as he walked. The way this gentle human being moved made it seem that with every step he was kissing the earth. He was totally immersed in the act of walking, nothing else—not even the hundred people following him in a walking meditation. Transfixed, I watched him savor every moment. I became acutely aware that his body was at one with each movement. Suddenly, I understood what it meant to be present—to be fully aware of each moment of one's life.

Later, as I was walking to dinner, I realized that my mind was going in a million different directions as my body charged toward the dining hall. Phone calls, appointments, to-do lists, and business discussed earlier that day yanked me from the present to the past and into the future. I felt anxious, unfocused.

At that moment I understood that instead of being aware of the present moment, I was oblivious to it. Unlike Thich Nhat Hanh, I was unconscious of the way I was walking, my breath, and what it felt like to be alive, here, now. So I stopped walking and made a conscious decision to drop the thoughts that were driving my head one place and my body another. I allowed myself to concentrate on my breath. As I did, I began to notice a peacefulness coming over me. My sense of time expanded. I felt at one with the moment and the positive nature of my life. Although I had walked over the spot on which I was standing so many times before, I knew that this time I was in a new place—a state called grace.

People feel drawn to the Wellness Program largely because they desire to be more in the flow of the present moment. Often the catalyst comes in the form of wake-up calls such as burnout, heart palpitations, panic attacks, or just plain exhaustion. Taught from the time they were little to view their bodies mechanically, many students admit to taking better care of their cars than of themselves. Some even add that they'd like to be able to deal with their bodies the same way: Drop them off for routine maintenance in the morning. Send the brain to work at the office. Have the mechanics do their thing. And, finally, pick up a tuned-up body on the way back home.

Sadly, their attitude reflects the prevailing state of our health-care system. Like society-at-large, it is not one that encourages us to learn preventive self-health skills. Indeed, at times it seems that our health-care institutions actually thwart our efforts to assume responsibility for doing that. From an early age we're taught our health comes from the outside, not the inside. It is just another purchasable product—something you get from an employer, if you're lucky, or buy off the shelf at a premium price. What we need to hear and understand more often is that the best health maintenance organization (HMO) around is not the one listed on your insurance card but *you*. Good health doesn't come from the outside. It comes from within and when it does, there are no deductibles. Everything is included.

A former patient of mine helped me to understand how automatically we look outside ourselves for good health. She made the appointment to see me because she was one of those people who "just wasn't feeling well." As I was gathering information, she started crying and told me that her husband had died, prematurely, of a heart attack. "You know," she said, "he was perfectly healthy until one day when he went out to shovel snow and just dropped over dead on the driveway."

The way in which this distressed patient told me that story, it sounded like her husband's sudden death was the snow shovel's fault. As far as she was concerned, he'd still have been healthy and alive twenty years from now if only he had used a better one. But the fact was his lifestyle, which included a high-fat diet and no exercise, indicated he was at risk for heart failure years before his fatal heart attack.

It's not surprising that my patient blamed both the paramedics for not responding fast enough to the 911 call and her husband's physician for not detecting the problem. It's typical of the passive attitude many people have toward their health. They expect others to take responsibility for it. It's as though diabetes, cancer, heart disease, fall out of the sky and hit them on the head. "Oh, God, why me?" they exclaim. They don't want to admit that whatever hit them might be the result of the lifestyle they've lived for the last ten years, not the last ten minutes.

Unfortunately, in the past, conventional Western health-care wisdom perpetuated that passive attitude by teaching us that health is characterized by the absence of disease. That, in turn, led us to believe that we shouldn't see our doctors until we are very ill. This approach makes sickness a black-and-white issue. You are either sick or you're not. "Don't worry," you're told when you have vague complaints and just don't "feel well." "There's probably nothing wrong. Take two aspirin, Excedrin, or Advil, and call in the morning if your symptoms get worse." In other words, call back only if things get bad enough to be differentiated, categorized, and named. Yet how many times have you hesitated to call your doctor because you feared "wasting" his or her time or dreaded hearing that your problem might be "all in your head"? How many times have you left a doctor's office feeling either frustrated because there was no diagnosis or greatly relieved because he or she attached a medical name to your symptoms?

Taking responsibility for your health is a call to be proactive and practical about learning how to live more healthfully. Tragically, many people with chronic and life-threatening diseases have taken this to mean that they are responsible for their poor health. They think they are the ones who caused their cancer or M.S. and now they are being punished. It's a popular and erroneous concept put forth by supposed experts who write books filled with lists of diseases and the problems in our lives that they believe cause them. Thus it's not unusual for people who are ill to blame themselves and believe that they caused their disease.

When we use the term *taking responsibility for one's health*, Marc Cohen and I mean something quite different. We believe we all must place the proper emphasis on prevention, knowing that there are many factors beyond our control which can affect the outcome. One of my patients, an octogenarian named Tony, is a good example. The first time he showed up in my office, Tony told me to punch him in the stomach because he wanted to prove how well he was. Of course I didn't punch him, but my examination, which included taking a thorough medical history plus listening to stories about Tony's life and family, proved he was right. He was in excellent health. In fact, he had the body of someone twenty years younger and his mind was as sharp as that of many people half his chronological age. The only reason he had come for a checkup was to check in and find out if he needed to do anything else to ensure he would have lifelong health.

Tony was a rare bird. As a wellness doctor, I see very few people who come to me because they are well and want to stay that way. Most patients show up at my office because wellness is a state to which they want to return.

Another factor that contributes to the way in which we view health in our society is the word *normal.* When I went to medical school, a "normal" cholesterol level was considered to be 200 plus your age. That wasn't "normal." It was *average.* Obviously, there's confusion about what these two words mean. In our culture *normal* is average. We perpetuate a myth that a level of health shared by large numbers of the population is somehow normal. But the fact is that it is *abnormal.*

For example, while I was in medical school I reviewed a barium enema report of a patient in his late fifties who had diverticulosis. This is a disease that causes little balloonlike pouches to form on the side of the colon. Without proper treatment sufferers run the risk of developing diverticulitis, an inflammation of the colon. It can also be a precursor of colon cancer. As I studied his case history, a radiologist remarked that it was normal for men of his age to have this. He was wrong. Biologically, if something is normal it occurs or functions in a natural way and lacks observable abnormalities or deficiencies. This man's colon didn't fit that definition. His condition wasn't *normal*; it was *common.* In other places in the world this man's condition would never be considered normal. In parts of Africa, for example, scientific studies conducted more than three decades ago show that people belonging to certain tribes never get diverticulosis or colon cancer. The reason, concluded Dr. Denis Burkitt, the famed researcher, is that high-fiber foods are the mainstay of the tribespeople's diets. Every day they eat enough of them to do an extraordinary job of cleaning out the colon, which helps it to function normally. Their average stool weighs 1.5 pounds. Our average stool weighs .5 pounds. For many of us just the idea of eating enough fiber to help prevent colon diseases in the way the Africans studied avoid them would be challenging. Not because high-fiber foods fail to be tasteful and appealing, but because it would require many of us to shift our view of what kind of diet is both healthy and normal.

The last reason why many of us have been tentative about taking more responsibility for our self–health care is the belief still held by many in the medical community that it is unnatural to endorse natural healing. Only recently did the prestigious *Journal of the American Medical Association (JAMA)* come out with an editorial urging physicians to "become more knowledgeable about alternative medicine and increase their understanding of the possible benefits and limitations." Until then conventional medical wisdom taught that it wasn't kosher to mix the words *alternative, complementary, nontraditional, nonconventional,* and/or *integrated* with the words *Western medicine.*

Not surprisingly, the editorial, which began:

> *There is no alternative medicine. There is only scientifically proven evidence-based medicine supported by solid data or unproven medicine, for which scientific evidence is lacking. Whether a therapeutic practice is "Eastern" or "Western," is unconventional or mainstream, or involves mind-body techniques or molecular genetics, is largely irrelevant except for historical purposes and cultural interest,*

raised the ire of many within the medical community. Why? Because even at a time when hundreds of scientific studies appearing in medical journals conclude that many nontraditional and noninvasive therapies such as meditation, guided imagery, yoga, certain supplements, and even prayer are safe and effective, many American doctors stubbornly disagree. One oft-cited reason is that their medical-school training to practice allopathic medicine did not prepare them (as it didn't prepare me) to integrate and/or recommend such treatments. Another is that many doctors believe, falsely and perhaps fearfully, that their patients will blindly substitute these techniques for conventional medicine or that they'll fall for the slick pitch of every snake-oil salesman who comes along. Yet from my years of experience as a physician who studied and then recommended many of these noninvasive therapies, I know that most of those fears are unfounded. Alternative medicine can serve our patients well—not as a substitute for treatments only conventional medicine can provide, but in partnership with it.

For example, if a person is having a heart attack or is bleeding to death from the impact of a car accident, it is not the time for him or her to consider taking vitamins and supplements, but to call 911. To its credit Western emergency medicine is extremely adept at treating those crises. However, once the patient begins rehabilitation, scientific studies tell us that it makes good sense to make him aware of complementary therapies. As you'll discover throughout this book, double-blind, controlled studies prove that yoga, biofeedback, guided imagery, group support, meditation, and supplementation can reduce hospital stays, pain, blood pressure, depression, and an ever-growing, lengthy list of other problems.

Ultimately, what I see is that although the winds of change are blowing in our health-care system, they are tempered by the message that the only time to be proactive is when we *know* we are ill. Just as everyone in a room knows that the dog hiding behind the curtain with his tail hanging out is really there, I know as a holistic physician and past board member of the American Holistic Medical Association that hiding from our responsibility for our health exposes our immune systems, psyche, emotions, spirits, and our society to all kinds of assaults that can potentially weaken and harm them.

What does it mean to be a holistic physician? We believe that our bodies, minds, emotions, and spirits function as an interdependent system in which the health of one part can affect the well-being and vitality of every other part. Rather than basing our health-care decisions about the health/disease status of an individual upon an isolated part of his or her body that might be ailing, we are committed to working with the whole person. In Chapter 1 you will learn more about why we, at Omega, believe that it's only when we take a holistic approach to self–health care that we can optimize our well-being.

My years of learning about and practicing holistic medicine taught me that each of us has a remarkable capacity for self-healing. It's a potential that's just waiting to be tapped. However, we have to be the ones to tap it. No one can do it for us. All that the best program, book, teacher, or doctor can do is guide you to the road leading to wellness and encourage you to move forward. The rest is up to you. From that point on the only thing that can make a difference is your choice to take the first step.

If that seems daunting, be assured that even the smallest changes that you make to take more responsibility for your health can make noticeable and positive differences. And while we know that we can't guarantee you a specific degree of health and vitality if you follow the guidelines set forth in this book, we can promise you unconditional support for your choice to seek wellness, vitality, and longevity.

So now we invite you to begin discovering new ways to creatively and healthfully balance your wellness equation. We will not suggest anything radical or fanatical, because we don't believe in traveling such narrowly defined routes. The path we describe is a safe **middle way** that has been thoroughly tested at Omega.

We also won't be giving you a specific prescription for optimal wellness. You are the best judge of what you need. For example, there are dietary programs that work for some people but not for others. Therefore, in the chapter on nutrition, we don't specify one diet for everyone. Instead, we will give you useful information about wholesome foods, good nutrition, and supplementation to help you decide what is best for you.

Helping us along the way will be other experts in the field of holistic health whose respected ideas and proven programs are already positively affecting the health of thousands of their patients, students, and readers. Some of them currently teach at Omega; many others have taught here in the past. We trust their thoughts, ideas, information, and exercises, and hope you will find them insightful and reassuring guides.

We also encourage you to use this book in a way that best meets *your* needs. Begin by exploring it in order to get a glimpse of the doors to optimal health that our staff and other experts with skilled hands can open for you. Many people say that they were drawn to take the Omega Wellness Program because it seemed empowering. Others admit that they wound up taking it because the catalog description called out to them while they were searching for something else. Some say they came because of a strong interest in stress reduction or because they wanted to learn how to make more time for themselves. Yet others chose it because they wanted to learn about a variety of health-enhancing practices before settling on one. As you begin reading this book, why not take a few moments to ask yourself: What draws me to this book, here, now?

Finally, we know that not all the information you read will be relevant to where you are at this time and place in your life. Feel free to use what information you can and put the rest aside. Perhaps, at another time or in another place, you may find it calls to you. Albert Einstein once said, "Listen to what the experts say, but always rely on your own judgment." It is our hope that as you begin to explore the road to optimal health and well-being you will feel empowered to do just that.

I.

Beginning the Journey

Joseph Campbell, the late mythologist, often said that he believed that people are not searching for the meaning of life, but seeking the experience of being alive. The reason, he explained, was "so that our life experience on this purely physical plane will have resonances within our innermost being and reality, so that we actually feel the rapture of being alive."

What do you imagine it would be like if your experiences on the purely physical plane resonated with your innermost self? What might it be like if you truly felt the "rapture of being alive"—not just occasionally, but throughout your life—every day, every year?

For most of us it would mean that we were living our lives in a way that allowed us to feel more passion, love, enthusiasm, and heart. We would be robust—full of vitality. We might even feel intoxicated—not from alcohol, drugs, sugar, and caffeine, but with the greatest natural excitement of all: life itself. It would also mean that we

Man is ultimately self-determining.

—VIKTOR E. FRANKL

wouldn't be living our lives passively. Instead, we would become advocates and champions of the most important cause of all—living our life to the fullest.

If you were to take Campbell's words seriously, how might you go about seeking the experience of "aliveness" that he refers to? What might prompt you to go on a hero or heroine's journey of self-discovery? How would you determine the cost and promise of staying versus the cost and promise of leaving a familiar and comfortable world to uncover another hidden below your surface life?

Try This

When you were a child, did your parents or teachers tell you that if you were going to make a change, it should be for "the better"? Of course, the thought of making a change for the worse sounds ridiculous. Yet we've all experienced a change planned for "the better" taking a turn for the worse. Sometimes, in order to make a change for "the better," we must first go "through the valley of darkness" or through a time that initially feels "worse" or "painful" before we get to the "better."

Throughout this book you will be invited to make all kinds of changes that can enhance your health and well-being. Here is a process for determining which of those invitations you might want to accept:

+ Name what you want to change. Is it a habit? A behavior? An attitude? An image of yourself? Then write it down.

+ Write down a statement that says why you want to make that change.

+ Write down all the obstacles that you believe you will face if you try to make that change.

+ Do a cost-and-promise analysis. Ask yourself:

—What is the cost of making this change?

—What is the promise of making this change?

—What is the cost of not making this change?

—What is the promise of not making this change?

- List all the costs and promises that you can.

- Now close your eyes and imagine your hands are the pans on either side of a scale. Fill one pan with the cost of making the change. Fill the other with the promise of making the change. Which hand feels heavier? Do the same with the cost and promise of not making the change.

- Ask yourself: What does "weighing" my options tell me about my readiness to make this particular change?

- If you're ready to move forward, write a commitment to yourself to do so.

- List your objectives and your goals.

- Consider the obstacles you are aware of and make a list of what you have to do to overcome them.

- Create a timetable or timeline that details where, when, and how you will take responsibility for staying on course and accomplishing your goal.

Should you decide to go on such a journey and cross the threshold separating the known part of your life from the unknown, what might you leave behind? What path would you follow? One that others have trod? Or would you blaze your own, as the knights of King Arthur's court did when they went in search of the Holy Grail? Would you prepare for this journey by first questioning yourself about your physical strengths and/or limitations to determine how your body would hold up? Or would you begin by mentally and mindfully "brainstorming" and considering how, when, where, why, what, and, especially, who this journey was about? Or might you start by sitting and listening, patiently, for your emotions to rise and your spirit to speak?

Whatever you pick as your starting point—your body, mind, emotions, or spirit—it's hard to imagine that you would take the first step of such an important journey without consulting all of the aspects of your "self" of which you are aware. You would want to gather all of the information you could about your needs, desires, limitations, yearnings, and strengths.

You might also want to know about some of the hardships you might endure.

The Call

David Spangler, an author and one of the cofounders of the renowned Findhorn Community in northern Scotland, teaches a workshop at Omega that's named after his book *The Call*. In both the book and workshop, Spangler explores the idea that each of us has "callings"—both great and small—throughout our lives. He believes that we are here because of a unique gift that only we can give to the world.

To help others discover their gifts and be responsive to their call, Spangler asks age-old questions: "Who am I?" "Why am I here?" "What is the meaning of my life?" Here he reflects on the first question:

> At any given time there are various ways you might answer this question: "I am a Democrat"; "I am a Republican"; "I am a man"; "I am _____" and you can fill in the blank with whatever you wish. Yet there is always, somewhere in the background, a lurking question that asks, "Yes, but . . . are you sure? Is this really the whole story of who you are? Do you really know who you are?" And this question is a quiet anxiety that can live within us and color our days.
>
> There are a couple of ways to respond to this inner question. One way is to deny that it is there and to hold ever more tightly to the particular answer with which you have filled in the blank. This defensiveness, though, may only increase the anxiety. . . .
>
> The other option is to say "Well, for right now, provisionally, to the best of my knowledge, I am this. But I am open to further information. I am open to further discovery. I have set boundaries with my answer, but they are permeable. They can be expanded toward new possibilities." This response can decrease the anxiety, or at least channel it constructively, for now the question behind it is seen as an opportunity. . . . "Let me explore. Let me go boldly where no identity has gone before. What are the endless reaches of who I am and who I can become? Let me go and see."

That's because it would be naive to set out expecting the road ahead to be straight and your quest to be filled with only joyous and rewarding experiences. Stories of such travels—both ancient and modern—tell us otherwise. Indeed, whether real or imag-

> The real voyage of discovery rests not in seeking new landscapes,
> but in having new eyes.
>
> —MARCEL PROUST

ined, tales about those who set out in search of themselves remind us that a pilgrimage for the sake of self-discovery is about living questions, not having answers. It's about a process and not an outcome, a *journey* and not a destination.

An old Hasidic tale about Eisik of Cracow, a pious but very poor rabbi, goes like this:

> *On three consecutive nights Rabbi Eisik had the same dream. In it a commanding voice told him to leave Cracow, the capital of Poland, and go to Prague, which was far away. Once there, the voice said, Rabbi Eisik should look under the great bridge that led to the royal castle. There he would find a treasure.*
>
> *After struggling with whether to stay or go, Rabbi Eisik went on the long journey by foot. When he got to Prague, he found the bridge, but sentinels who guarded their posts day and night surrounded it. Fearful, he did not dig. Instead, he loitered day after day trying to figure out what to do. Finally, when one of the guards asked him if he kept returning because he had lost something, the rabbi told him his dream.*
>
> *"You poor man," the guard said, laughing. "You traveled all that way and wore out your shoes because of a dream. Why, I once had a foolish dream like that too. In it a voice commanded me to go to Cracow and search for the home of a Rabbi Eisik, son of Jekel, where I would find a great treasure buried in a dirty corner behind the stove. Can you imagine believing such a dream?"*
>
> *Bowing politely, Rabbi Eisik said good-bye to the guard, who was still laughing. Then he returned to Cracow as fast as he could. When he got home, he dug under the neglected corner behind his stove and found the treasure, which put an end to his poverty.*

Not surprisingly, in order to make a genuine commitment to quest for wholeness, one must weigh, carefully, the costs and promises. The road ahead may be challenging, unfamiliar, and, at times, scary. In her poem "The Journey," Pulitzer Prize–winning poet Mary Oliver describes how it feels to become aware that it's time to take the journey, make a commitment to it, and then have the tenacity needed to stay the course:

> *One day you finally knew*
> *what you had to do, and began,*
> *though the voices around you*
> *kept shouting*
> *their bad advice—*
> *though the whole house*
> *began to tremble*
> *and you felt the old tug*
> *at your ankles.*
> *"Mend my life!"*
> *each voice cried.*
> *But you didn't stop.*
> *You knew what you had to do,*
> *though the wind pried*
> *with its stiff fingers*
> *at the very foundations—*
> *though their melancholy*
> *was terrible.*
> *It was already late*
> *enough, and a wild night,*
> *and the road full of fallen*
> *branches and stones.*
> *But little by little,*

as you left their voices behind,
the stars began to burn
through the sheets of clouds,
and there was a new voice,
which you slowly
recognized as your own
that kept you company
as you strode deeper and deeper
into the world,
determined to do
the only thing you could do——
determined to save
the only life you could save.

If it feels risky and radical to try to live the question "Who am I?" you are not alone. For many of us, the changes in our lives and lifestyles that can empower us to be self-healers may, in fact, appear radical.

Hopefully, this book will help reassure you that although the changes you may make might appear extreme to others, you don't have to be radical while making them. You don't have to do everything at once to reap the benefits of journeying toward holistic health. Walking to the beat your particular drummer allows you to find a sense of balance and sustain it. The pilgrimage ahead is about being sensible, sane, and authentic, so that as you make a pilgrim's progress you can feel as rewarded by the journey as you are by the destination.

One way to quell any resistance you may harbor toward your journey is to recall significant changes that have already taken place in your life. Think back for a moment on the events, planned or unplanned, that have had an important impact on you. What invited, nudged, or coerced you to give up old ways of being in the world? Perhaps the catalyst was a major event like the birth of a new baby or the death of a loved one, the diagnosis of a life-threatening illness or a remarkable recovery, or the acceptance of a new job or the unexpected loss of a needed one. It may have even been something as minor as the passing remark of a stranger. Could it have been some "thing" that happened in such a subtle way that in another time or place you might never have noticed it? However, in this time and place it became something quite noticeable that made you stop, think, and say "aha."

Invariably, when the right conditions prevail, seeds of change germinate whether we expect or even want them to. Moreover, as these seeds take root and their shoots break new ground, they may cause our world to tremble. That doesn't mean it has to crumble. Change can be wonderful too. For example, walking up the aisle for a diploma or down the aisle for a lifelong union; seeing a loved one for the first time in years or falling in love at first sight.

When we make choices that move us in the direction of the gifts that optimal health, vitality, self-discovery, and inner healing bestow upon us, we put into action our desire to embrace change, to see beauty in our lives, and to be better stewards of ourselves and the world around us. Anne Frank wrote in the famous diary she kept during the years she and her family hid from the Nazis: "I don't think of all the misery, but of all the beauty that still remains." We can learn a lot from the simple words that twelve-year-old wrote just months before dying at the hands of her captors. In making a choice to see the positive side to our circumstances, we begin to:

- feel in, rather than out of, control
- see the events in our lives in lively colors instead of black and white
- take responsibility for our health and healing
- live in the moment instead of the past or future

No matter what part of your life may be the focus of your desire to change, it's important to think about your body, mind, spirit, and emotions **holistically.** Although we often talk about the parts of the body as separate, especially when illness strikes, they are interconnected. They comprise a dynamic system in which no one part, not even the smallest cell, functions in a vacuum. That means that even though every or-

---

At first sight it is odd that the laws governing life's responses at such different levels
as a cell, a whole person, or even a nation, should be so essentially similar.

—HANS SELYE

---

gan, nerve, muscle, bone, and cell has a specific task, it does its job only by functioning in relationship to other parts of the body. Additionally, the whole of a system cannot be understood by simply understanding the individual parts. No matter how scientific our understanding of the biology of the brain, heart, and the rest of our physiology may be, it still can't explain why something makes us cry. For this we need to examine our emotions too.

To get a better idea of how systems function, think about your car. Without the proper connections to the other parts an engine is just a piece of metal. It can't go anywhere or do anything. However, when connected to the body of the car, the drive train, and the fuel and exhaust systems, the car is able to get you from point A to point B smoothly without faltering or breaking down. In other words, it's a healthy system.

The natural world offers innumerable examples. For example, it is said that a butterfly flapping its wings in a South American rain forest sets off a chain reaction that affects the weather hundreds of miles north. Just looking at a beehive, a school of fish, or an anthill gives you a snapshot of the way a self-contained living system works. Each element does its part to try to ensure not only its own survival but that of the whole system. The sun, moon, stars, and planets that surround us are also a system, a solar system that's part of a galaxy that joins with all the other galaxies to form the universe.

Once we begin to think in terms of systems, it changes our perspective on our personal health and the well-being of the planet. We begin to see clearly why it's so important to strive for optimal health and, in turn, help to prevent the destruction of the ozone layer, the rain forests, and all endangered forms of life, including us. We realize that when we fail to preserve our inner and outer worlds, we fail to preserve that which gives us life. "People did not weave the great web of life, we are merely a strand in it," said Chief Seattle. "Whatever we do to the web we do to ourselves."

Thich Nhat Hanh, a revered Vietnamese Buddhist monk mentioned earlier, sums it up this way in his book *Touching Peace: Practicing the Art of Mindful Living:* "Your body belongs to your ancestors, your parents, and future generations, and it also belongs to society and all other living beings. All of them have come together to bring about the presence of this body. Keeping your body healthy is an expression of gratitude to the whole cosmos—the trees, the clouds, everything."

Reflection

The legendary dancer Martha Graham once wrote:

You will know the wonders of the human body because there is nothing more wonderful. The next time you look into the mirror, just look at the way the ears rest next to the head; look at the way the hairline grows; think of all the little bones in your wrist. It is a miracle.

Now ask yourself:

+ When was the last time I looked, mindfully, at the different parts of my body and considered each a miracle?

+ When was the last time that I stopped to think about the gift of life they give me with every breath, heartbeat, and bowel movement?

+ Have I ever thanked my heart for not attacking me—even when I don't exercise or watch my diet?

+ Have I ever thanked my back for carrying real and imagined burdens?

+ Have I ever thanked my lungs for knowing what to do day in and day out?

+ What about my uvula—that funny little pendulum at the back of my throat? Have I ever thanked it for being a traffic cop that's directed all the food I've ever eaten down the right lane?

What about all the parts of me, both seen and unseen? Have I thought about them and thanked them for dancing with each other all these years?

The natural healing force within each one of us is the greatest force in getting well.

—HIPPOCRATES

> Health is a consummation of a love affair of all the organs of the body.
> —PLATO

Today, the cutting-edge scientists and physicians who study and treat the human body from a systems perspective use the phrases *mind/body* or *body/mind* to describe the interactive relationship between the two. Either is a shortcut for saying that our mind, body, emotions, and, as many believe, the spirit mutually influence each other or that they have a "cocausal" relationship.

Conversation with Candace Pert, Ph.D., author of
MOLECULES OF EMOTION *and Omega teacher*

Q: Neuroscience is now one of the hottest fields in the academic world. You're a neuroscientist who spends most of her time searching for groundbreaking discoveries. Yet you also teach ordinary people about hard-to-grasp concepts such as psychoneuroimmunology, biomedicine, and molecular theory. Why?

A: Many of the people who come to my lectures feel deeply disappointed and disillusioned by the failure of science to cure major diseases. I believe I have a responsibility to help them understand a new biology in which information is the bridge between the mind and body. I've seen the most basic understanding of this empower people to see ways in which they can be more responsible for their health and feel more control in their lives.

Q: Back in the 1980s your laboratory experiments laid the foundation for the discovery of endorphins, the body's own pain suppressors and ecstasy inducers. What do you tell people today about the body/mind connection?

A: The most important thing is that there is a biochemical link between the mind and body that unites them inextricably. It's a new concept of the human organism as a communication network that redefines health and disease and the role emotions play in health and disease.

Q: You once said that as a culture, we are all in denial about the importance of psychosomatic causes of illness. Why did you say that and what is that denial all about?

A: The word *psychosomatic* has two parts: *psyche,* meaning mind or soul, and *soma,* meaning body. The fact that they form one word suggests a connection between them. However, in our culture we treat that connection like a curse. One reason is that it threatens the legitimacy of any particular illness by suggesting it may be imaginary, unreal, and unscientific. Another reason is that unless we, as scientists, can measure something, our peers won't concede it exists. That's why science typically refuses to deal with "nonthings" such as the mind, the soul, or our emotions.

Q: What do you believe about these "nonthings"?

A: Because I've watched and participated in the process of unraveling clues about the mind/body connection, I now believe that virtually all illness has a psychosomatic component. I now understand how the molecules of our emotions share intimate connections with and are inseparable from our physiology. To me that suggests our emotions are the links between our minds and bodies.

Q: What are the benefits of being able to consciously tap into this communications network?

A: I believe it can affect many of the problems that the mainstream medical model deals with ineffectively. For example, the problem of unhealed feelings, the accumulation of bruised and broken emotions that leads to a diagnosis of "depression." Modern medicine prescribes "talk and dose" therapy—lots of talking about problems and pills that alter our chemistry. But that doesn't heal us—they are merely Band-Aids. . . . What's not given much attention is what it means to be antidepressed—happy. I believe that happiness is what we feel when our biochemicals of emotion are open and flowing freely throughout the psychosomatic network and integrating and coordinating our systems, organs, and cells in a smooth, rhythmic movement. Physiology and emotions are inseparable. I believe that happiness is our natural state and that bliss is hardwired—a birthright. Only when our systems get blocked, shut down, and disarrayed do we begin to experience the mood disorders that add up to unhappiness in the extreme. By learning how to consciously tap into the body/mind and know ourselves better, we can begin a healing process unlike any other.

Although this way of looking at the causes of illness and stress may seem new to us, it's old news to other cultures. For example, among native peoples such as the Native Americans in our country or the aborigines in Australia, healers believe that illness doesn't occur in just the body or the mind. To them the root of illness is a spiritual problem. Therefore, indigenous healers don't just treat the ailing part of a patient's body but focus instead on the whole person and use a variety of modalities to treat what is both seen and unseen. Sometimes those treatments even include Western medicine.

Other medical systems, such as those used throughout Asia and India, also look at the body/mind relationship when treating illness. For centuries physicians practicing Chinese, Tibetan, and Ayurvedic medicine have recommended daily doses of stress-reducing practices such as yoga, tai chi, qigong, and meditation (see Chapters 3 and 7) to their patients. They consider them important ways to calm busy minds and help free up blocked *chi, ki,* or *prana,* which are names used to describe a vital life-force that travels along meridians that branch throughout the body.

Body/Mind Medicine

Every year, more and more doctors acknowledge the therapeutic value of body/mind medicine. Most of the complementary and alternative therapies listed below are now being studied in hospitals and laboratories worldwide. Physicians and other health-care professionals routinely offer many to patients who face surgery or must deal with chronic pain or rehabilitation from heart attacks, stroke, cancer, and other life-threatening conditions. This list is adapted from *The Complete Guide to Alternative and Conventional Treatments* by Time-Life Books and other sources. Many of these therapies will be discussed in more detail in Chapters 3 (meditation) or 7 (fitness). The study results come from professional journals and other reports.

+ **Biofeedback** uses computers and other instruments to measure and monitor bodily functions and states such as heart rate, brain activity, muscle tension, and skin temperature. Patients see or hear the changes and learn to control them.

—At the University of Pittsburgh Medical Center, children aged seven to seventeen who suffered from migraine headaches were taught one of two biofeedback techniques. Overall, 57 percent of the children using one form and 40 percent using the other reported at least a 50-percent improvement in the frequency and intensity of their migraines.

+ **Guided imagery** uses the power of the imagination to help heal the body. Patients usually listen to a prerecorded script that helps them imagine healing possibilities. Guided imagery is not limited to "seeing" a scene in the mind's eye. Patients may experience sights, sounds, tastes, and other sensations.

—Alice Domar, Ph.D., director of women's health at Boston's Deaconess Hospital, found that while 20 percent of the infertile women got pregnant with standard medical treatment, 57 percent did when their medical regimen included support groups, anger management skills, and guided imagery.

+ **Hypnotherapy** induces a relaxed, focused state of awareness that can help patients change their psychological and physiological reactions to illness, pain, anxiety, or habits. In clinical settings a professional always administers hypnotherapy. However, patients can learn self-hypnosis.

—At the School of Medicine at the University Hospital of South Manchester, England, 25 patients with irritable bowel syndrome who were treated with hypnotherapy had less severe abdominal pain, bloating, nausea, flatulence, urinary symptoms, lethargy, and backache than a control group that did not receive the treatment. Researchers concluded that the hypnotherapy also improved the patients' quality of life and reduced absenteeism from work.

+ **Meditation** is a practice that can help quiet the mind and calm the body. It can relieve stress and its symptoms. It requires the person to rest quietly and focus their attention on their breathing and/or a word or a phrase.

—A report of a three-month study of 111 hypertensive African-American men and women that appeared in the August 1996 journal *Hypertension* concluded that Transcendental Meditation lowered their blood pressure substantially.

+ **Spirituality** includes prayer and healing rituals.

—In 1983 one of the most definitive studies of prayer at a distance and healing was conducted. For ten months a group of people nationwide prayed for a group of cardiac care patients in San Francisco. They did not know the people for whom they were praying. A control group of patients were not prayed for. The patients who were prayed for experienced fewer medical complications and lower incidences of pneumonia. They also required fewer antibiotics and diuretics and less mechanical breathing assistance.

—In a 1994 study conducted at Kaplan Hospital in Israel, 53 postoperative hernia patients were randomly assigned to one of three groups. The first group received verbal suggestions that they would recover rapidly. Another served as a control group. The final group, another who were prayed for, recovered faster from hernia operations than those who did not receive prayers.

+ **Support groups** bring people together who suffer from the same illness or condition. In this setting they build a sense of community as they share their experiences and feelings.

—A study of the medical records of 292 women aged sixty-five and over who were hospitalized for heart failure showed that those who lacked emotional support had an eightfold risk of suffering additional cardiac complications in the year after being hospitalized.

+ **Yoga, tai chi, and qigong** are ancient Eastern practices that use body positions, slow movement, and breathing to calm and condition the mind, body, and spirit.

—One study of elderly patients who took up tai chi showed that they experienced the same drop in high blood pressure as a group doing vigorous aerobic exercise. Another showed increased stamina.

Why do we in the Western world divorce the mind from the body? Blame it on the Enlightenment and René Descartes, says Candace Pert, Ph.D., a leading neuroscientist whose pioneering research in the field of psychoneuroimmunology shows how emotions and health are linked at the molecular level. When you start talking about the mind and body and then bring in the spirit, you're going where scientists have been officially forbidden to tread ever since the seventeenth century, she explains. "It was then that Descartes, the philosopher and founding father of modern medicine, was forced to make a turf deal with the pope in order to get the human bodies he needed for dissection," she explains in her spirited way. Descartes's part of the bargain was to abandon the soul and have nothing to do with it as well as the mind or the emotions. Those were aspects of human experience under the exclusive jurisdiction of the church at the time, and all Descartes wanted was to claim the physical realm as his own. "Alas," Pert concludes, "this bargain set the tone and direction for Western science and separate spheres that could never overlap, creating the unbalanced situation that is mainstream science as we know it today."

Ironically, says William Collinge, M.P.H., Ph.D., author of *The American Holistic Health Association Complete Guide to Alternative Medicine*, the very scientific methods championed by mainstream medicine, especially in the area of testing drugs, offer the greatest scientific evidence for the existence and power of the body/mind connection. Collinge, who has conducted research in behavioral medicine for cancer, AIDS, and chronic fatigue syndrome, as well as a study on the effects of breath therapy on the immune system, explains that when drugs are tested "the mechanisms are so formidable that the standard research procedure requires separating out their effects from those of the drug. Hence, the power of the body/mind mechanisms has been examined and measured in virtually thousands of drug studies. It is in this sense that they have been verified and acknowledged by medical research to be a real and powerful phenomenon."

The interest in and power of this phenomenon called body/mind medicine is not to be underestimated. A 1993 study that was published in the prestigious *New England Journal of Medicine* announced that 34 percent of the health-care consumers were seeking medical treatments outside their regular doctors' offices. Today, it is estimated that over $14 billion is spent annually on treatments that allopathic (traditional) medicine calls "alternative," "complementary," or "integrated." As a result, mainstream doctors and researchers are now beginning to focus more of their attention and research dollars on the efficacy of guided imagery, hypnosis, mindfulness, meditation, massage, breathwork, biofeedback, and other adjunct treatments.

Herbert Benson, M.D., author of *The Relaxation Response* and president and founder

Today, stacks of scientific research and anecdotal evidence demonstrate the efficacy of body/mind practices and techniques. Although medical professionals give credence only to studies conducted according to the scientific method, anecdotal evidence is both interesting and convincing. The following story of what's called a spontaneous remission or remarkable recovery is a legendary example of the body/mind relationship. Bruno Klopfer, Ph.D., chronicled it in an article that appeared in a 1957 issue of the *Journal of Projective Techniques.*

According to Klopfer the man he dubbed "Mr. Wright" suffered from terminal lymphosarcoma. Quoting Mr. Wright's physician, Klopfer reported that the patient's cancer had spread throughout his body. His tumors were the size of oranges, he needed an oxygen mask to breathe, and his chest was filled with a "milky fluid."

Clearly, Mr. Wright had nothing going for him except tremendous hope that Krebiozen, a new drug that was being touted worldwide and tested at the clinic, would work for him. However, when he asked his doctor about getting the treatment, Wright learned that he didn't qualify. Tenaciously, he continued to press for this "golden opportunity." Finally his doctor agreed.

Much to everyone's surprise, within days of receiving his first shot Wright not only rallied, he got out of bed and walked around the ward. But what was even more amazing was that as Wright's tumors "melted like snowballs on a hot stove," the drug wasn't having any effect on other patients. Days later the tumors disappeared completely and Wright was sent home.

About two months later Wright heard a news report suggesting Krebiozen was ineffective. Almost immediately his tumors returned and he was back on his deathbed. Knowing how Wright had held out hope once before, his physician told Wright that a new, super-refined update of the drug would be there the next day. It was a lie, the physician admitted, because he wanted to see what would happen. The next day the doctor began giving Wright placebos, injections containing only water. Again, Wright improved, went home, and stayed healthy. However, seven months later, when the American Medical Association announced that Krebiozen was a worthless cancer treatment, Wright lost all hope. He died two days later.

of the Mind/Body Medical Institute at New England Deaconess Hospital, Boston, sees this as a very positive outcome of work on the body/mind paradigm that began in the early 1970s. Back then he, his colleagues, and a handful of other physicians and scientists nationwide pioneered research that focused on the impact body/mind interventions could have upon cancer, hypertension, and heart disease. Today, Benson, like a growing number of other physicians, sees medicine that factors in the mind, body, and the spirit, too, as an integral part of his health-care equation.

"I believe the ideal model for medicine is that of the three-legged stool," Benson writes in *Timeless Healing: The Power and Biology of Belief.* The stool is balanced by the appropriate application of self-care, medications, and medical procedures. "One leg, that which patients can do for themselves, is the most disparaged and neglected aspect of health care today." It's the reason, he adds, that the stool is unbalanced. "We rely far too much on pharmaceuticals and surgery and procedures. We must embrace self-care to optimize medicine, health, and well-being as well as to balance the stool."

To embrace the responsibility for our self-care, we must first foster the belief that health is much more than the absence of disease. It's not a light that's controlled by a switch that's either on or off. Instead, our health functions more like a light that's on a dimmer switch. When we want to optimize the light we give it all it needs to shine its brightest. Conversely, when we want it to be faint, we take away its light-giving resources. In this way health is a continuum. At one end is optimal health, and we get there by maximizing the resources we can use to take care of our bodies, minds, emotions, and spirits. These resources include eating well, exercising, and attending to our inner life so that we can enjoy a quality of life that doesn't feel compromised.

Larry Dossey, M.D., author of *Healing Words: The Practice of Medicine and the Power of Prayer*, is one of the world's leading authorities on the healing power of prayer. His groundbreaking book looked at the results of over 150 scientific studies that showed a positive relationship between different forms of prayer and healing. One form was prayer offered at a distance. In some cases the prayers were on one coast and those prayed for on another.

As a result Dossey now divides the practice of medicine into three evolutionary stages or eras. The one we call mind/body medicine he calls "Era II."

+ Era I medicine was launched in the last third of the nineteenth century. It is based solely upon a mechanical model of the body. Practitioners use surgery, drugs, radiation, and other physical interventions. Included in this model are acupuncture, homeopathy, herbs, and other treatments that are often used to complement traditional medicine or as an alternative.

+ Era II medicine incorporates Era I. It began in the 1940s and includes mind/body and psychophysiological approaches. It teaches that the mind within the individual has causal power—that our thoughts, emotions, and physical bodies are linked. Therapies such as biofeedback, relaxation, hypnosis, that emphasize the effects of consciousness solely within the individual belong in this category.

+ Era III medicine views consciousness from a "nonlocal" perspective. That means consciousness breaks the bounds of the body and is no longer constrained by time and space. Dossey maintains that Era II is nonlocal (or transpersonal) because it acknowledges the ability of one person's consciousness to affect the mind/body of other distant persons. In Era III medicine, intercessory prayer, shamanic practitioners, and other remote healers and healing practices can influence a patient's health.

At the other end of the continuum is horizontal health. This, being the polar opposite of optimal health, is where we feel resource-*less*. Horizontal health can be a chronic or an acute care state in which pathology prevails. We may feel incapacitated because we are flat on our backs due to an accident or other emergency. We may also be permanently disabled or close to death because of a chronic or life-threatening disease. Certainly, this is a place where traditional emergency medicine truly shines and often saves lives by providing triage and resources the patient cannot provide.

In the Western world most of us begin our lives at the optimal end of the continuum. Before and shortly after birth we develop a formidable internal pharmacopoeia that functions to keep us healthy. When something happens that assaults our system, our innate ability to self-heal mobilizes to remedy the situation and restore **homeostasis.**

Sadly, because we live in a demanding, busy, and materialistic society we become habituated to other ways of being in the world. We live with high, ongoing levels of stress and anxiety that impede our natural healing system and prevent it from functioning efficiently. That creates a tension for our immune system, which may make it feel like it's doing triage twenty-four hours a day. Instead of acting seamlessly as our first line of defense against disease, it now struggles. Finally, it reaches the point where it becomes impossible to sustain the ongoing tension any longer. As our immune system lets go, we not only become ill, we may also have to face the reality that we may not fully recuperate. We're now in an in-between state called "vertical health."

We spend most of our lives in vertical health. It's the middle ground between the optimal and horizontal poles of the continuum. Whether we spend it in sickness or in health is, for the most part, up to us. Vertical health is a state of flux.

Hopefully, most of what we do while in vertical health gets accomplished with lots of vigor and enjoyment. But for many people that's not the case. They move along, hoping for "the best" healthwise, while living with a gnawing feeling that all is not well. They complain of vague symptoms and just not "feeling good," but instead of listening to their body's wisdom, the only action they take is to pop an over-the-counter drug and hope "it" will go away.

The antidote, as we all know, is not to be passive and merely tolerate the minor aches, pains, illnesses, and stresses that assault us. As we've said before, we are called, instead, to take action that can permanently reduce and possibly eliminate those symptoms, by:

- ◆ changing our diet
- ◆ reducing high stress levels

- learning how to manage our emotions
- getting in better shape

However, it's not unusual for us to resist making those changes, because our way of life has become familiar and comfortable. The following story about a group of patients with multiple sclerosis (M.S.) demonstrates just how strongly and unconsciously people spiral down toward horizontal health because they resist changing a particular comfort level and their "set ways."

Case Study

There were about fifty people gathered to hear one of the Omega Wellness Program teachers speak about a new, low-fat diet that was proving to slow down the debilitating physical deterioration that occurs with M.S. For half the morning the group listened to his lecture on the diet and the importance of incorporating regular exercise and a daily stress-reduction practice into their lifestyle. Then the group took a break. Suddenly, everybody made a beeline to some desserts sitting on a table. The instructor commented, "Was I here the last two hours? Did I miss something? Didn't I just say this stuff was incompatible?"

Only two women in the entire group looked healthy. Interestingly, they were the only ones who reported that they were following the diet and that they were experiencing very positive results. In fact, they were the only two people overtly saying "Wait a minute. I have responsibility for my life and I'm going to do something about it." Everyone else believed that they were a victim of M.S. That there was nothing that they could do to change their outlook or the outcome. "Why me?" they asked. "I guess I better get whatever gratification I can out of life right now." They really believed the jingle that says "Things go better with Coke."

> The greatest revolution of our generation is the discovery that human beings, by changing the inner attitudes of their minds, can change the outer aspects of their lives.
>
> —WILLIAM JAMES

Of course, the two women who were following the diet didn't stop having M.S. But they did significantly change how it affected their lives—and have lived well with fewer symptoms.

As this chapter pointed out earlier, by reading this book, pondering the questions raised, and doing the exercises, you have already begun to chart a course that can help you make positive changes in your life. What are those changes? That's up to you. Perhaps it's time to change your diet or to get more exercise. Maybe you're thinking that you need to give up addictive behaviors or reduce the amount of emotional upheaval and chronic stress you experience. Maybe it's one of these things. Maybe it's all these things. Whatever it is, know that in taking the first steps to really get to know you and your relationship to your thoughts, feelings, behaviors, and overall health, you've crossed a threshold and opened a door to new possibilities. In so doing, what do you leave behind? Only you know. But also know that whether it is a burden of belief or behaviors, you leave carrying a lighter load as you move closer to the rapture of being alive.

RESOURCES

BOOKS

Benson, Herbert, M.D. *Timeless Healing: The Power and Biology of Belief.* New York: Simon & Schuster, 1996.

Campbell, Joseph. *The Hero with a Thousand Faces.* Princeton: Bollingen, 1990.

Collinge, William B. *The American Holistic Health Association Complete Guide to Alternative Medicine.* New York: Warner Books, 1997.

Dossey, Larry, M.D. *Healing Words: The Power of Prayer and the Practice of Medicine.* San Francisco: Harper San Francisco, 1994.

Golan, Ralph, M.D. *Optimal Wellness.* New York: Ballantine Books, 1995.

Locke, Steven E., and Douglas Colligan. *The Healer Within: The New Medicine of Mind and Body.* New York: NAL-Dutton, 1987.

Moyers, Bill. *Healing and the Mind.* New York: Doubleday, 1993.

Pert, Candace, Ph.D. *Molecules of Emotion: Why You Feel the Way You Feel.* New York: Scribner, 1997.

Spangler, David. *The Call.* New York: Riverhead, 1998.

The Complete Guide to Alternative and Conventional Treatments. New York: Time-Life Books, 1996.

MAGAZINES AND JOURNALS

The following magazines are available at many libraries and on most newsstands. If you cannot find them or the journals, contact their offices.

Advances: The Journal of Mind-Body Health
The Fetzer Institute
9292 W. KL Avenue
Kalamazoo, MI 49009
Phone: 616-375-2000

Alternative Therapies in Health and Medicine
InnoVision Communications
101 Columbia Avenue
Aliso Viejo, CA 92656
Phone: 800-899-1712

Intuition
275 Brannan Street
San Francisco, CA 94107
415–538–8171

Natural Health
70 Lincoln Street
Boston, MA 02111
800-526-8440 (subscription)

New Age Journal
42 Pleasant Street
Watertown, MA 02472

617-926-0200 (editorial)
815-734-5808 (subscriptions)
www.newage.com

Positive Health (British)
Positive Health Publications, LTD
51 Queen Square
Bristol BSI 4LH, UK
E-mail—mike@positive.u-net.com

Psychology Today
Sussex Publishers, Inc.
49 E. Twenty-first Street, 11th Floor
New York, NY 10010
212-260-7210

Spirituality and Health
P.O. Box 54151
Boulder, CO 80321-4151
800-876-8202
www.spiritualityhealth.com

Vegetarian Times
P.O. Box 420235
Palm Coast, FL 32142-0235
800-829-3340
www.vegetariantimes.com

Yoga Journal
California Yoga Teachers Association
2004 University Avenue, Suite 600
Berkeley, CA 94704
510-841-9200
www.yogajournal.com

BOOK CLUBS

One Spirit: Resources for the Spirit, Mind, and Body
800-348-7128

VIDEOTAPES

Mystic Fire Video
P.O. Box 442
New York, NY 10012
800-999-1319

AUDIOTAPES

New Dimensions Radio
P.O. Box 569
Ukiah, CA 95482-0569
800-935-8273

Sounds True
P.O. Box 8010
Boulder, CO 80306-8010
800-333-9185

WWW

All of these sites on the World Wide Web have links to other sites. Most allow you to search for information about a specific topic or condition such as body/mind, stress, tai chi, alternative medicine, et cetera. Most search engines such as Snap, Yahoo, Infoseek, et cetera, have health-related links on their homepage.

Achoo Healthcare Online—www.achoo.com

Alternative Therapies in Health and Medicine—www.alternative-therapies.com

Ask Dr. Weil—Q & A—cgi.pathfinder.com/drweil

At Health—www.athealth.com

Back to Health—www.bth.4the.net

Health Journeys—www.healthjourneys.com

Healthy Way—www.sympatico.ca/healthyway

HealthWorld Online—www.healthy.net/Index.html

Medscape—www.medscape.com

Medsite—www.medsite.com

Thrive—www.thriveonline.com

2.

Stress Awareness

Do you ever wake up in the morning feeling anxious and worried that the day ahead is little more than a "stress rehearsal"? And then do you then find it hard to sleep peacefully at night because you've spent the last twelve hours racing around like the juggler at the circus who frantically tries to keep a dozen spinning plates from crashing?

If you do feel that way—either occasionally or often—you're not alone. According to the American Institute of Stress in Yonkers, New York, in the late 1990s as many as 75 to 90 percent of visits to doctors in this country were due, in part, to stress.

Although a large and growing body of scientific evidence indicates that today many of us may be living in the throes of a stress epidemic, take heart. Despite the fact that almost daily headlines in the media tell us how harmful stress can be for our health, we don't have to accept their pronouncements as immutable forecasts of

There's nothing basically wrong with you that what's right with you can't cure.

—ANONYMOUS

> The mind is its own place, and in itself,
> can make heaven of Hell, and a hell of Heaven.
> —JOHN MILTON

gloom and doom. Hans Selye, the Canadian physiologist who pioneered stress research in the 1940s, put it this way: "It's not stress that kills us, it is our reaction to it."

Think about the way you react to stressful news. Do actual headlines such as "Marital Stress Linked to High Blood Pressure," "Personality Type Linked to High Risk of Heart Attack," and "Earthquakes, Sudden Stresses Can Cause Death" push buttons that make you feel stressed and anxious? Or do you feel hopeful that this information can help you change your life? Remember, you are the chief administrator of your health-care team who can either:

+ passively get caught in the undertow of a stressful lifestyle, or
+ actively and consciously learn to respond to stress in order to deal better with the ebb and flow of life's uncertainties and the unpredictable tides of change

By choosing the latter, we begin to make positive lifestyle and self–health-care readjustments. These help us to manage and reduce stress by cultivating:

+ awareness of the present moment
+ nonjudgmental awareness of ourselves and the world around us, and
+ acceptance of "what is"—good, bad, or neutral

Mother Teresa of Calcutta knew the devastating impact of social, political, economic, and biological stresses upon the human mind, body, emotions, and spirit in ways most of us never will. She said, "Yesterday is gone. Tomorrow has not yet come. We have only today. Let us begin."

So let us begin. Throughout this chapter and the rest of this book, we will describe practical ways to begin enjoying a less stressful lifestyle. At the heart of these techniques are five universal principles of stress reduction that serve as basic tenets of Omega's Wellness Program. Consider copying them onto an index card and carrying it with you to read while waiting for the next red light that never seems to change.

+ As we think, so we become. *The mind is everything: what you think, you become.*

THE BUDDHA

+ It's not the events in our lives that make us miserable, but our view of them. *You create your own reality.*

JANE ROBERTS

+ What we put out to others always comes back to us (karma). *The way you prepare the bed, so shall you sleep.*

YIDDISH PROVERB

+ We don't see people or things as they are—we see them as we are. *Why do you see the speck in your neighbor's eye, but do not notice the log in your own eye?*

JESUS (MATT. 7:3)

+ The only person we can really change is ourself! *Nothing can bring you peace but yourself.*

RALPH WALDO EMERSON

Before going further we offer you a small caveat. You may be surprised to discover that after putting some of these stress management techniques into action, you may feel even *more* stressed than you did before you began. Responding to change this way is normal. It's much easier to intellectually acknowledge that a change is in our best interest than it is to embrace it emotionally. More often than not our emotions take longer to align with a change even when the promise it offers far outweighs the cost.

Finally, know that if you stay the course the day will come when you will reap the benefits of your hard work. One day that new way of being will begin feeling like a natural, joyful, and positive affirmation of the desire for health and wholeness to which your mind, body, emotions, and spirit beckon you.

What Is Stress?

Stress is a physiological and psychological reaction to something we perceive to be either a challenge or a threat. Despite the belief that all stress is bad, research shows it can be either positive or negative. Good stress may cause us to feel happy, more productive, and really on top of things. Bad stress is just the opposite. It can make us feel like we're anxious or wallowing in a dark, gloomy, moody, vulnerable, and unproductive place.

Although good stress may make us feel better than bad stress, both upset our balance and resilience. So in either case we can wind up feeling like a rubber band that has gotten so stretched out, it finally loses its elasticity or breaks.

One reason that stress impacts us so dramatically is that our response to it is rooted in a primitive behavior called the fight-or-flight response. Back then it ensured our ancestors' survival by kicking in automatically whenever a threat could mean the difference between their having dinner or being dinner.

Today, the fight-or-flight response still serves the same purpose. For example, if a strange, growling pit bull appeared out of nowhere and headed for you, you would probably consider that a real threat to your well-being. You might also feel that way if your boss was on a rampage and you were the target of his or her rage. Upon becoming aware that danger loomed, your body would mobilize the forces it needed to prevent an assault. First your adrenal glands would release epinephrine (also called adrenaline), the hormone that turns on other survival mechanisms. Following that surge your:

+ blood pressure would rise

+ heart would pound

+ blood would rush to your skeletal muscles

+ muscles would tense

+ level of oxygen (fuel) consumption would rise

+ pupils would widen

+ sweat glands would soak you

and you would make a decision whether to stand your ground or flee for your life.

Clearly, this primitive response is not useless. It can still serve us well today. However, it does so in a stress-filled world that our ancestors could never have imagined. Daily, ongoing stresses—not just those generated by an emergency—impact our lives. If we choose to live with that kind of stress over a long period of time and not manage it appropriately, it will contribute to the psychological and/or physiological breakdown of our bodies. This is evidenced by studies that conclude that ongoing stress can:

- weaken our immune system

- cause chronic fatigue, depression, and hypertension

- set the stage for heart disease, stroke, cancer

- exacerbate autoimmune diseases and other conditions

Remember, be gentle on yourself. This is not about being perfect. It's about becoming more conscious of:

- stressors at home, at work, in relationships, and in other aspects of your life

- how those stressors make you feel

- how you feel about them

and then choosing to move forward at your own pace to live as fully as possible in the only moment you have—the present one.

The five tenets of the Omega Wellness Program, the discussion in the last chapter about how we "see" events in our lives, and Shakespeare's wise words below are all

---

There is nothing either good or bad, but thinking makes it so.

—WILLIAM SHAKESPEARE

> The only thing we have to fear is fear itself.
>
> —FRANKLIN DELANO ROOSEVELT

variations on the recurring theme that it is not the events in our lives that make us miserable, but how we view them.

Today, scientific and social studies on stress, resiliency, and other factors that can either bolster or break down the body/mind demonstrate the truth of that statement. For example, a 1991 joint study conducted by a psychologist at Carnegie-Mellon University and scientists working on a cold research team in Sheffield, England, found that the more stress a group of robust people were feeling in their lives, the greater their susceptibility to coming down with the common cold when exposed to the virus causing it. Only 27 percent of the people with little stress came down with colds, as opposed to 47 percent of those who were living very stressful lives.

The news appeared in headlines worldwide. Perhaps you saw it at the time. But how did you see it? Did the words "Stress Linked to Catching Colds" become a dire warning that a study proved adults who face high levels of interpersonal or work-related stress are likely to get a cold if they're exposed to the virus? Or did you mentally *reframe* that negative headline about stress into a positive one that perhaps read: "Cutting Stress Cuts Colds"?

Reframing is one way to turn the lemons in our life into lemonade. Reframing is a process by which we can begin to:

+ see our problems as opportunities and challenges

+ focus on our strengths not our weaknesses, and

+ transform negative thoughts and ideas into positive realities and self-talk

Instead of *reacting* to a stressful situation, reframing helps us to *respond*. For example, if you reacted negatively to the headline stating "Stress Linked to Catching Colds," then the message you may have given your mind and body was: "I'm working overtime, feeling tired, my stomach is tied in knots, and I'm feeling depressed. I guess I'm destined to get the first cold (flu, bug, et cetera) that comes along." In contrast,

> The mind, in addition to medicine, has powers to turn the immune system around.
>
> —JONAS SALK

if you reframed the message you probably gave yourself this wholesome advice: "I'm glad I read that. It reminds me that I've been working extra hard lately and the stress I've been feeling is an early warning signal to take better care of myself."

Reflection(s) with Omega Faculty

Wonder what the "experts" who teach others about optimal health, self-awareness, and self-healing do to take care of themselves when they get stressed out? Do they follow the biblical injunction Physician, heal thyself? To find out we asked several of Omega's faculty two questions:

+ How do you know you're under a lot of stress?

+ How do you reduce stress and regain a sense of balance?

Here are their replies:

Larry Dossey, M.D., author of ***Healing Words: The Power of Prayer and the Practice of Medicine*** and executive editor of the journal ***Alternative Therapies in Health and Medicine***

+ I know I'm under stress when the "joy level" of my work takes a nosedive. Tasks take on a sour note and feel out of key, oppressive, and unfulfilling. This stress signal is emotional and spiritual, rarely physical. It's infallible too.

+ I regain balance and reduce stress immediately by:

   —establishing priorities among outstanding projects

   —saying no to further demands

—reminding myself of the value of my work and why it is worth great effort

—putting my ego aside by asking "Who is this 'I' who feels stressed?" This helps me take the larger view—that my work is not about me, but something universal and immensely important

Barbara Dossey, R.N., M.S., author of *Rituals of Healing* and *Holistic Nursing: A Handbook for Practice*

✦ I know I'm under stress/being stressed/feeling stressed when I feel tense in my left shoulder, have shallow breathing, and experience being rushed.

✦ I regain my sense of balance by walking in the garden, sitting on a stone bench, or listening to the water flowing down the water rocks that I have all around my home. It is a time to just be present, do nothing, look at the colors, sounds, textures, and feel the wind, and, most of all, to engage in prayer, meditation, relaxation, and imagery.

Belleruth Naparstek, M.S., L.I.S.W., creator of **Health Journeys** guided imagery tapes and author of *Staying Well with Guided Imagery* and *Your Sixth Sense*

✦ When I get cranky, mean spirited, and find everyone is annoying me, I know I'm stressed. In fact, I'm probably stressed when I'm annoyed at more than two people on any given day—'cause when I'm balanced that usually doesn't happen. I do know that I will get this way if I've been surrounded by people for too long, even lovely people. I also get really stressed when I spin into "hurry sickness," as the cardiology mavens say . . . when I'm racing around, very intent on ticking items off my to-do list—as if they were really important.

✦ I regain a sense of balance by, first and foremost, snagging some solitude (which is essential to a closet introvert like myself) and also by:

—doing a walking meditation in beautiful outdoor surroundings

—listening to fifteen minutes of heart-opening guided imagery

—practicing yoga

—doing some intensely aerobic exercise for about twenty-five minutes

Candace Pert, Ph.D., neuroscientist and author of ***Molecules of Emotion***

+ I know I'm stressed when I secretly buy cigarettes and candy bars and eat the candy in the closet.

+ I reduce stress and regain my sense of balance by going back to basics. I meditate twenty minutes twice a day and follow a regime of early to bed and early to rise.

Rick Jarow, Ph.D., author of ***Creating the Work You Love: Courage, Commitment, Career*** and developer of the "anticareer" workshop

+ I'm stressed when a phone call sounds like chalk screeching on a blackboard or when I walk into a room and forget why I walked in. I also know I'm stressed when I feel an incessant "pushing" in my system.

+ Reducing stress? Playing basketball really does it for me. I also walk on grass because it's a grounding exercise. I call it "green breath"—walking, breathing, and releasing. Another thing I do is remind myself it's all a dream.

Although scholars and dictionaries agree on a few objective definitions of stress, subjective definitions are another story. As the definition of stress that says *"Stress. Everybody knows what it is, no one knows what it is"* points out, it's difficult to zero in on all its particularities. For example, one definition describes stress as "a particular relationship between the person and the environment that is appraised by the person as taxing or exceeding his or her resources and endangering his or her well-being." Another tells us that "stress is a force that when applied to a system modifies its form." And so it goes.

Sadly, many people don't realize how affected they are by stress until they crash,

> The way people cope with incipient illness may be at least as important
> as the biological pathogens in determining health and illness.
>
> —KENNETH PELLETIER

physically, psychologically, emotionally, or even spiritually. Typically, this happens when people:

+ live an overstimulated, overactive life that habitually attracts rather than repels stress

+ fail to take time to be with themselves and stay apprised of what they are really feeling and needing, and

+ fail to pay attention to the early warning signs that stress may be putting them at physical and emotional risk

Adapt: Synonyms for the word *adapt* are: *accommodate, adjust, conform, fit, reconcile.* The central meaning shared by these verbs is "to make suitable to or consistent with a particular situation or use."

In an Omega wellness workshop one student told the following story. It points out how extraordinary our ability to adapt to ongoing stress can be.

I grew up in a neighborhood adjacent to La Guardia Airport in New York. The planes would fly so low over my parents' house that we could wave at the pilots. The noise never bothered me. It was just always there. In fact, I never thought about it until people would come to visit and ask my parents: "How can you stand it?"

"What's there to stand?" they would answer.

Later, when I was in college, I had a friend who lived in a town in New Jersey. The first time I visited him, I finally understood why people visiting me were so bothered by the noise the planes made. It smells unlike any other place I've ever been to. It's a sickening chemical smell that can make you feel nauseous. I'm convinced it's toxic. When I walked into my friend's house, the first words out of my mouth were "How can you stand it?"

"What are you talking about?" he said.

Often we don't recognize stress until it affects our health. Spend a moment reflecting upon your answers to the two questions asked at the beginning of this chapter:

• Do you usually wake up feeling even mildly anxious and worried?

• Do you usually find it hard to fall asleep or to sleep peacefully at night?

If you said yes to one or both questions, see if you can remember what was going on in your life when those cycles got started. Along with anxiety and sleeplessness are you experiencing other stress-related symptoms?

When we are unaware that we are living with stress the pressure on our minds, bodies, emotions, and spirits begins to feel "normal." Even though it's not normal, our ability to *adapt* in order to survive makes it seem as though it is. Daily, the level of our overactivity and overstimulation remains critical as we frantically race around doing for others while remaining oblivious to the fact that we are undoing ourselves.

Today, most holistic physicians believe that almost all illnesses—ranging from headaches to life-threatening ones—are either related to or aggravated by stress in one way or another. For example, medical professionals believe the following conditions and illnesses are stress related. You may want to check off any that apply to you. If you can recall when you first noticed any symptoms and the circumstances that brought it on, note it. You may also want to rate each condition on a scale of 1 to 5, with 1 being "rarely" and 5 being frequently:

• muscle tension

• backache

• neckache

An XYZ Theory of Stress

In the course of conducting studies to answer the question "What promotes health?" Israeli social scientist Aaron Antonovsky looked at what influences health instead of what prompts disease. He knew that germs alone were not the instigators because earlier studies showed that 25 percent of the population in any area had 75 percent of the illnesses. To find other underlying causes Antonovsky studied Holocaust survivors—a populace who had suffered enormous amounts of stress in the Nazi death camps. Because a reasonable number of these people went on to live meaningful lives after their liberation he determined that stress alone was not enough to cause illness.

From this and other research Antonovsky developed a theory that three strengths—*meaningfulness, comprehensibility,* and *manageability*—lead to increased health. He called these strengths "a sense of coherence" (SOC) and described them this way:

+ *Manageability* means a person has confidence in his or her ability to deal with life. Such persons believe that they can influence or control events and do not act like victims.

+ *Meaningfulness* means that an individual has an overall sense of purpose and that life matters. People with this strength make commitments, get involved, take up challenges, and shape their destinies.

+ *Comprehensibility* means a person can make cognitive sense of what is happening. People with this strength are less fearful and cautious; their ability to see events objectively gives them a clearer view of things and a more hopeful approach. They deal with change effectively because they see it as a norm. They seek clarity, not certainty.

When Antonovsky studied people with a low SOC versus those with a high sense, he found they functioned differently in stressful situations. Stressful situations paralyzed those with a low SOC. They became diffused, more reactive, and defensive. They also blamed others for their circumstances, and felt abandoned.

Those with a high SOC responded just the opposite. Stressful and anxiety-provoking events motivated them. They became focused, sought clarity and specificity, exhibited coping behaviors, took action, and worked through grief.

Ultimately, Antonovsky noted that all living things seek balance, integrity, coherence, and stability. When challenges from outside stressors threaten homeostasis, the unbalance causes tension and possibly disease. Plants and animals can use only their automatic responses to deal with these threats. However, he said, human beings also have XYZ, which will determine whether or not they move toward distress (disease) or eustress (health).

X, he explained, is how a person appraises the situation. Y is how he or she handles the situation, and Z is the confidence he or she has in resources to deal with it. Not surprisingly, a solid sense of coherence leads to a more positive appraisal as well as effective handling and increased confidence in the resources available.

+ sexual dysfunction

+ indigestion

+ stomach ulcers

+ bowel problems

+ menstrual problems

+ skin disorders

+ temporomandibular joint disorder (TMJ)

+ alcohol/use and abuse

+ recreational drug use and recreational drug abuse

+ depression

+ asthma

+ hypertension

+ stroke

+ heart disease

+ some cancers

+ autoimmune diseases (e.g., HIV/AIDS, lupus, chronic fatigue syndrome)

Now take a few moments to review your list and take another look at the discussion of horizontal, vertical, and optimal health in Chapter 1. You may also want to write down the answers to the following questions:

Try This

This is a journaling exercise called a "dialogue." You can use it whenever you want to help bring into awareness information you may have buried in your unconscious about your relationship to yourself, others, and the world around you. In this case, dialoguing can help you learn more about a particular stress you feel. Knowing something more about it expands the number of choices you can make to help manage or eliminate that stress. You can do this exercise by writing in a journal with a pen or pencil or you can also "write" in any other way that's comfortable for you—on a legal pad or on a computer or by speaking into a tape recorder.

◆ Find a quiet place and close your eyes for a few moments. Take some deep breaths.

◆ Let your eyes scan the signs-and-symptoms-of-stress list. Does one condition draw your attention more than another?

◆ Pick one that's "calling" you. That's the one with which you will dialogue.

◆ Imagine that since this symptom of stress is present in your life it's trying to tell you something.

◆ Begin the conversation as though you were writing a play. Let your voice ask the stress a question. It could be "Why are you here?" or "What do you want to tell me?" or any other question that comes to mind. Write it down.

◆ Listen for an answer. Be patient. One will come. Write down whatever comes. Make no judgments about it. Then respond to it. Listen again and then write again.

◆ Allow the conversation to continue until it seems to naturally end.

◆ Reread your dialogue to see if it offers you new insight into what your mind/body might be saying to you about the form and function of a particular stress in your life.

Until I accept my faults I will most certainly doubt my virtues.

—HUGH PRATHER

- ✦ What do the numbers you assigned to these twenty conditions tell you about the ways in which stress may be impacting your life?

- ✦ How do you feel about any conditions to which you gave a 3, 4, or 5?

- ✦ What do you know about any of the chronic or life-threatening diseases to which you gave a 3, 4, or 5?

- ✦ Do you see any patterns in your life or family history that might be related to the conditions or their symptoms? Did either of your parents, grandparents, or a sibling suffer or die from any of these illnesses? What stresses are you aware of that might have affected their health? Are you aware of any healthful measures your relatives took to improve their well-being?

If you've already made one or more commitments to make lifestyle changes, ask yourself how the above information may help you to envision and accomplish your objectives and goals. Also use it as a baseline reading of the places in your body that may be feeling lots of pressure and/or manifesting stress. Bookmark this page so you can easily reference it. As you begin making changes to better manage any stresses you feel, see if your signs and symptoms remain the same. Is the rating for each condition stagnant or is it changing?

The results of studies on ongoing stress show that its impact upon our bodies, minds, emotions, and spirits can be likened to a rubber band that gets so overstretched that it either loses its elasticity or breaks. How does that image strike you? Does the thought of those consequences make you wonder why someone might allow him/herself to get to that point? What, you might ask, prevents that individual from being proactive about managing and reducing stress? And why do he or she or so many of us go so far as to actually deny that this systemic *dis*-ease can have such an effect?

The answer to those questions rests with whom you know or don't know. If you spend all your time giving pieces of yourself away to others and leaving little time, energy, and space for your "self," then your levels of "self-awareness" and "stress

> I care not what others think of what I do, but I care very much about
> what I think of what I do. That is character!
>
> —THEODORE ROOSEVELT

awareness" may be critically low. You may be doing a great job of knowing who you are in relation to other people, but do you know who are you in relation to your self?

According to psychologist Nathaniel Branden, Ph.D., the "father" of the concept of self-esteem, "Chronic tension conveys the message of some form of internal split, some form of self-avoidance, or self-repudiation, some aspect of the self being denied or held on a very tight leash." In contrast, he adds, "relaxation implies that we are not hiding from ourselves, not at war with who we are."

Because we live in a society where accolades get heaped upon those who can multi-task, compartmentalize their minds, bodies, emotions, and spirits, and find twenty-eight hours in a twenty-four-hour day, many of us find it difficult to relax and not be at war with who we are. We become habituated to living with a worldview that is based upon illusions of the past, fears about the future, and others' expectations, but not upon the reality of who we are or what we feel in the present moment. Buddhist monk Thich Nhat Hanh puts it this way: "We are very good at preparing to live, but not very good at living. We know how to sacrifice ten years for a diploma, and we are willing to work very hard to get a job, a car, a house, and so on. But we have difficulty remembering that we are alive in the present moment, the only moment there is for us to be alive."

Similarly, one of the guiding lights of American spirituality, Ram Dass, says that the antidote for the stress we feel from living our lives somewhere else in time and apart from ourselves is, quite simply: "Be here now." But is it really that simple? If it were, wouldn't more of us "be here now"? Rather than putting our psychic energies into reliving the past or projecting them onto an unknown future, wouldn't more of

> A man cannot be comfortable without his own approval.
>
> —MARK TWAIN

> The curious paradox is that when I accept myself just as I am, then I can change.
>
> —CARL ROGERS

us be focused on getting in touch with our thoughts, feelings, emotions, and the yearnings of our souls in this moment?

How about you? Do you find it difficult "to be here now"? That's another way of asking whether you find it difficult to just be a human being and not be a human doing. If you find it challenging to answer that question, is it because you don't know? Has it been such a long time since you've been with yourself that you find it tough to remember what it might be like?

"What do you see when you turn off the lights?" singer John Lennon once asked. Then, answering his own question, he replied, "I can't tell you, but I know it's mine." One way to get your own answer to Lennon's question is to begin spending enough time with yourself to know what's yours. But can you? The following exercise will help you find out. Start by sitting on a couch with no distractions. Now ask yourself:

+ What is it like to sit here?

+ What would I rather be doing?

+ Why would I rather be doing it?

+ What feelings and emotions am I experiencing?

While the first and last questions may seem similar, they are different. Answers to the first question may include words that reflect your relationship to the outer world—words like *uncomfortable, restricted, imprisoned, comfortable,* or *relaxing.* Words that come up in response to the last question may reflect more of your inner world—*anxiety, pain, guilt, boredom, joy,* or *happiness.* Now take some time to ponder all your words.

If you are really focusing on those words and what each one is saying to you, you may notice that you become stressed only when tensions generated by your thoughts, feelings, and emotions pull you toward the future or back into the past. Since studies show that we may have as many as fifteen thousand to fifty thousand thoughts a day and a high percentage of them are about the past and future, ask whether the words you're looking at are causing you to trip off to either of those places and feel stressed. Or are you so focused on the task itself that you experience that in-the-moment state called "flow"?

Sir John Marks Templeton, whose philanthropic foundation is funding major research bridging spirituality and medicine, believes some simple spiritual principles have helped him to live his life more fully, deeply, and joyfully.

Many of Templeton's prescriptive principles have the power to help us think more carefully about our lives and our relationships. In so doing they help us to become more self-aware and less stressed by events and situations that can trigger negative emotions and anxiety. Here are five of those principles from his book *Worldwide Laws of Life:*

✦ **All sunshine makes a desert**—without variety, another way of saying balance, in our life, we would never improve our lives or ourselves. We will always have to face problems. The key is recognizing that every problem has a solution. Remember that a desert cannot support life without some rain. Look for the balance in your life. If it is not there, then it's time to create it.

✦ **Minds are like parachutes**—they function only when open; otherwise they remain tightly packed and inactive. Open minds make us free agents who can receive unexpected insights and information. Open minds enable us to grow, learn, and encounter new ideas and people. The key here is to be responsive instead of reactive by not jumping to conclusions. Instead, see opportunities at every turn.

✦ **Laughter *is* the best medicine**—laughter not only soothes the savage beast, it benefits the mind, body, and soul. See Chapter 6 for a detailed discussion of the healing power of laughter.

✦ **Defeat isn't bitter if you don't swallow it.** Failing at something is very different from seeing yourself as a failure. The former relates to action, the latter is who you are. Once you accept defeat you can use it as a stepping-stone on the path to success. B. F. Skinner said, "A failure is not always a mistake; it may be simply the best one can do with the circumstances. The real mistake is to stop." Take Thomas Edison, for example. He at-tempted more than a thousand times to invent the lightbulb. When someone asked him, "Did you ever become discouraged?" Edison answered, "Those were steps on the way. In each attempt I was successful in finding a way not to create a lightbulb."

- ✦ **You get back what you give out.** When you get up on "the wrong side of the bed," and find other people seem to be in that same grumpy place, it may be because you're getting back what you were giving out. You may especially notice it if your mood changes to a more positive one and suddenly people seem to respond in kind. Your level of self-awareness and manner of expression can determine the quality of living you experience. So begin cleaning out those things in your mind that you know make for more problems. Things such as resentment, anger, self-pity, and blaming others. Become aware of the emotions you broadcast. And remember you are present in your life on earth at this moment for the purposes of living, loving, learning, and growing. Your level of self-awareness and manner of expression can determine the quality of living you experience.

Before "getting up," ask yourself what your answers to the above questions might tell you about your willingness to be in the present moment while sitting on the couch. Did you resist being there or enjoy it? Now that the exercise is finished, where are you? Are you here now—"the only moment there is to be alive"?

Why is it so difficult to be in the present moment? Could it be related to low self-esteem? "At its root self-esteem is the immune system of consciousness, the ability to trust one's mind, and the belief that one is worthy of happiness," says Nathaniel Branden. Fully realized, self-esteem is the experience that we are appropriate to life, to the requirements of life, and that we have confidence in our ability to think, assert our needs and wants, and cope with the basic challenges of life.

One of the ways we can develop stronger self-awareness that enhances self-esteem and reduces the impact of stress is to practice meditation and/or use the body/mind modalities that are described in the next chapter. Another is to become more con-scious of what psychologist Daniel Goleman calls our "emotional intelligence."

In Goleman's best-selling book *Emotional Intelligence*, he discusses abilities that build our self-esteem. These include self-control, zeal, persistence, and self-motivation. All are needed for real emotional intelligence, he explains, because even sociopaths possess one or two. They are skills that each of us has either learned or not learned while growing up. Studies also show that these skills can be taught to the youngest children and that they can play an even more important role than IQ in determining a child's "success" on the playground, in school, and, later, at work and in the world.

For example, studies in the 1960s conducted by psychologist Walter Mischel, Ph.D., demonstrated that four-year-old children who delayed an impulse for immediate gratification instead of acting on a whim greatly benefited from their "emotional intelligence." When Mischel followed up on his cohort as they graduated from high school, he found that those who could delay gratification to meet a goal as preschoolers scored an average of over 210 points higher on their SAT exams in high school than those who couldn't. "What shows up in a small way early in life blossoms into a wide range of social and emotional competencies as life goes on," observes Goleman. One's ability to delay an impulse is at the root of many of the efforts we make as adults. This can range from staying on a diet to pursuing a Ph.D.

Citing road rage and random shootings as increasingly common examples of what happens when emotions go awry, Goleman says we're living in a time when "the fabric of society seems to unravel at ever-greater speed, when selfishness, violence, and a meanness of spirit seem to be rotting the goodness of our communal lives."

Goleman says we are often victims of emotional hijacking. It usually nabs us when we react to anxiety-provoking incidents from the emotional parts of our brain instead of the "neocortex," or thinking part, of the brain. For example, you may remember the incident in which Mike Tyson, the infamous heavyweight boxer, bit an inch out of his opponent's ear during a championship fight. In an interview with *Psychology Today* Goleman said that the fight-or-flight reaction is so powerful that it still initiates the same primitive response that was quite useful back in Stone Age days. However, today, we're reacting to symbolic or perceived emergencies, not actual ones. When

Tyson got enraged and bit his opponent, the boxer said, "I'm taking the blows for my children." Commenting, Goleman adds, "He clearly has a deeply felt sense that he's boxing to help his family and he reacted as if he were actually in a life-and-death struggle to protect his kids. That's a dramatic example of the kind of thing that happens to us every day." Tyson had clearly failed to master some basic emotional skills that in Aristotle's words help us "to be angry with the right person, to the right degree, at the right time, for the right purpose and in the right way."

Unlike Tyson, when we become aware of our emotions, respond instead of reacting to them, and put them at the center of aptitudes for living, Goleman believes that we become better equipped to rein in emotional impulse, read another's innermost feelings, and handle relationships smoothly. It also helps to disempower toxic emotions, which can, in the long run, put us at risk for a whole spectrum of *dis*-ease ranging from depression to violence to eating disorders and substance abuse.

"We must look at the fact that our passions, when well exercised, have wisdom," concludes Goleman, because they guide our values, thinking, and survival. But they can also easily go awry. "As Aristotle saw, the problem is not with emotionality, but with the appropriateness of emotion and its expression. The question is, how can we bring intelligence to our emotions—and civility to our streets and caring to our communal life?"

Goleman's last question is an important one. Selye taught us that stress can be challenging and useful up to a point. However, at times when our bodies can't cope or the stress is chronic, our emotional response to what is a real or an imagined threat can get skewed. Not knowing the difference, our body reacts to both. As a result we find ourselves in a place where we are distressed and at greater risk for immune deficiencies and illness. So how can we raise our emotional IQs and self-awareness in order to respond to stress positively and thoughtfully? What do we need to do to turn emotional situations into health-enhancing opportunities to demonstrate our emotional intelligence instead of excuses for going ballistic?

To begin we can develop skills that will help to make us become "stress hardy." That's a term that psychologist Suzanne Kobasa, Ph.D., used to describe the employees of a giant corporation she studied whose positive approach to stress made them less vulnerable to stress-related illness and absenteeism from work than others. Her research at the University of Chicago in the early 1980s demonstrated that stress-hardy individuals have "Three C's," which are characteristics that include:

+ *control*—people who felt in control of their lives exhibited a greater degree of stress-hardiness because they knew they could make sound choices and exert a positive influence on stressful events

+ *challenge*—those who saw stress as a challenge instead of a threat were more apt to use it as an opportunity for learning and personal growth

+ *commitment*—committed people felt connected to important people in their lives as well as to their work and found it easier to be engaged in the world and people around them

In his fascinating book *Why Zebras Don't Get Ulcers,* Robert M. Sapolsky, Ph.D., a MacArthur Fellow and professor of biological sciences and neuroscience at Stanford University, compares the ways in which we live our lives to those of our ancient ancestors. In the Western world we now get different diseases than we used to with different causes and consequences, he notes. "A millennium ago a young hunter-gatherer inadvertently eats a reedbuck riddled with anthrax, and the consequences are clear—he's dead a few days later. Now a young lawyer unthinkingly decides that red meat, fried foods, and a couple of beers per dinner constitute a desirable diet, and the consequences are anything but clear—a half century later maybe he's crippled with cardiovascular disease, or maybe he's taking bike trips with his grandkids."

The outcome for this modern carnivore will depend on several obvious factors, says Sapolsky. How his liver deals with cholesterol. The level of fat enzymes in his fat cells. Whether the walls of his blood vessels harbor congenital weaknesses. However, he adds, "the outcome will also depend heavily on such surprising factors as his personality, the amount of emotional stress he experiences over the years, whether he has someone's shoulder to cry on when those stressors occur."

It's not just about the body but its interaction with the mind, he concludes. "It is about the role of stress in making some of us more vulnerable to disease, the ways in which some of us cope with stressors, and the critical notion that you cannot really understand a disease *in vacuo,* but rather only in the context of the person suffering from that disease." The best way to begin to understand that "context" better, says Sapolsky, is to make a list of the things you find stressful such as traffic, deadlines, relationships, and money. If you come up short, think of your stresses in terms of these three categories:

+ *acute physical stressors*—extremely stressful events that demand immediate physiological adaptations if you are going to live.

+ *chronic physical stressors*—those stresses that plague you over a long period of time. For our ancestors they were drought, locusts, and food shortages. Sometimes they're the same things for us today.

+ *psychological and social stressors*—the stressful events we generate in our heads by worrying and the wild, strong emotions linked to mere thoughts.

Later, a fourth *C, closeness,* was added to Kobasa's list of stress-hardy characteristics by three clinicians who wrote about her work in *The Wellness Book.* Their article, which

---

Rule 1: Don't sweat the small stuff.

---

appeared in the collection of essays compiled by cardiologist Herbert Benson, M.D., and the staffs of the Mind/Body Institute of New England Deaconess Hospital and Harvard Medical School, reported: "People who have relationships and social support feel considerably more stress hardy than their counterparts who feel isolated from personal contact. If those same individuals also exercise regularly and maintain a healthy diet, the incidence of illness falls even more markedly." Clearly, by approaching life with the positive attitudes now identified as the "four C's" we optimize our potential for reducing stress and for lifelong health.

An important aspect of learning to manage or release stress is to become aware of your stress triggers. What is a stress trigger? You name it—it's just what it sounds like: a thought, memory, event, or feeling that sends a bulletlike fight-or-flight reaction surging through our system. They are the events of daily living that we perceive as threatening, or that require considerable adaptation. If you are a student failing a course, an upcoming test that will determine your grade can be a stress trigger. Words that typically lead to a fight with a spouse are a common stress trigger. So is money, whether it's having too little or too much. And the list goes on to include anything that can set us off—from the weather to a lightbulb blowing at the wrong time to getting a flat tire to not having a camera handy at a picture-perfect moment. In other words, we all have stress triggers that get pulled or buttons that get pushed, but not all of us know what they are, what sets them off, or what to do about them. Do you?

When we can't name what triggers our anxiety we are more apt to get thrown into emotional upheaval. Conversely, when we take measures to become more aware of what triggers our stress and anxiety, we take more responsibility for our lives. This, in turn, helps us to feel more in control. The following story by a participant in an Omega wellness workshop points that out:

Case Study

When we won a state lottery for over $1 million, we were sitting on top of the world. Since we couldn't get the whole amount at once, it wasn't going to produce a lot of annual income. But we had been struggling for years to make ends meet, and this assured us that we would be comfortable and have some added money for retirement. It also meant we could buy some things we had only dreamed of having.

Never did we imagine that extra money could be so stressful. Some family members were annoyed that we didn't share the entire pool with them. Mail and phone calls asking us to donate to all kinds of things tripled. Friends teased us mercilessly. And we didn't agree on ways to spend the discretionary part of our windfall.

It didn't take long for our daily walks to turn into battlegrounds. Most of the time whatever we argued about had nothing to do with the lottery. However, I have no doubt now that even passing comments about the money were stress triggers. It wasn't until we stopped talking about the lottery and started talking to each other about the feelings we each had around the money issue, that the load we each felt lightened. Eventually, the lottery did become a blessing, but for a long time it was a stress trigger in disguise.

As mentioned earlier, stress triggers, whether major financial issues or something minor, do not, in reality, cause a stress reaction. It is not the events in our lives that make us miserable, but the view we take of them and how we describe these events to ourselves. And many of us describe minor problems and normal challenges of daily living in rigid, exaggerated, and catastrophic terms.

When we're out of control we tend to react emotionally instead of thoughtfully to what squeezed the trigger—automatic thoughts and irrational beliefs that may be

---

Rule 4: If you don't mind, it don't matter.

—AUTHOR UNKNOWN

---

exaggerated, mistaken, and negative. Typically, once an unknown, unnamed stress trigger fires, it diminishes our ability to cope and raises our anxiety.

Of course, occasional bouts of such distress are normal, especially at times when we're faced with death, divorce, life-threatening illness, the loss of a job, and other traumatic events. As mentioned before, we can feel it on happy occasions too. Birthdays, holidays, and weddings can all be both joyous and stress-filled. However, lingering distress, especially when our stress-hardiness and self-esteem are at chronically

Let us assure you that the stress you feel doesn't always have to be some monster lurking behind a corner ready to hijack you. It can effect you positively, according to Kenneth Pelletier, Ph.D. In *Sound Mind, Sound Body*, a book that was based on his five-year study of how personal health practices and a sense of meaningful purpose played a major role in the lives of fifty-one prominent men and women, he wrote:

> One of the world's best-kept secrets is that most truly successful people are not overburdened by stress. Nor do they achieve success at the expense of their physical and emotional health. In fact, many individuals in high-demand situations actually thrive on stress.

In the course of his study Pelletier turned to a Gallup poll conducted in the 1980s that showed only 8 percent of the top executives in the *Fortune* 500 companies reported stress to be a problem. And, surprisingly, a whopping 60 percent reported that they were sometimes or often exhilarated by stress.

"Stressors can actually assume a positive role in a person's life," Pelletier writes. "They can prepare us to deal with emergencies. They can also provide an opportunity for accomplishment that leads to gratification and an enhanced sense of control and productivity." Stress can be positive, he says, when the person being stressed:

- sees stress as an opportunity for learning and achievement
- exerts an appropriate level of control so the stress may actually be health enhancing
- possesses a disciplined self-awareness and the flexibility to handle excessive amounts of stress appropriately
- has factored techniques for managing stress into his or her lifestyle

At the end of his study Pelletier concluded that those who found benefits to stress were people with a positive attitude. "It is this attitude that is the real stress management, not the techniques themselves. There is a Buddhist koan that says we should not confuse the finger with that to which it points. The same applies to stress management strategies, which should not be confused with the ultimately important state to which they lead."

low levels, can trigger an emotional chain reaction that may play itself out daily in inappropriate ways. It can show up anywhere along a continuum that includes rage, abuse, a lack of focus, blaming, bullying, depression, and illness. Although outwardly those suffering from it can usually get through the day at work or school or taking care of the children standing on their feet, inwardly they feel exhausted. Moreover, once they leave those tasks behind it doesn't necessarily mean they've let go of the stress, fear, and anxiety those tasks generated.

Earlier, you looked at a list of signs and symptoms of stress and possibly identified one or more of the events that may have triggered your own experience. By naming what caused you stress and how you experienced it in your body, you opened the door leading to greater self-awareness. You also took one of the most important steps in learning to manage and release stress in healthy ways.

To help expand your assessment of how stress may be affecting your health, look at the following modified version of the Social Readjustment Rating Scale. This is a long-standing inventory that was developed in the late 1960s at the University of

Washington School of Medicine by some of the earliest researchers to note a correlation between the intensity of life changes and the onset of illness. Check off the ones that apply to your life over the last year.

Event	Value
Death of a spouse	100
Divorce	73
Marital separation	65
Jail term	63
Death of a close family member	63
Personal injury or illness	53
Marriage	50
Fired from work	47
Marital reconciliation	45
Retirement	45
Change in family member's health	44
Pregnancy	40
Sex difficulties	39
Addition to family	39
Business readjustment	39
Change in financial status	39
Death of a close friend	38
Change to different line of work	36
Change in number of marital arguments	35
Mortgage or loan for a home or other significant purchase	31
Foreclosure on a mortgage or loan	30
Change in work responsibilities	29
Son or daughter leaving home	29
Trouble with in-laws	29

Outstanding personal achievement	28
Spouse begins or stops work	26
Starting or finishing school	26
Change in living conditions	25
Revision in personal habits	24
Trouble with boss	23
Change in work hours, conditions	20
Change in residence	20
Change in schools	20
Change in recreational habits	19
Change in church activities	19
Change in social activities	18
Mortgage or loan for a small purchase	17
Change in sleeping habits	16
Change in number of family gatherings	15
Change in eating habits	15
Vacation	13
Holidays	12
Minor violation of the law	11

Now add up your score.

The scientists who developed this scale found that if your score was 150, your chances of developing an illness or some other health change would be about fifty-fifty. A score that skyrocketed to over 300 in a twelve-month period would increase the odds of becoming ill to almost 90 percent. Additionally, the higher the score, the greater the risk of the illness being serious or life threatening.

You can use your score like a barometer or thermometer. If you do, what might it tell you? If yours is a high score does it automatically stir up negative thoughts and cause you to worry and blame external events for your stress? Or have you begun to reframe a high score into helpful information that you can use to decide how to proactively reduce stress and take better care of yourself? If your score is low, does that automatically mean your level of stress is low? Not necessarily, although it might

Breathing can profoundly influence emotional and mental states. Erratic breathing patterns and shallow chest breathing often point to emotional stress, upset, and instability.

Diaphragmatic breathing is the most efficient, least taxing way to breathe. Learning to breathe this way may prevent stress and disease. It also helps to balance and reintegrate the mind and body.

To try breathing diaphragmatically, find a quiet spot where you can sit comfortably. If you sit in a chair, keep both feet on the floor and your back comfortably straight.

+ extend your abdomen as you inhale

+ pull the air deep into the lungs without moving your chest

+ flatten your abdomen gently while exhaling

+ always breathe through the nose

+ breathe rhythmically and deeply, yet effortlessly

+ do not pause between breaths

+ concentrate on the breath

+ acknowledge and release any extraneous thoughts

+ refocus on the breath

Try practicing for five minutes three times a day. Some people find it helpful to imagine they are inhaling a relaxation "force" and exhaling tension, anger, frustration, etc., with each breath. You may want to slowly repeat the word "I am" on each inhalation and the word "relaxed" on each exhalation.

To get the full benefit of this technique, practice it daily. Be consistent about the times you choose to practice. Within a few weeks, it should become habitual. Notice any changes you experience.

if you are already using the five universal principles of stress management described earlier.

There are many things in life that we can't change. We can't change the weather or stop the clock. Both are beyond our control. Perhaps one of the most important aspects of stress reduction is this: We change what's reasonable to change in our lives. For those many stressors beyond our direct control, we must learn to openheartedly accept them and to open to their presence.

In essence, we create much of our stress. In a lighthearted way the following story shows us how important it is to believe and recognize the truth of that saying, if we are going to transform the depredations of stress into opportunities to enjoy our life and health more.

Ever since Joe joined the company three years ago, he and his coworkers would meet weekly for a brown bag lunch in the cafeteria. Like clockwork, every Wednesday Joe would come in late, open his bag, and moan, "Oh, no. Not another peanut butter sandwich." He would then spend the next few minutes complaining how much he hated the smell of peanut butter and the fact that it upset his stomach.

This went on for several months. Finally, a coworker couldn't stand listening to Joe's complaints any longer. "Why don't you tell your wife to make you something different?" he yelled across the table.

Joe looked puzzled. "What wife?" he finally asked. "I make my own sandwiches."

⟋ RESOURCES ⟋

BOOKS

Benson, Herbert, M.D., and Eileen M. Stuart, R.N., M.S., *The Wellness Book: The Comprehensive Guide to Maintaining Health and Treating Stress-Related Illness.* New York: Fireside, 1992.

Borysenko, Joan. *Minding the Body, Mending the Mind.* New York: Bantam Books, 1987.

Branden, Nathaniel. *The Six Pillars of Self-Esteem.* New York: Bantam, 1994.

Covey, Stephen. *The Seven Habits of Highly Effective People.* New York: Simon & Schuster, 1989.

Goleman, Daniel, Ph.D. *Emotional Intelligence.* New York: Bantam, 1997.

Goleman, Daniel, Ph.D. (ed.). *Healing Emotions: Conversations with the Dalai Lama on Mindfulness, Emotions, and Health.* Boston: Shambhala, 1997.

Goleman, Daniel, Ph.D., and Joel Gurin (eds.). *Mind Body Medicine: How to Use Your Mind for Better Health.* New York: Consumer Report Books, 1993.

Hanh, Thich Nhat.

Being Peace. Berkeley: Parallax Press, 1996.

Peace Is Every Step: The Path of Mindfulness in Everyday Life. New York: Bantam, 1992.

Pelletier, Kenneth R., Ph.D.

Mind as Healer, Mind as Slayer: A Holistic Approach to Preventing Stress Disorders. New York: Delta, 1977.

Sound Mind, Sound Body. New York: Simon & Schuster, 1994.

Sapolsky, Robert M. *Why Zebras Don't Get Ulcers: An Updated Guide to Stress, Stress-Related Diseases, and Coping.* New York: W. H. Freeman and Company, 1998.

Templeton, John Marks. *Worldwide Laws of Life.* Philadelphia: Templeton Foundation Press, 1998.

Weil, Andrew, M.D. *Spontaneous Healing.* New York: Alfred A. Knopf, Inc., 1995.

WWW

See listings in Chapter 1. Go to those sites and then do a search for "Stress" or "Stress Management." You will get multiple pages of links.

3.

Time-shifting

For most of us the rare occasions when time seems to stand still are precious. So much so that in retrospect we refer to them as "moments of grace" or "heavenly" and sense that something deep in our psyche and soul yearns for more. One reason that longing is so great is that we usually feel like time is a scarce resource and that we're suffering from a "time famine." The idea that there could be an abundance of this intangible, priceless commodity seems absurd. After all, as we rush from one event in our lives to another, every glance at a clock or our watch is a reminder of how steadfastly time "marches on," "flies by," or "slips away" before running out and disappearing forever. Clearly, such a perception leaves us believing that the maxim "Use it or lose it" applies not only to our brains and muscles, but to time as well. But does that have to be the principle guiding our relationship to time? Hardly.

In this chapter we will show you how to transform the ways in which you relate

---

The paradox of time is that people rarely consider they have enough when,
in fact, all of it is available to everyone.

—JEAN-LOUIS SERVAN-SCHREIBER

Half our life is spent trying to find something to do
with the time we have rushed through life trying to save.

—WILL ROGERS

to, perceive, and use your time. Here you will learn about "time-shifting," a process that:

+ shifts the gears that may be spinning you toward bouts of "time sickness"
+ releases the mounting stress of "time pressure"
+ counters the negative effects that "time stress" can have upon your lifestyle, health, and longevity

As an antidote for time pressure, time sickness, and time stress, time-shifting helps us to feel more balanced because it synchronizes the rhythms in our inner and outer worlds. When we practice using it, we're making a choice of how to respond, actively and positively, to time pressure instead of merely reacting to it either passively or negatively. That's why time-shifting is not a one-time or quick fix. Instead, it helps us to speed up *or* slow down the pace of our lives in response to what's happening around us.

During a wellness workshop at Omega participants discover that the benefits of time-shifting include calm, peace, happiness, and a fullness of life and most return home knowing, firsthand, that every day can be filled with magic moments that have a feeling of timelessness within time. You can too.

Remember learning how to ride a bike? At first it seemed awkward and difficult because you had to concentrate on pedaling, shifting gears, maintaining your balance,

An eternity is any moment opened with patience.

—NOAH BEN SHEA

> Time is but the stream I go a-fishing in.
>
> —HENRY DAVID THOREAU

watching the road ahead, and putting on the brakes. Then, one day, everything changed. Suddenly you and the bike were one. Your muscles "remembered" what they were supposed to do and riding the bike seemed effortless. Instinctively, you pedaled, steered, braked, and felt balanced. And in the days that followed, the conscious awareness that you needed to maneuver the bike faded as you began automatically "reading the road." Gearshifting remained the only action that still required a thoughtful response.

Although time-shifting helps to give us a more balanced view of the world, it's rare that we get to sit back and just roll along on autopilot. Instead, as we focus, mindfully, on the present moment—not the future; not the past—we begin to consciously shift our breath, our thoughts, and other internal gears in order to reconcile the paces at which our inner and outer worlds are moving. In some cases that may mean speeding up in order not to get trampled by those around us. Other times it may mean slowing down long enough to discover whether or not we really want to be marching with the band or to the beat of our own drummer.

If that task seems daunting at first, remember to mix patience in with your perseverance and practice. As you become more conscious of where and how your time is being spent, you'll begin to see that even the smallest shifts, like the one described below, can be a refreshing pause.

For this simple time-shifting technique, think about the way in which you answer the telephone. Ask yourself, "What do I do when this 'time thief' steals me away from whatever else I'm doing? Do I respond to this intrusion? Or do I react?"

Like most of us, you probably *react* to the phone's ring by anxiously grabbing the

> Hurry? I have no time to hurry.
>
> —IGOR STRAVINSKY

receiver as fast as you can. What would it be like, you might ask yourself, if you were to practice what Buddhist monk Thich Nhat Hanh teaches and pause to let your phone ring three times? Most likely, you would soon discover that *response* gives you lots of extra time to make a "time-shift" and take three deep breaths before picking up the receiver. With practice it won't be long before you realize that doing this feels so natural, you are actually relaxed and focused when you finally say "Hello."

Time-shifting and time management are not synonymous. Time-shifting heightens your awareness of time and affords you more time to enjoy your life. Time management programs focus only on doing more in less time—in other words, making your use of time more "efficient." Time management experts teach people how to break up their time into manageable segments. Doing this, according to experts in the field, makes them more efficient, because each piece becomes a miniproject. For those who apportion their time wisely there's a reward—as soon as they complete one project, they're assured there's time for the next one on the list. As a result they can increase productivity and meet goals set by themselves and others.

Not surprisingly, such success can be seductive and easily lure us into believing that there are enormous personal and financial benefits to be gained by working this way. After all, in our culture, time *is* money. However, over time, what most people learn is that the cost to their health versus the promise of this form of increased efficiency, productivity, and on-the-job success may be disproportionately high. That's because time management subtly increases the speed on the treadmill of our lives. As those around us applaud our efforts, we respond by running faster. Like gerbils in

I recommend to you to take care of the minutes;
for hours will take care of themselves.
—LORD CHESTERFIELD

wheels we stay on track and run as fast as we can, until one day, in a state of exhaustion, we succumb to "time sickness." Only then do we finally realize that the real reward for "managing" our time so well was simply getting more to do.

"Time awareness," however, promises a radically different outcome—more time to enjoy your life by *living life in the now*. Think back to our previous discussion of stress. Recall that in the present moment—in the now—there is no time stress or any other kind of stress. We only begin to react to, and even get overcome by, the effects of time pressure from the world when we stuff our feelings down and/or get distracted by "shoulds" that make us feel anxious about the future or guilty about what has happened in the past. However, we can counter those effects by following the basic principles of time-shifting, which include:

- slowing down
- noticing what's happening in our inner and outer worlds, and
- taking time to experience our physical *and* emotional states

The following story about Vicki illustrates the tension between making a choice to be in the present moment and the stress we feel repeatedly when we're not.

Case Study

Every winter Omega sponsors workshops on a Caribbean island. The last leg of the participants' journey to the idyllic tropical island of St. John is on an open-air ferry. Several years ago the ferry got held up because of a schedule change. As the group waited, the sun warmed them and the boat rocked gently. From the deck they could see the lush green island off in the distance. Several people took slow, deep breaths and gazed dreamily at the ocean.

Although most seemed content to just be far away from home or wherever they came from, Vicki didn't. Instead of taking in the ocean air, blue sky, and vast turquoise sea, Vicki was staring straight ahead and repeatedly beating her fists on her knees. She seemed tense and impatient—completely unaware of her extraordinary surroundings. Eventually, one of the leaders went over to her and asked if anything was the matter.

Anxiously, she asked, "When are we going to get there?"

Startled, the leader told her there was no rush because there was no "there." "What could be more beautiful than where we are right now?" he asked. Vicki, however, couldn't see it that way. For her sitting still meant she was wasting precious time and being nonproductive. Like a rolling stone this fast-paced city dweller was not going to gather any moss—even while attending a wellness workshop to find ways to deal with stress in her life.

When we're so fearful that time and tide will wait for no man or woman, we, like Vicki, find it difficult to embrace the present moment and feel at peace, internally, with the world around us. Max Lerner, the twentieth-century intellectual and gadfly, explained, blatantly, the consequences of living our lives that way: "We all run on two clocks. One is the outside clock, which ticks away our decades and brings us ceaselessly to the dry season. The other is the inside clock, where you are your own time-keeper and determine your own chronology, your own internal weather, and your own rate of living. Sometimes the inner clock runs itself out long before the outer one, and you see a dead man going through the motions of living."

As we "mature" and take on the never-ending responsibilities of adulthood, it's so easy for us to forget that as children we were in touch with the flow of time and that it felt natural for us to meander, to pause, to play, and, most important, to be in the present moment. Back then we never worried about stress or whether the rhythms in our inner and outer worlds meshed. Summers seemed endless and childhood, we believed, would last from here to eternity.

For most of us that way of being in the world eroded, quickly, as others imposed

---

For tribal man space was the uncontrollable mystery.
For technological man it is time that occupies that same role.
—MARSHALL McLUHAN

---

their sense of time upon us. Vacations from school were short-lived reprieves from focusing on future success or past failures that were regimented by schedules, the clock, or someone else's priorities for the next hour, day, or week. Time, which once seemed eternal, was now measured, precise, and always running out.

However, that way of being is not the norm everywhere. Reflecting upon the twelve years he lived in a monastery, a place where eternal time is always out of synch with ordinary calendar time, psychotherapist Thomas Moore writes in *Meditations on the Monk Who Dwells in Daily Life*, "In monastic life time is not measured by a clock. The day may be set out according to the parts of Divine Office, a set of psalms and songs chosen according to the remembrance of the day—a saint, a liturgical season, a holy event." He says that such qualities of time are also evoked by chants. For example, sometimes while chanting, monks will land upon a note and sing one syllable of text for fifty notes of chant. It's a time-shift called *melisma.* Moore reflects that if we were to live a melismatic life in imitation of plainchant, we might stop on an experience, a place, a person, or a memory and rhapsodize in imagination. Living our lives one point after another is one form of experience that can be emphatically productive, he concludes. "But stopping for melisma gives the soul its reason for being."

Indeed, today, there are still many places, worldwide, where people like Moore are in the world, but not of it. These are places where native people's lives are not governed by Timex. For them the passage of time is not linear and marching along from one hour to the next, one year to the next, and one millennium to the next. Instead, time is experienced as a natural cycle with cues about what to do when, that come from internal biological clocks and rhythms. By doing what comes naturally to every other species on the earth, indigenous people living outside the boundaries of our industrialized world continue to feel connected to, not distanced from, the flow of the natural world around them.

Take the Machiguenga Indians of Peru as an example. To the Machiguengas, who survive by hunting, gathering, gardening, and fishing, time is circular. There are no fifty-minute hours—only, as the Bible and a once popular song remind us, "a time for every purpose under heaven." Unlike those of us in the "civilized" world, the Machiguengas don't need to look at a watch or calendar to know whether it's still morning or February. Instead, throughout the day, night, seasons, and years, they intuitively shift their rhythms to the beat of the world as they know it. In so doing they

Q: It's easy to talk about the ways in which time affects our minds and bodies, but what about the soul?

A: The soul has its own sense of time as well as its own odd forms of clock and calendar. I've always felt that the sundial and hourglass picture the passage of time in imagistic ways that engage the soul—much more than a quartz or digital clock.

Q: What is the most dangerous quality of our modern notions—perceptions—of time?

A: Its distance from nature. The second hand is running, so we gobble down lunch instead of slowing down to time our meal with the ascendant sun. The workday, we've been told, should run from nine to five instead of in accordance with the natural rhythms of the moon or our own biological clock.

Q: What happens when we "time-shift" in order to become more attuned to those rhythms?

A: We invite more spirit and soul into our lives.

Q: Do you have to remind yourself to do that or does it come naturally?

A: I'm influenced by habit and the society around me. I find that my days can be full of busyness that I didn't initiate, projects that may not be "worth my time," and deadlines that others find more important than I. Sometimes those influences make it difficult to keep the promise that I made to myself to exercise, play, and cut back on travel in order to stay home with my family. When I realize that busyness is a fantasy—a story that I tell myself—it reminds me that life is the gift of time, and time calls for artful attention.

awaken with the rising sun, go to sleep with the waxing and waning moon, and throughout the day respond to the natural world around them in the only moment there is—the present one.

Interestingly, one would think that living this way would never allow enough time for "things" to get done. Yet social scientists John P. Robinson and Geoffrey Godbey report in *Time for Life: The Surprising Ways Americans Use Their Time* that in a study comparing the way in which French men and women and the Machiguengas spent their time, anthropologists discovered that the Peruvian Indians had four more hours of free time a day despite the fact that they had to labor to produce *everything* they consumed. This led the researchers to make two observations:

✦ While modern industry and technology provides us with more goods, those goods don't give us more free time.

✦ The pace of life for the Machiguengas was leisurely and their daily activities never seemed hurried or frenetic.

"Each task was allotted its full measure of time, and free time is not felt to be boring or lost but is accepted as being entirely natural," the anthropologists concluded.

A scientific way to describe what happens to the Machiguengas and other indigenous peoples is to say they become "entrained" or synchronized to the rhythms of the sun, moon, planets, and seasons. To get a hands-on experience of what that shift feels like, put down this book and take a few minutes to relax and listen to one or more favorite pieces of music. While the music plays, don't relegate it to being background "noise." Instead, stay with it and do nothing except listen and observe the ways in which it affects your body and mind.

Can you think of times when you've been so present in the now—so focused on what you were doing—that concentration was effortless and clock time disappeared? Throughout the sports world the experience of the time-shift that produces those exceptional moments is called "the zone"—that state where a runner, for example, is so focused on the movements of his or her body that there's no room for the past or present, only the now.

Psychologist and author Mihaly Csikszentmihalyi, Ph.D., uses the term *flow* to describe the exceptional moments that produce the athlete's experience of "the zone." For religious mystics this experience is called "ecstasy"; for artists or musicians it's "aesthetic rapture." Overall, this time-shift is a total immersion in the moment that can happen while doing anything—reading, singing, dancing, working, playing, rock climbing, folding laundry, gardening, he says in his book *Finding Flow: The Psychology of Engagement with Everyday Life.* Because flow is an experience that usually happens during a favorite activity, it is shared by swamis and plumbers. Rarely do people report having such an experience during passive leisure activities such as watching television.

Csikszentmihalyi surveyed thousands of people to get information about flow. He concludes one in five people report having flow experiences one or more times a day. Fifteen percent say it never happens. Those who experience flow tend to have the following characteristics:

+ A clear set of goals that require appropriate responses. That's why it's easy to be in the "now" while playing sports or "mind games" such as chess. The goals are compatible, clear, and provide immediate feedback.

+ Skills that can overcome manageable challenges. These skills function like a magnet and attract new skills that increase challenges. When challenges are too low, one can engender flow by increasing them. When they're too great, one can return to flow by learning new skills.

+ A habit of doing what needs to be done—even the most routine tasks—with concentrated attention and care.

In 1990, *American Demographics* reported that 32 percent of the participants in the Americans' Use of Time Project said they *always* felt rushed to complete tasks and stressed for time. For the study five thousand people kept diaries in which they recorded all their activities on a single day and said whether they "always," "sometimes," or "almost never" feel rushed to get it all done. In general people aged thirty-five to fifty-four felt the most rushed and classic "Type A" personalities who always cram everything in were most likely to feel time stress.

Most who said they "always" felt rushed spent more hours:

+ working per week than the average person
+ caring for children
+ doing housework than the average person
+ washing and grooming themselves than the average person
+ participating in organizational activities
+ attending cultural events
+ attending sports events and participating in sports activities
+ talking to people face-to-face and on the telephone

and less time:

+ watching television
+ going to parties
+ working on hobbies
+ grocery shopping (than those who felt less stressed)
+ eating than average (especially meals at home)
+ sleeping at night and/or napping
+ just doing nothing

Now ask yourself the following questions:

+ How did you feel inside?

+ Did your body respond automatically and harmoniously to both the tempo and sound?

+ Did you find yourself gently swaying or dancing exuberantly?

+ Was your foot tapping rhythmically or were your hands and arms conducting an imagined orchestra vigorously?

+ Did soothing sounds help to calm the savage beast within? Or did driving sounds provoke that "beast"?

+ What about any joyful sounds you might have heard? Did they "lift" your spirits?

+ Did melancholy sounds stir heartwarming or painful memories of other times; other places?

Although we can't reach out and touch the phenomenon that causes entrainment, we can see it in action by simply placing two out-of-sync pendulum clocks side by side. For a while each will tick and tock at its own pace. However, eventually a "time-shift" takes place as the ticking of one clock enters into the current of the other. Suddenly their movements become synchronized.

More examples of this powerful force that causes our internal rhythms to shift abound in the world around us. For example, since ancient times, medicine men and women called shamans have used drums, other monotonous-sounding instruments, and human voices to synchronize the bodies, minds, and spirits of their tribespeople during healing, battle, or celebration ceremonies. In places of worship such as churches and synagogues the hymns at the beginning of the service do the same as they call in holy spirits and help worshipers shift from ordinary to sacred time. Entrainment is also the reason why women living in college dormitories experience a time-shift in their monthly cycles and begin to menstruate simultaneously.

Sadly, in contemporary society we find it very difficult to follow in our ancestors' footsteps to commune with the bucolic, rhythmic sounds heard throughout the natural world. Instead, we are bombarded and distracted by their replacements—frenetic, demanding noises produced by beepers and other electronic devices that can, at any moment, arrest our attention and make us prisoners to the ticks and tocks of others' clocks. Like parts on an assembly line we succumb to the time pressure that modern technology exerts upon us. "Keep moving," it bellows. And we do—even when it feels counter to the still, small voice in our psyches and souls reminding us that there are other ways to be in the world.

Even after we acknowledge that we can't "do it all," because there isn't enough time, the ingrained perception that we can often lingers. Time-shifting can help reframe that idea by pulling us out of the future and encouraging us to focus on what's happening in the present moment, be it joyful or painful, making us conscious observers of just one life—ours.

Jon Kabat-Zinn, founder of the Stress Reduction Clinic at the University of Massachusetts Medical Center, reminds us that mindfulness means being awake and knowing what you are doing. All too often we go unconscious and fall back into an automatic-pilot mode of unawareness when we begin focusing on what our mind is up to, he writes in his book *Wherever You Go, There You Are*. "These lapses in awareness are frequently caused by an eddy of dissatisfaction with what we are feeling in that moment, out of which springs a desire for something to be different, for things to change."

Time-shifting is a positive way to address that desire for things to be different, for

Try This

Over the next few days, make a list of all the wonders of modern technology at home, at work, and in the world around you that arrest your attention by beeping, buzzing, ringing, and whirring. When the list is complete, ask yourself:

+ Which of these "alarms" can I do without?
+ Which am I willing to give up?

The following transcription appeared in *Time for Life: The Surprising Ways Americans Use Their Time* by John P. Robinson and Geoffrey Godbey. It is from an actual radio interview to determine the amount of time people spent working:

Q: So, for last week, how many hours did you actually work at your main job?

A: I just figured this out for my time card. So, not including that one hour off and the nine hours off I think I worked, like, forty-one and a half, including that time off. So minus nine, is—thirty-two. I think I worked thirty-two and a half—something like that. Okay. Oh, God, and for #@$%*&^, oh, my God. My schedule goes from Thursday to Wednesday. I need to fall back on. Let me do it backwards. Did I work Saturday? Yes, I worked Saturday to Saturday or Saturday to Sunday? Sunday to Saturday. Saturday I worked from—six to ten, and I worked Friday—no, Thursday—yes, I worked twelve to four-thirty. Wednesday—yes I worked—When did I work? I worked five to eleven. And Tuesday, did I work? Nnnooo. Monday, did I work? Na, I volunteer worked that night. No, I didn't work. Sunday did I work? Oh, gosh, Sunday night, November— What day was that? November twenty-fourth. Gosh, did I work that day? I think I may have worked that day— What did I do? I watched the football game? That day I was with a friend all day. I watched the football with XXX. We stayed over there until about—I don't think I did any work that day. So that's four, four and a half, and six, ten and a half—I'll say fourteen and a half hours.

things to change. It awakens us to the fact that as our day moves along, we often feel out of sync with the world around us. Actually, that's not surprising when you consider the fact that most Americans organize their priorities in the following way:

+ work
+ family and children
+ mundane chores
+ social responsibilities
+ ourselves

> Time is a circus always packing up and moving away.
> —BEN HECHT

Clearly, this list suggests that we may, in fact, be out of control because the time we allot for ourselves is at the bottom of the pecking order. If we viewed that list as a food chain, there's no doubt that we're getting gobbled up first. That, of course, raises the question: Why do we put ourselves last on the list?

To answer that question, let's look at two different types of time that operate at varying speeds. One is called "mental time" and the other is "emotional time."

We spend most of our day in mental time during which anywhere from fifteen thousand to fifty thousand thoughts can flow or fly in, around, and out of our heads. Mental time is an important place to be because we need to simultaneously process those thoughts, use or store them, stay on task, and relate to others around us. For example, when you're in mental time, if someone asked you to picture a friend, your

Try This

One reason we find it difficult to be in the present moment is we're tugged and nagged by the past and future. Often the most distracting tugs from the past can be those that remind us of what we *woulda, coulda, or shoulda* been if only we had time.

The following exercise will help you to focus on the present moment better by shifting those distractions out of the past and into the present.

- ◆ Reflect upon the things you wanted, hoped, or planned to do that never happened.
- ◆ Write each of them down.
- ◆ Spend some time looking at your list.
- ◆ Ask yourself: "Do I still really want to do these things or are they just ghosts that haunt me?"

childhood home, a merry-go-round, a yellow sea, and even a pink penguin, you could do so easily and know which were relevant to whatever you were doing at the time.

Emotional time is the counterpart of mental time. We don't enter emotional time through a conscious effort. In other words, if someone told you to *instantly* feel sad or happy or scared, or the way you felt the first time Cupid's arrow struck, you might exclaim that it's impossible to do that. Like an actor who's been told to cry on cue, you'd probably ask for some time out to recall certain events and get in touch with your feelings. That's another way of saying that you needed some space in order to shift from mental time into its counterpart emotional time.

It's probably no surprise that we habitually stay in mental time throughout the day. That's because it functions as a control tower that helps us make decisions, get things done, and recall needed information. But what if an event happens that causes us to feel anger, annoyance, sadness, or loneliness? Stopping to deal with it can interfere with the flow of mental time. Exactly. That's why most of the time the control tower sends a reactive message that tells us to stuff those feelings in order to avoid pain and not lose precious time thinking about those feelings.

For example, just think what happened the last time you got upset with an irritable spouse or angry with a coworker. Did you stop what you were doing to experience your feelings? Or did you push them down deep inside so you could get on with what you were doing? Additionally, when an opportunity to have some peace and quiet finally presented itself, did you sit down by yourself in order to spend emotional time with the painful, annoying, or anxiety-provoking feelings you neglected earlier in the day? Or did you find ways to avoid going there by turning on the television, pouring a drink, or doing the dishes?

If you did whatever was necessary **not** to allow your feelings to resurface so you could reexperience them, take heart, for you're not alone. The urge to resist the discomfort we can feel in emotional time is powerful. A sampling of participants who attended time-shifting and wellness workshops at Omega demonstrated that point when they did the "sitting on a couch" exercise in Chapter 2. Their responses to how it felt included: bored, fearful, apprehensive, unproductive, guilty, sleepy, anxious, restless, morose, antsy, and just plain uncomfortable. Most reported feeling more comfortable as human "doings" than as human "beings" and admitted they wanted to be distracted by the television, the radio, a newspaper, a book, a phone call from some-one, or by housework, schoolwork, or job-related work.

Before reading on, why not flip back to Chapter 2 and see how you responded to those questions. What kind of experience was it for you? Of course, there's no right or wrong answer to that question. Just *your* answer. Yet it does raise another question: What in us wants to act so counter to just "being" with ourselves in one of the ways described in Chapters 4 and 5—especially when it's proven that resisting the present moment causes stress and that showing up allows for lots to happen?

The resistance comes not just because we're in a hyperactive, hyperproductive state so much of the time, but because we rarely get immediate gratification from hanging out with feelings that are disturbing or painful. Ads in the media lead us to falsely believe that if the only time is now, we should never experience pain and there are thou-

Try This

Find a spot in nature where you can sit and be alone for what "feels" like an hour. Take off your watch and put it away. Now, take several slow, deep breaths and begin to use your senses to observe everything around you. As you do ask yourself:

- ✦ How does the air smell?
- ✦ What is the air doing?
- ✦ What does the ground feel like?
- ✦ What sounds do I hear?
- ✦ How do I feel?
- ✦ Can I name my feelings? What are they?

Acknowledge your feelings and thoughts as they come up. Try to stay focused on the present moment as long as you can. Observe thoughts that take you out of it. When you get ready to leave, note how much time has passed. How much time actually passed that *felt* like an hour to you?

sands of ways to resist it. Sadly, the only thing that attitude avoids is the truth that
any and every feeling—pain, joy, sorrow, anger, ecstasy—is like a searchlight that can
illuminate some dark place or ignored part of our mind, body, or spirit.

The great novelist Hermann Hesse once said, "Nothing in the world is more dis-
tasteful to a man than to take the path that leads to himself." When we welcome the
messages our feelings bring us and embrace them the moment they arrive, we begin to
shed light on the only path we can take to go home.

Clearly, we can't always time-shift on the spot in order to stop what we're doing in

"If I Had My Life to Live Over" is just one version of a "generic" story. This one appeared in
a book of the same name and was attributed to Nadine Stair, an eighty-five-year-old woman
from Kentucky. It's a poignant reminder of the fact that when we time-shift we give ourselves a priceless gift.

> I'd dare to make more mistakes next time. I'd relax, I would limber up. I would be
> sillier than I have been this trip. I would take fewer things seriously. I would take more
> chances. I would climb more mountains and swim more rivers. I would eat more ice
> cream and less beans. I would perhaps have more actual troubles, but I'd have fewer
> imaginary ones.
>
> You see, I'm one of those people who live sensibly and sanely hour after hour, day
> after day. Oh, I've had my moments, and if I had it to do over again, I'd have more of
> them. In fact, I'd try to have nothing else. Just moments, one after another, instead of
> living so many years ahead of each day. I've been one of those persons who never goes
> anywhere without a thermometer, a hot water bottle, a raincoat, and a parachute. If I
> had to do it again, I would travel lighter than I have.

mental time and sit quietly with our feelings in emotional time. However, the next time you become aware that you are stuffing a feeling instead of being with it, use a moment or two of your mental time to acknowledge that emotional time. Then commit yourself to returning that call in a "timely" manner later in the day.

The difficulty we may have switching from mental time into emotional time raises the question of how to begin time-shifting wherever you are, whenever you become aware that you're not living in the now. Here are a few tips:

- by remembering that time-shifting is a variation on the Buddhist theme of mindfulness that you will explore in the next chapter

- by making a commitment to yourself to gradually and patiently incorporate one or more of the following time-shifting techniques into your life

- by remembering that Buddhists call mindfulness a practice, and time-shifting is a practice that will take practice

You can also begin time-shifting by experimenting with some of the techniques and exercises below or coming up with and experimenting with ideas that are uniquely yours.

- **Set boundaries.** How often do you make short appointments with yourself that allow you to segue from the pace of one activity into another or from mental time into emotional time? Blocking out some time for yourself creates boundaries that keep others out and give you time to refresh or recharge yourself. In order to begin experiencing the benefits of these appointments or "dates," it's important that you try to make one at the same time every day. Look at creative ways to adjust your daily routine so you have time to read a trashy novel, walk, play, exercise, take a bubble bath or even a nap. Can you get up a little earlier in the morning to meditate, journal a dream, or muse? Might you consider getting to work fifteen minutes early to relax or stopping at a park on the way home to mark the transition from work to home life? One participant in an Omega workshop decided she would no longer race into the house after work to cook, care for the kids, and catch up with her husband's day. Now when she pulls into the driveway, she sits in the car for at least ten minutes. Everyone knows this is her time and doesn't bother her.

+ **Use ritual.** Historically, monks and mystics have taught us that participating in rituals can be one of the most effective ways of time-shifting. In their religious communities they use music, prayer, chanting, beads, incense, bells, and food to engage the senses and evoke a sense of timeless mystery that causes a shift from ordinary to sacred time. You can make that time-shift too. Moreover, your rituals don't have to be elaborate. Worldwide, people time-shift by meditating or praying upon awakening in the A.M. or retiring in the P.M. A variation on those rituals would be to contemplate a random passage from the Bible or the I Ching or to pick a rune or some other oracle. Visiting a spiritual community, attending religious services, or participating in a drumming circle are other ways to experience the time-shifting benefits of ritual. You can even use ritual as a way to periodically time-shift during your workday. Begin by putting a favorite picture, rock, shell, crystal, fossil, or just a single flower on your desk. When, in the midst of your busyness, your eye catches your relic or icon, take a moment to contemplate something beautiful that sits before you in the present moment. Or put a small chime on your desk and periodically stop what you're doing to tap it. Breathe deeply while you listen to its sound going off into the universe. Follow Thich Nhat Hanh's recommendation to smile each time you breathe out.

+ **Honor the mundane.** What's mundane for a skydiver might be thrilling for someone taking her first plane ride. Ask yourself what's mundane in your life. Too often we judge the value of our time in terms of how much we've accomplished by other people's standards. In reality, ironing, washing dishes, sweeping the floor, weeding the garden, and every other act that you might call "mundane" can be meditative acts. That's because when we fully engage in the act of *mowing* the lawn instead of just cutting the grass, we're apt to experience the sensation of being outside of time. Try giving a "mundane" daily activity—brushing your teeth, combing your hair, slicing and dicing vegetables, et cetera—your full attention. See if this concentration changes not only your perception of time but the activity as well.

+ **Be spontaneous.** Remember shouting "Yeah!" when you heard it was a snow day and school was canceled? That's because you didn't know about it in advance—it was so "in the moment" that suddenly you felt you had more time to enjoy your life. Though you weren't aware of it, you immediately began time-shifting. Were those snow days the last time you can remember having "spontaneous" time? If so, consider giving yourself permission to occasionally have a snow day. You don't have to do something outrageous—although you could. You don't even have to take a whole day. Spontaneous time can last for a few moments, a day, a weekend, or a week or more. It may mean getting in the car and letting the car take you where it wants to go. It could also mean calling in to work for a "personal day," not to get things done but to get "undone." Perhaps it's as simple as opening the telephone book to "Restaurants," closing your eyes, and going to one your finger lands on. You get the idea. Now—as the popular ad says—"Just do it!"

+ **Take care of yourself.** If you're reading this book, you have a desire to do that. But once again we ask the question: How often do you take care of you by putting yourself first? Can you say no to others' requests and demands for your time? Do you get run down running around for others? Sometimes you can't say no, but you can time-shift when saying yes raises your anxiety. Try taking some deep breaths between the request to do something and the next thing you have to do. If you feel like you're giving all your time away and saving none for yourself, ask: What needs to change and where and how can I consciously begin time-shifting to make that happen?

+ Time Retreats—as explained in Chapter 5.

In *The Art of Time,* Jean-Louis Servan-Schreiber suggests that if we want to find more time, we should try falling back in love with our lives. He reminds us that no matter how full life seems to be, when we fall in love we feel completely willing to devote hours to the new relationship.

> For everything there is a season, and a time for every purpose under heaven.
>
> —ECCLESIASTES 3:1

Describing what typically happens to those in love, Servain-Schreiber says, "You found yourself making long telephone calls several times a day, dreaming of the image of the other person, walking together aimlessly through the streets, leaving work early." You had time for all that, he explains, because "you canceled what had suddenly become less important and gratifying." In other words, your priorities changed so you reordered them. You discovered that time could shift, could be flexible, and that you had some to spare.

Whether each of us will ever feel like we have enough time is a choice. When we choose to time-shift in order to synchronize our bodies, minds, and spirits with the present moment, our perception of time changes in response. We no longer feel as though we're suffering from a time famine. Instead, we feel less fearful and anxious and begin to see the world through a new lens—one that focuses on the many ways in which we can joyfully create more time to enjoy our lives now.

✍   RESOURCES   *✍*

BOOKS

Hanh, Thich Nhat. *Peace Is Every Step: The Path of Mindfulness in Everyday Life.* New York: Bantam Books, 1992.

Kabat-Zinn, Jon. *Wherever You Go, There You Are.* New York: Hyperion, 1994.

Moore, Thomas.

    Care of the Soul. New York: HarperCollins, 1994.

    Meditations: On the Monk Who Dwells in Daily Life. New York: HarperCollins, 1994.

Rechtschaffen, Stephan, M.D. *Time Shifting: Creating More Time to Enjoy Your Life.* New York: Doubleday, 1996.

Servan-Schreiber, Jean-Louis. *The Art of Time.* Reading, MA: Addison-Wesley Publishing Company, Inc. 1988 (out of print).

AUDIOTAPES

Dass, Ram. *Spiritual Practices and Perspectives for Daily Life.* Louisville, CO: Sounds True (800-333-9185).

Moore, Thomas. *Soul Life.* Louisville, CO: Sounds True (800-333-9185).

Rechtschaffen, Stephan, M.D. *Time Shifting: Creating More Time to Enjoy Your Life.* New York: Bantam Doubleday Dell Audio Publishing, 1996.

4.

Meditation 101 and Other Healthful Practices

What do prisoners in a maximum-security facility, high school students in an inner-city classroom, a support group for women with breast cancer, white-collar executives at a *Fortune* 500 company, monks in monasteries, and students in a wellness workshop at Omega have in common? If the chapter title tipped you off and your answer is that these diverse people all meditate, you're right. Because they meditate, they also share several traits. These include:

+ the motivation to make positive, creative, and healing changes in their lives

+ a commitment to risk reaching in, not out, to touch and foster the growth, creativity, and serenity of their minds, bodies, spirits, and emotions

---

Underneath the superficial self, which pays attention to this and that, there is
another self more really *us* than *I*. And the more you become aware of the
unknown self—if you become aware of it—the more you realize that
it is inseparably connected with everything else that is.

—ALAN WATTS

Many Westerners consider meditation to be a complex, mysterious modality shrouded in an Eastern cloak. Actually, we're more familiar with it than we think. For example, while meditation is not a religion, almost every religion—including Judaism, Islam, and Christianity—teaches a particular variation on the theme (even if they don't call it "meditation"). And while meditation can't be purchased or popped like a pill, more and more doctors are prescribing it to their patients. And although some advanced practices require one to sit for hours at a time, many of the healthful benefits of meditating can be reaped by taking just a few moments to quiet one's mind and b-r-e-a-t-h-e.

The following informal "meditation" helps Omega participants to be more in touch with the process of eating. It is based upon an exercise that Jon Kabat-Zinn uses in his stress-reduction program at the University of Massachusetts Medical Center.

Take just one raisin and bring your full attention to seeing that raisin. Observe it carefully, curiously, as though you have never seen a raisin before. Feel its texture and notice its color and surfaces.

Be aware of any thoughts you are having about raisins as you do this. Do you have thoughts of either liking or disliking raisins?

Smell the raisin for a few moments and then, with awareness, bring it to your lips. Be aware of your arm moving your hand and of salivating as the mind and body prepare for eating.

Take the raisin into your mouth but don't bite into it. Feel its texture with your tongue and move it around other parts of your mouth.

Now bite into it and chew it slowly enough to experience the taste of just one raisin. Notice the process of chewing, the movement of the tongue and the teeth.

When the desire or impulse to swallow the raisin arises, be aware of that as the raisin leaves your mouth.

Imagine or "sense" that your body is now one raisin heavier.

Jot down some of your thoughts about eating a raisin mindfully—from moment to moment.

A Zen saying goes like this: If you find something boring after two minutes, try it for four. If it's still boring after four minutes, try it for eight. If it's still boring, try it for sixteen, thirty-two, sixty-four, et cetera. Eventually, one will discover that it's not boring after all—that it is interesting.

If meditation is a road not yet taken, spend a few moments mulling over your reasons. At Omega some people say they tried a class and found it boring. Others comment that it seemed too difficult. A few confess that the idea of meditating scares them. Many say they just haven't gotten around to it or doubted they'd stick to it. Maybe you have similar reasons, or maybe you haven't even come to a sign pointing you in that direction.

In the pages that follow, we will help to demystify meditation so that you can get a better understanding of its healthful and healing benefits and, perhaps, begin to see *your* path with new eyes. Furthermore, because not everyone sees things or benefits

If meditating is not a part of your lifestyle, rest assured that you are not alone. Despite the fact that every year more and more studies prove that meditation is a healthful practice in our busy time-consumed lives, meditation is usually not on our to-do lists until a really good reason comes along to discover how balanced and peaceful we can get doing it.

For some people who now meditate, many of their "good" reasons for getting started were rooted in the fact that they were feeling "bad" mentally, emotionally, physically, and/or spiritually. For example:

+ They felt stressed out, burned out, or just out of it no matter what "it" happened to be, before learning that meditation could help reduce their stress, anxiety, depression, irritability; improve mental functioning, increase stamina, and restore balance to their lives.

+ They suffered from intractable pain, hypertension, heart disease, or asthma before learning that scientific studies concluded that meditation could help them to gain a measure of control over their condition.

> Mr. Duffy lived a short distance from his body.
>
> —JAMES JOYCE

from them in the same way, we will also briefly discuss related practices such as guided imagery and affirmations. In so doing, may this chapter become one of those practical tools and resources that can help you to expand *your* vision for optimal health and well-being and then make it a reality.

When Jon Kabat-Zinn wrote his best-selling how-to book on a practice called "mindfulness," he picked the title *Wherever You Go, There You Are.* For him it was a way to remind readers that wherever we are on this journey called life, the only moment we have is this one. All too easily we go about our lives as if forgetting, momentarily, that "we are *here,* where we already are, and that we are *in* what we are already in," he observes. "In every moment, we find ourselves at the crossroads of here and now. But when the cloud of forgetfulness over where we are now sets in, in that very moment we get lost. 'Now what?' becomes a real problem." At those times we lose contact with our deepest potentials for learning, growth, and creativity and our *modus operandi* becomes robotlike. When that happens, he warns, "we must be careful not to allow those clouded moments to stretch out and become most of our lives." The antidote to moving through life shrouded in a fog is to pay more attention to the present moment—the only time in which we can live, feel, grow, and change. Meditation, Kabat-Zinn teaches, can help us do that, because it is "simply about being yourself and knowing something about who that is. It is about coming to realize that you are on a path whether you like it or not, namely, the path that is your life."

Although you may not be confined to a cell in a maximum-security prison like the group of meditators mentioned earlier, that doesn't mean that you're not doing time. Day after day any of us may feel imprisoned by the ways in which our inner and outer worlds impact our lives. When our bodies hurt, or we can't forgive ourselves or others,

> Know who you are and do it on purpose.
>
> —DOLLY PARTON

the pain can hold us hostage. When worries and fear flood us with panic and doubt diminishes our confidence, we may feel sentenced to a dismal future. And when a lack of time stresses us to the max, we may truly feel under the gun.

Perhaps no one knows that laundry list better than journalist Larry Bratt, who received a double life sentence in a Maryland correctional facility for murdering two people. In an article for *Natural Health* magazine titled "Doing Time—Inside the

You have to trust your inner knowing. If you have a clear mind and an open heart,
you won't have to search for direction. Direction will come to you.

—PHIL JACKSON

Mind," Bratt, the author of over fifty other articles that he's published from prison, confesses that shortly after his incarceration he felt suicidal. Only by chance did he discover that a combination of yoga, meditation, and self-expression through writing could become a lifeline that would save him from the depths of despair and despondency. For example, the more he practiced meditation, the more his practice became a vehicle that was leading him to the images and memories he would later write about. One such image was that his life resembled an onion and that his practices were the implements that peeled away one layer after another to expose what lay underneath. Patiently, as he worked his way down to core issues that had driven him to commit murder, Bratt could plainly see what in his past caused him to make "so many wrong choices." He sums up his discoveries with a quote by Swami Vishnu-devananda:

> When body, mind, and soul are healthy and harmonious, the higher mind can easily triumph over the vicious instinctive lower mind. Obstacles become stepping-stones to success, and life is a school for the development of character, compassion, and realization of the Divine All-pervading Self.

According to Wes Nisker, a renowned lecturer on Buddhist meditation, Bratt's experience is a common one for those who meditate regularly. "As meditators go inside to explore and experience the nature of their bodies and minds, the insights slowly begin to seep into the marrow of their being (perhaps resetting what the neuroscientists call the resonating neuronal assemblies)," he writes. "What is discovered and per-

God, grant me the serenity to accept the things I cannot change, the courage to change
the things I can, and the wisdom to know the difference.

—REINHOLD NIEBUHR

> Be a light unto yourself.
>
> —THE BUDDHA

ceived is finally 'realized,' a word used by many spiritual traditions to mean that one is starting to live and experience life according to his or her deepest understanding."

Today, after almost two decades behind bars, Bratt believes meditation and writing remain "keys" to his personal freedom that continually open doors that expand his view of "changes for the better."

Acknowledging that he will probably spend the remainder of his life behind bars, yet sounding like one who has been recently liberated, Bratt concludes: "I am convinced that I have changed. I feel like a lighthouse keeper. I hope that by sharing my experiences I can act like a beacon, guiding others safely through some of life's treacherous shoals. And I pray every night that my efforts might make it easier for somebody else to deal with his or her own struggles."

What struggles do you deal with? What casts you onto treacherous shoals, leaving you searching for a beacon to guide you to safety? Is it physical or emotional pain; endless worries about the future; guilt about the past, or the tension of living with the question "Is this all there is?" Do your struggles tend to be petty annoyances, soap operas, or big-screen blockbusters? And as you struggle, do you tend to endlessly mull the problems, options, possible solutions, and "what if" scenarios in your head? What does this chatter and self-talk sound like? Perhaps it's an ongoing sermon in your head filled with judgments, shoulds, and mustn'ts concerning school, work, kids, parents, problems, and so forth and so on. When you can actually tune in to that

Reflection

What in your world imprisons you? Your job? Responsibilities to your family? An addiction? Anxiety attacks? A chronic or life-threatening illness? A painful experience from your past? Take a few moments to ponder that question and then make a list of what you believe incarcerates you. Then date and sign it.

> Look inward, thou art Buddha.
>
> *—THE BOOK OF THE GOLDEN PRECEPTS*

inner din, whose voice do you actually hear? Is it always yours? Or do other judgmental voices belonging to your parents, siblings, friends, teachers, children, relatives, bosses, or a spouse rise up?

When our inner voice helps us to judge a situation by presenting us with wisdom and options for determining the cost and benefit, pros and cons, of making particular choices, it's constructive. However, at other times, when that same voice acts like a critical nag, it can actually be destructive. For example, when you finally get to the part of your day when you might have nothing to do, does the chatter inside your head get busy reminding you how you need to be much ado about "something"? From the time many of us wake up in the morning, an unthrottled inner voice commands the driver's seat. As we travel from one obligation it tells us we *should* meet to another, we add more things to do, places to be, people to see, and other "stuff" to our already busy lives. All too often many of us find that as days whiz by and sleepless nights seem to get longer, we feel stressed, out of control, or even depressed. "Will I ever get done all that nagging, complaining voice tells me I *should* get done?" we wonder.

Unrestrained, it becomes a cycle, perpetuating itself day in and out. Those of us caught in it awaken in the morning and in our rush to do all we must in the hours remaining we immediately and unconsciously begin stuffing away:

- feelings we don't want to deal with

- worries about how to deal with and do all the stuff we've taken on

- anxieties about when and if all our stuff can get done, and

- questions and doubts about whether the stuff we're stuffing or we, ourselves, are the right stuff

> A day spent judging another is a painful day. A day spent judging yourself is a painful day.
> You don't have to believe your judgments; they're simply an old habit.
>
> —THE BUDDHA

If that sounds like a frenetic, unbalanced way to be in relationship to yourself, you're right. Our survival as a species calls for us to take time out to intentionally reflect on our actions and deeds and become consciously aware of our innermost thoughts and feelings. For example, most world religions call for a day of rest, or sabbath. Traditionally, the word *sabbath* suggests a complete, twenty-four-hour work stoppage during which we table our toils. Once free of the labors of our lives, we are called to rest, relax, reflect, reduce stress, and restore a sense of balance by

George Carlin, the comedian, once posed the question, "If you had all the stuff in the world, where would you put it?"

Make a list of all the stuff you stuff into your life on a typical weekday. Include activities, people, and even any self-talk that regularly takes up space. Look over your list. Now ask yourself: How much of this stuff is really important?

Looking at your list, put a *p* next to items that make a positive contribution to your health, happiness, and survival; put an *n* next to anything that has a negative impact. If you're not sure, jot down a question mark and let it be.

Look at your list of *n*'s and see if you can trace some of your negative stuff back to its origins by asking yourself:

+ Where does this stuff come from? (i.e., a person, place, thing)

+ Why do I own it right now?

+ Was my choice to take it on a conscious choice?

+ Now that I have this stuff, do I really want it?

reestablishing touch with a higher power, who may get lost, forgotten, or unconsciously put on hold in all our busyness. Meditation—both religious and nonreligious—can be a way to fulfill our ancient and innate longing for a sabbath without having to take an entire day to be in that space.

However, as Daniel Goleman points out in his book *The Meditative Mind*, it's important not to confuse meditation and relaxation. While the most common use of meditation is as a quick-and-easy relaxation technique, it's not the same thing as relaxation. Echoing others, Goleman points out that at its core meditation is the effort to retrain attention. "This gives meditation its unique cognitive effects such as increasing the meditator's concentration and empathy." In turn, these effects contribute to the meditator's ability to:

+ gain access to otherwise blocked memories and feelings
+ use meditation as a general prescription for handling garden-variety stress, and
+ reduce the severity of hypertension and the frequency of colds, headaches, and a whole host of stress-related illnesses

If that makes meditation sound like good medicine, you're right. James Gordon, M.D., author of *Manifesto for a New Medicine* and director of the Center for Mind/Body Medicine in Washington, D.C., reminds us that the word *meditation* comes from the same Greek and Latin roots as *medicine* and words meaning "to take one's measure." Gordon explains that in indigenous societies, physicians were and still are spiritual guides as well as a temporal healers who customarily prescribe meditative techniques. He also admits that over the years it has become a vital and integral part of his medical practice. "It provides a physiological and psychological 'time out.' It is also something more: a direct route to the awareness that helps us make the deep change that is necessary for healing."

Finally, psychologist and meditation teacher Jack Kornfield notes that meditation is not *just* a practice for awakening a clear mind. It is also a practice for reaching into a wise and open heart that can that guide us to our original or Buddha nature. In *A Path with Heart*, Kornfield writes:

Many of the great sorrows of the world arise when the mind is disconnected from the heart. In meditation we can reconnect with our heart and discover an inner sense of spaciousness, unity, and compassion underneath all the conflicts of thought. The heart allows for the stories and ideas, the fantasies and fears, of the mind without believing in them, without having to follow them or having to fulfill them. When we touch beneath all the busyness of thought, we discover a sweet, healing silence, an inherent peacefulness in each of us, a goodness of heart, strength, and wholeness that is our birthright.

Although Kornfield's particular practice is grounded in the precepts of **Theravada Buddhism,** which he studied in Burma, Thailand, and India, he teaches that all forms of meditation are to be viewed as an "art" that can help you to:

+ relax and remain alert in the midst of the problems and the joys of life

+ rest in the moment with ease

+ pay respectful attention to your body

+ move through life wakefully, with your whole body, heart, and mind together in harmony

+ evoke a loving-kindness and friendliness toward oneself and others

+ bring wisdom and joy alive in your life

+ awaken the best of your spiritual human capacities

+ forgive yourselves and others and, in so doing, ease the burden of pain in your heart

+ hold and transform the sorrows of life into a great stream of compassion

By now you may be saying "All this information gives me good reasons to think seriously about meditating. But how do I get started?"

Begin by remembering a time when you were totally riveted on a blazing sunset, mesmerized by a glowing candle, captivated by a tank full of fish, absorbed in just being, not doing, focused on the patter of raindrops on a windowsill, or so immersed in a mundane activity like polishing a doorknob that nothing else mattered. Although

> If an Arab in the desert were suddenly to discover a spring in his tent, and so would always
> be able to have water in abundance, how fortunate he would consider himself; so too,
> when a man who . . . is always turned toward the outside, thinking that his happiness
> lies outside him, finally turns inward and discovers that the source is within him.
>
> —SØREN KIERKEGAARD

you were probably far from a specific place set aside for meditating, you were, in fact, in a state similar to that experienced by meditators. In those moments you were *awake* in the classic Buddhist sense of the word. You were, in Kabat-Zinn's words, "an eternal witness"—one who was watching the moment without trying to change it at all.

According to Victor N. Davich, the author of *The Best Guide to Meditation,* "*Awake* as used by the Buddha does not simply mean alert. *Awake* means a new, more joyous, enriching and happier way of being. As the powerful sun of clarity burns off our individual fog of delusion, we find ourselves in a new, bright, happier place where the sun always shines. Moreover, meditation helps us connect with the universe in a new way."

For that reason Davich, a meditator, attorney, creative consultant, and movie producer for Paramount, Fox, and Universal studios, suggests writing out a simple definition of meditation and putting copies wherever you post memos—on your bathroom mirror, your refrigerator, your computer monitor, et cetera. The one he uses is:

Meditation is the art of opening to each moment with calm awareness.

However, he also encourages you to write out your own definition, since the only way to understand what meditation means is to meditate. He also advises developing a meditation practice slowly in order to avoid our national tendency to "plunge into new activities with a gung-ho, take-no-prisoners attitude." While meditation is not hard to learn and is accessible to everyone, Davich cautions us to also remember that it is a skill and, therefore, cannot be mastered overnight.

The very presence of Thich Nhat Hanh is often a reminder that you don't have to be sitting on the floor like a cross-legged yogi or even on a chair to meditate. For ex-

Before you read on, why not pause to take a moment to do this exercise that can help you get out of the doing mode and into the being mode. It is based upon Kabat-Zinn's teachings in Wherever You Go, There You Are:

+ *Think of yourself as an eternal witness, as timeless.*

+ *Just watch the moment. Don't try to change it at all.*

+ *What is going on?*

+ *What do you see?*

+ *What do you feel?*

+ *What do you hear?*

+ *Throughout the day, try stopping, sitting down, and occasionally becoming aware of your breathing.*

+ *Just breathe and let go.*

+ *Again, don't try to change anything—give yourself permission to allow this moment to be exactly as it is and you as you are.*

ample, do you remember the story in the introduction to this book about Thich Nhat Hanh teaching a walking meditation to a group of retreatants in the garden at Omega? With each step it seemed that this gentle Vietnamese monk "kissed the earth." Hear what he has to say about what he experiences during a walking meditation:

I like to walk alone on country paths, rice plants and wild grasses on both sides, putting each foot down on the earth in mindfulness, knowing that I walk on the wondrous earth. In such moments existence is a miraculous and mysterious reality. People usually consider walking on water or in thin air a miracle. But I think the real miracle is not to walk either on water or in thin air, but to walk on earth. Every day we are engaged in a miracle which we don't even recognize; a blue sky, white clouds, green leaves, the black, curious eyes of a child, our own two eyes. All is a miracle.

Reflections on Meditation

Bernie Siegel, M.D., author of *Love, Medicine & Miracles* and *Peace, Love, & Healing:* Someone once said, "Prayer is talking, meditation is listening." Actually, it's a method by which we can temporarily *stop* listening to the pressures and distractions of everyday life and thereby be able to acknowledge other things—our deeper thoughts and feelings, the products of our unconscious mind, the peace of pure consciousness, and spiritual awareness. I know of no other single activity that by itself can produce such a great improvement in the quality of life.

Joan Borysenko, Ph.D., author of *The Power of the Mind to Heal: Minding the Body, Mending the Mind,* and *Guilt Is the Teacher, Love Is the Lesson:* So what is meditation? Essentially, it's about being spacious and bringing the mind home. Meditation is a type of mental martial arts training in which we learn to sidestep the ego and its incessant judging. Every time you let go and return to your concentration, the mental muscles of awareness and choice are being exercised. Remarkably, even when most of a meditation exercise is spent thinking, beneficial bodily changes still occur. I think of that as a sort of grace. Even the intention to let go produces a near magical result.

Dean Ornish, M.D., author of *Dr. Dean Ornish's Program for Reversing Heart Disease:* The *concept* of meditation is very simple. Anyone can do it. The *practice* of meditation can be very challenging, though, because it is not very easy to quiet one's own mind. You cannot force your mind to be quiet, any more than you can smooth out the waves in a tray of water by running your hand across its surface. And if you look at your reflection in a disturbed tray of water, then your face looks distorted. You don't have to do anything to smooth out the waves other than to stop disturbing them. When you do, then you can see your true self more clearly in the reflection. Similarly, meditation doesn't smooth out the disturbances in your life, as a tranquilizer might. Meditation allows you to go deeper, to where the disturbances begin. It helps you become more aware of how your mind becomes agitated and gives you more control to stop these disturbances. It doesn't *bring* you peace, for the peace is already there once you stop disturbing it.

Jon Kabat-Zinn, Ph.D., author of *Wherever You Go, There You Are* and *Full Catastrophe Living* and founder and director of the Stress Reduction Clinic at the University of Massachusetts Medical Center: It's not anything exotic. Meditation just has to do with paying attention in a particular way. That's something we're all capable of doing. One way to look at meditation is as a kind of intrapsychic technology that's been developed over thousands of years by traditions that know a lot about the body/mind connection. The mind that has not been developed or trained is very scattered. That's the normal state of affairs, but it leaves us out of touch with a great deal in life, including our bodies.

Stephen Levine, author of *Gradual Awakening; Guided Meditations, Explorations, and Healings; Who Dies;* and *One Year to Live:* Meditation is a means to an endlessness. It allows us to directly experience our true nature—the ever-healed, the unconditioned, the deathless. From that unimaginable vastness and clarity comes the peace and wisdom that we so long for. The space to accept ourselves "as is" and recognize our enormous power for healing, which is our birthright. Meditation allows us to directly participate in our lives instead of living life as an afterthought.

Sharon Salzberg, author of *Lovingkindness: The Revolutionary Art of Happiness* and founder of the Insight Meditation Society in Barre, Massachusetts: Freeing ourselves from the illusion of separation allows us to live in a natural freedom rather than be driven by preconceptions about our own boundaries and limitations. The Buddha described the spiritual path that leads to this freedom as "the liberation of the heart which is love," and he taught a systematic, integrated path that moves the heart out of isolating contraction into true connection. That path is still with us as a living tradition of meditation practices that cultivate love, compassion, sympathetic joy, and equanimity. These four qualities are among the most beautiful and powerful states of consciousness we can experience. . . . By practicing these meditations, we establish love, compassion, sympathetic joy, and equanimity as our home.

Thich Nhat Hanh, author of *The Miracle of Mindfulness* and *Being Peace*: Why should you meditate? First of all, because each of us needs to realize total rest. Even a night of sleep doesn't provide total rest. Twisting and turning, the facial muscles tense, all the while dreaming—hardly rest! Nor is lying down rest when you still feel restless and twist and turn. Lying on your back, with your arms and legs straight but not stiff, your head unsupported by a pillow—this is a good position to practice breathing and to relax all the muscles; but this way it is also easier to fall asleep. You cannot go as far in meditation lying down as by sitting. It is possible to find total rest in a sitting position, and in turn to advance deeper in meditation in order to resolve the worries and troubles that upset and block your consciousness.

Venerable Henepola Gunaratana, author of *Mindfulness in Plain English* and president of the Bhavana Society in the Shenandoah Valley of West Virgina: The purpose of meditation is personal transformation. The you that goes in one side of the meditation experience is not the same you that comes out the other side. It changes your character by a process of sensitization, by making you deeply aware of your own thoughts, words, and deeds. Your arrogance evaporates and your antagonism dries up. Your mind becomes still and calm. And your life smooths out. Thus meditation properly performed prepares you to meet the ups and downs of existence. It reduces your tension, your fear, and your worry. Restlessness recedes, and passion moderates. Things begin to fall into place and your life becomes a glide instead of a struggle. All of this happens through understanding.

With each step Thich Nhat Hanh practices what he calls not just "mindfulness" but "the miracle of mindfulness." The instructions upon which he bases the practice that he teaches come from **sutras**—ancient discourses that contain the teachings of the Buddha.

The original sutras were first published five hundred years after the Buddha's death. In his workshops, Thich Nhat Hanh refers to a collection of seventeen-hundred-year-old sutras that teach sixteen methods of using one's breath to maintain mindfulness.

The secret of happiness . . . is to be in harmony with existence, to be always calm, always lucid, always willing to be joined to the universe without being more conscious of it than an idiot, to let each wave of life wash us a little farther up the shore.

—CYRIL CONNOLLY

He reports that everyone in a Buddhist monastery studies these precepts and learns to use his or her breath as a tool to stop mental dispersion and build concentration power. Concentration power, he explains, is the strength that comes from mindfulness and is one of the things that can help one to obtain the Great Awakening.

"We must be conscious of each breath, each movement, every thought and feeling, everything which has any relation to ourselves," Thich Nhat Hanh says. He emphasizes that we should know how to breathe to maintain mindfulness, because

Meditation brings "the scattered mind back home," according to Lama Sogyal Rinpoche, author of *The Tibetan Book of Living and Dying*. He explains that mindfulness, which is called "Peacefully Remaining" or "Calm Abiding" in Tibetan Buddhism, can accomplish this three ways:

First—
The fragmented aspects of ourselves, which have been in conflict, dissolve and become friends. As a result, we begin to understand ourselves more and even have glimpses of our fundamental nature.

Second—
The practice of mindfulness diffuses our negativity, turbulent emotions, and aggression. At the same time, it also fosters acceptance and generosity of any thoughts or emotions that arise. Consequently, we begin to feel well, which leads to a feeling of release and self-healing.

Third—
Mindfulness unveils our essential "Good Heart" because any unkindness or harm in us is dissolved. This allows our real nature—fundamental goodness and kindness—to shine through. In turn, this leads to the true practice of nonaggression and nonviolence.

> Wisdom is intuitive knowledge of the mind of love and clarity that lies beneath one's ego-driven anxieties and aggressions. Meditation is going into the mind to see this for yourself—over and over again, until it becomes the mind you live in. Morality is bringing it back out in the way you live.
>
> —GARY SNYDER

breathing is a natural and extremely effective tool which can prevent dispersion. "Breath is the bridge which connects life to consciousness, which unites your body to

Early in the meditation sessions that Thich Nhat Hanh teaches, he introduces a method called "following the length of the breath." Here are a few suggestions from his workshop at Omega and book *The Miracle of Mindfulness:*

Lie down on a mat or blanket on the floor. Keep your arms loosely at your sides. Don't prop your head on a pillow.

When you inhale allow the stomach to rise. At the beginning of the breath the stomach begins to push out, but after you take in about two thirds of the breath, the stomach will start to lower again.

Focus your attention on your exhalation and count how long it lasts, 1, 2, 3, 4, 5 . . .

When you get to 5 (or whatever number), instead of inhaling try to extend the exhalation by one or two counts more to empty your lungs of more air.

Pause for a moment to let your lungs take in fresh air on their own. The inhalation will be "shorter" than the exhalation.

Keep a steady count in your mind and measure both. Try using a clock with a loud tick to keep track of the length of those breaths.

Instead of using numbers, you can also use phrases with a certain number of words.

Also measure your breath while doing other things—walking, sitting, standing.

Stop at once if you feel tired during your practice.

your thoughts. Whenever your mind becomes scattered, use your breath as the means to take hold of your mind again."

Thich Nhat Hanh also recommends that we practice smiling while meditating. "During walking meditation, during kitchen and garden work, during sitting meditation, all day long, we can practice smiling," he says in *Being Peace*. "Smiling means that we are ourselves, that we have sovereignty over ourselves, that we are not drowned into forgetfulness. This is the kind of smile that can be seen on the faces of Buddhas and **Bodhisattvas**."

If you wonder where you might find the time to practice meditation, think about using some of the spaces in your life when you rob yourself of the present moment by worrying about the future. What if you were to look at that pause in your day's occupation as an opportunity to breathe mindfully and let the corners of your mouth curl up in a smile? What are other opportunities? A traffic jam? A red light? A doctor's waiting room (it is, after all, called a "waiting" room)? A long line at the supermarket? In the morning when you stare into the bathroom mirror?

Lama Sogyal Rinpoche, in *The Tibetan Book of Living and Dying*, says:

> *Everything can be used as an invitation to meditation. A smile, a face in the subway, the sight of a small flower growing in the crack of a cement pavement, a fall of rich cloth in a shop window, the way the sun lights up flowerpots on a windowsill. Be alert for any sign of beauty or grace. Offer up every joy, be awake at all moments to "the news that is always arriving out of silence" (Rainer Maria Rilke).*

Benjamin Franklin once said, "Observe all men; thyself most." Of course, he wasn't the only one to express a variation on that theme. For example, Leo Tolstoy said, "Everybody thinks of changing humanity and nobody thinks of changing himself." Ann Landers said, "Know yourself. Don't accept your dog's admiration as conclusive evidence that you are wonderful." And Lao-Tzu put it this way:

> *It is wisdom to know others;*
> *It is enlightenment to know oneself.*

Lama Sogyal Rinpoche says meditation is the greatest gift you can give yourself in this life, because it is only through this practice that you can undertake "the journey to discover your true nature and so find the stability and confidence you will need to live, and die, well." In other words, he believes meditation is a royal road that leads us to awareness of and sensitivity to what lies within. However, that also means that as wonderful as this gift called meditation may be, not everything that we become aware of is going to be wonderful. Indeed, like any journey, this one may take us to unexpected places where, in existentialist Jean-Paul Sartre's words, you will discover that you can become what you are only by the radical and deep-seated refusal of that which others have made you. Therefore, it takes a certain amount of courage and a sense of adventure to embark upon a journey that may lead us to deconstruct and then reconstruct the person that the late Christian mystic Thomas Merton described as the one we think we are, here and now, but "who is at best an impostor and a stranger."

If you are ready to begin this practice in an informal way, the instructions in this chapter will certainly help you get started. So will an audio- or videotape and other books. However, to develop a more formal, sitting practice, you may want to find an experienced teacher who offers either private lessons or classes in a particular form of meditation such as Transcendental Meditation, Zen, or Theravada (see sidebar).

Recommendations from friends who meditate regularly can direct you to local teachers and classes. Other sources of information include your local library, hospitals, community centers, and the World Wide Web. You may also want to jump-start your practice by taking a weekend or week-long workshop at Omega or one of the

Awareness Meditation

This meditation technique is designed to help you be more aware of what you are experiencing in the present moment. As you become more aware of your body, mind, emotions, and external environment in a nonjudgmental and detached way, you will begin to experience a new clarity and self-acceptance that often triggers deep relaxation and healing.

You can tape-record this script and play it back at your convenience or have a friend read it to you. Read the script very slowly with long pauses between sentences. Sit straight in a chair comfortably with both feet on the floor, or lie on your back on a bed or mat on the floor. If you are reclining, please try to stay awake.

Begin by slowly closing your eyes. . . . Notice how the closed eyes feel. . . . Now take a moment to bring awareness to the sounds in the room. . . . Notice the temperature of the air against your skin. . . . Notice the smell of the air. . . . Notice how your body feels as it rests against the surface beneath it. . . . Notice what pleases you in this environment. . . . Notice what displeases you. . . . Take a moment now to bring awareness to your breath. . . . Notice the sensation of the cool air as it is inhaled through the nostrils and the warm air as it is exhaled through the nostrils. . . . There is no need to make the breath do anything special. . . . Just allow yourself to breathe naturally, noticing each breath as it flows in and flows out. . . . Rivet your attention to the breath. . . . The breath is the anchor for the mind. . . . If the mind drifts off to worry, fear, confusion, or any thought or image, just notice and name where it is straying and gently bring it back. . . . Over and over again, bring the mind gently back to the breath. . . . Now focus your attention on your feet and toes. . . . Notice how the feet and toes are feeling. . . . And allow the feet and toes to relax, release, and let go. . . . Focus your attention on the legs. . . . Notice how the legs are feeling. . . . Now allow all of the leg muscles to relax and release. . . . Focus your attention on your buttocks. . . . Notice how the buttock muscles are feeling. . . . Allow the buttock muscles to relax and release and let go. . . . Now bring your mind back to your breath, noticing the air as it is being breathed in through the nostrils and the air as it is breathed out. . . . Where is your mind right now? Is it calm or is it restless? Is it focused and involved or distracted and bored? Just notice without judgment. . . . Bring your attention now to the abdomen and chest. . . . Notice how those parts of the body are feeling. . . . Notice if there is any tightness, tension, or pain. . . . And allow the abdomen and chest to relax and release and let go. Notice the lower, middle, and upper back. . . . Simply observe how the back is feeling. . . . And now allow all of the muscles of this part of your body to relax and release and let go. . . . Bring your attention to the arms, hands, and fingers, and notice how they feel. . . . Allow them to relax, release, and let go. . . . You might even notice that your hands are getting heavier and warmer. . . . Bring attention to your neck and shoulders. . . . Notice how they are feeling. . . . Allow the muscles of the neck and shoulders to relax, release, and let go. . . . And now notice how your face is feeling. . . . Notice any tightness or tension or pain. . . . And with the mind focused on the face, allow all of the muscles to relax, release, and let go. . . . Feel the mouth droop and the eyelids get heavier and heavier. . . . Allow all the muscles of your body to relax, release, and let go as you breathe slowly, deeply, and effortlessly. . . . Notice the cool air as it is being breathed in and the warm air as it is breathed out. . . . Rivet your attention on the breath. If the mind strays gently, bring it back, over and over again. . . . With each breath, feel your body and mind become more and more relaxed, comfortable, and peaceful. Keep awareness on your breath as long as you would like, and whenever you're ready, you can slowly open your eyes.

centers listed at the end of this chapter and Chapter 5. Even a half-day or day-long workshop sponsored by a local YMCA, church, temple, hospital, or meditation society can be a very productive start-up motor.

As a beginner you will probably have lots of questions that can be answered through the resources at the end of this chapter. In the meantime here are answers to some typical questions:

+ *What should I wear?* Usually loose, comfortable clothing. In some cases a group or organization may request that your comfortable clothes be 100 percent cotton.

+ *Where is the best place to meditate?* It depends upon the system you are learning. For example, people do Transcendental Meditation in lots of locations—at home, at the office, in classes, and in other places. However, very strict Zen

Confused about all the different kinds of meditation out there? Sometimes even those who practice one form are mystified by others. According to Daniel Goleman, the mechanics that each meditation system uses determines whether it's classified as:

(a) *concentration*—the mind focuses on a fixed mental object. As the mind wanders, the strategy is to return one's focus to the object. For example, Transcendental Meditation.

(b) *mindfulness*—in which the mind observes itself—full watchfulness of each successive moment. For example, Theravada.

(c) *integrated*—a combination of concentration and mindfulness that makes allowances for individual needs. For example, Zen or Tibetan Buddhism.

practices usually take place in monasteries, where students may do sitting meditations for long periods of time. If you mean where in your home should you meditate, you will be told to find a quiet place, even if it's just a corner of a room. What's important is not how much space you have but what happens in it. Is it peaceful? Is it far enough away from phones, computers, televisions, blaring boom boxes, and doorbells, as well as any individuals or madding crowd that may have a different agenda?

✦ *What do I need to do besides breathe?* You can use an inspirational word, phrase, or prayer; repeat slowly with intense concentration on each word. If your mind wanders, acknowledge where it's gone and bring your mind back to the place it left off. Be aware of the judging quality of your mind. You don't have to try to stop it. Just observe it and let it go. Also have patience, which is considered a form of wisdom. Have trust in yourself and your own authority more than others and their authority. Don't strive for results—it's the antithesis of being present to the moment. Be accepting of who you are—all that you are—and what is happening for you in the moment. And finally, let go—of all the thoughts, feelings, and situations that the mind wants to hold on to—that have a hold on your mind.

✦ *What else is expected of me?* Come with a beginner's mind.

◆ *What's a beginner's mind?* You may get dozens of different answers. Lao-Tzu said that one with a beginner's mind sees himself as a beginner, totally empty and ready to receive. Here is the answer Kabat-Zinn gives in *Full Catastrophe Living*:

The richness of present-moment experience is the richness of life itself. Too often we let our thinking and our beliefs about what we "know" prevent us from seeing things as they really are. We tend to take the ordinary for granted and fail to grasp the extraordinariness of the ordinary. To see the richness of the present moment, we need to cultivate what has been called "beginner's mind," a mind that is willing to see everything as if for the first time.

And here is one by the late Shunryu Suzuki-roshi, a Japanese Zen priest who established Zen centers in the United States and author of *Zen Mind, Beginner's Mind*:

If you try to calm your mind, you will be unable to sit, and if you try not to be disturbed, your effort will not be the right effort. The only effort that will help you is to count your breathing, or to concentrate on your inhaling and exhaling. We say concentration, but to concentrate your mind on something is not the true purpose of Zen. The true purpose is to see things as they are . . . and to let everything go as it goes. This is to put everything under control in its widest sense. Zen practice is to open up our small mind. So concentrating is just an aid to help you realize "big mind" or the mind that is everything.

Affirmations, guided imagery, hypnosis, yoga, or tai chi are other modalities, in addition to meditation, that you can use to help balance your health-care equation. All help you to shift your awareness from your outer world to your inner one and discover the body's wisdom. Studies show that all these modalities can have positive effects on the body/mind that are similar to those experienced by meditators. Yoga and tai chi, which use movement and breathing to harmonize the body/mind and produce positive effects, will be discussed in Chapter 7. Affirmations, guided imagery, and self-hypnosis use the positive power of the mind's ability to help reinforce, gain awareness, and heal our bodies and emotions.

Affirmations are positive thoughts, phrases, or sayings. Essentially, affirmations

> When you meditate, sit with the dignity of a king or queen;
> when you move through your day, remain centered in this dignity.
> —THE BUDDHA

put into practice the phrase As we think, so we become. Just as negative thoughts re-peated over time create their own negative reality, positive thoughts can and do cre-ate positive outcomes. That's why repeating a simple affirmation such as "I accept myself as I am" can reframe negative self-talk into a positive and health-enhancing message.

According to psychotherapist Belleruth Naparstek, M.A., L.I.S.W., author of *Staying Well with Guided Imagery*, a series of guided imagery tapes and CDs called Health Journeys, "Guided imagery is a kind of directed daydreaming, a way of focusing the imagination to help the mind and body heal, stay strong, and perform as needed." She says for some people guided imagery is easier than meditation because you do not have to pay perfect attention to it. Yet guided imagery acts like meditation because it clears the mind, slows it down, and calms and strengthens the person practicing it.

Like meditation, guided imagery is an altered state of consciousness—a state of reverie, which in this case produces a dreamy kind of awareness. "Floating in and out of it is frequently sufficient and even typical of the process," explains Naparstek. When it is most effective, guided imagery encourages you to be imagining with all of your senses—hearing, touching, taste, smell, and sight. Visualization, a form of guided imagery, engages only the sense of sight.

Studies show that by regularly practicing guided imagery one can bolster emo-tional resiliency and coping ability, sports performance, and produce changes in the biochemistry of the body. For example, recent research concludes that like meditation, guided imagery can:

+ lower blood pressure

+ reduce anxiety, depression, and physical pain

+ heighten immune functioning

Studies show guided imagery can also:

+ ease nausea during chemotherapy
+ lower allergic responses
+ speed up recovery from surgery, cuts, burns, and fractures

All the affectionate feelings of a man for others
are an extension of his feelings for himself.
—ARISTOTLE

> Our discontent begins by finding false villains whom we can accuse of deceiving us.
> Next we find false heroes whom we expect to liberate us. The hardest,
> most discomfiting discovery is that each of us must emancipate himself.
>
> —DANIEL J. BOORSTIN

Case Studies

In *Mind/Body Health: The Effects of Attitudes, Emotions, and Relationships,* authors Brent Q. Hafen, Keith J. Karren, Kathryn J. Frandsen, and N. Lee Smith, M.D., relate the following stories about the effect that guided imagery had on two people with cancer. They also point out that guided imagery is a complementary modality and it should never be used as a substitute for appropriate medical treatment:

Biochemist Nicholas Hall began teaching positive imaging to his patients at George Washington University. Among them was a man with prostate cancer that had spread to the bone marrow. Hall taught positive imaging to this patient and then tested him once or twice a week while he was practicing it. While the patient was doing imagery, his white blood cell count was up and his body produced greater amounts of thymosin, a hormone that might help the immune response.

When the man was told to stop imaging, his white blood cell count dropped precipitously. Moreover, Hall could barely detect any thymosin in his body.

The second case is an example of what's commonly called a "spontaneous remission" or "remarkable recovery" by a cancer patient who was practicing imagery:

When psychologist Patricia Norris, clinical director of the Biofeedback and Psychotherapy Center at the Menninger Foundation in Topeka, Kansas, met Anna, the young mother had a malignant tumor growing rapidly at the back of her neck. Doctors had given her only three months to live. The cancer had virtually crippled her: She was hunched over, her head was forced painfully to one side, and her right arm was paralyzed and contracted. Her doctor had instructed her to go home and make the necessary arrangements for the futures of her children.

After Norris instructed her in positive imaging, Anna began to visualize her tumor as a dragon on her back; she imagined her white blood cells to be knights that were attacking the tumor with swords.

A year later, Norris saw Anna again. A remarkable change had taken place. Her arm was fully mobile, and the tumor had shrunk. The next time the two met, Anna was in total remission.

Naparstek observes that whether you invent your own imagery or listen to scripts on prerecorded audiotapes depends upon your preference. Each has pros and cons, and in either case your own imagination will eventually take over. Since guided imagery is a skill, it will get better and be more effective with practice. It also tends to work best in an unforced atmosphere and can be more powerful when experienced in a group, and when accompanied by music.

No amount of meditation, yoga, or diet will make our problems go away, says Jack Kornfield. But when we can transform our difficulties into a practice, little by little they will guide us on the path that leads to self-acceptance and inner peace.

Perhaps one of the most difficult roadblocks to self-acceptance is our resistance to forgiving ourselves and others, for real and imagined hurts and betrayals. Often we endure personal suffering instead of offering forgiveness or asking for it as a means to move beyond it. One way to overcome resistance to forgiving someone, asking for their forgiveness, or forgiving yourself is to do the dialogue exercise in Chapter 2. Journaling can be a very powerful way to uncover many of the thoughts and feelings you may still harbor about the issue or issues that separated you.

The following meditation by Stephen Levine, who is internationally known for his work in the field of death and dying, appeared in *Medical Self-Care* magazine. It is prac-

How unhappy is he who cannot forgive himself.

—PUBLILIUS SYRUS

Reflection with Belleruth Naparstek, author of
STAYING WELL WITH GUIDED IMAGERY, YOUR
SIXTH SENSE *and an Omega teacher*

Q: What effect does guided imagery have on the body/mind?

A: Images are events to the body and can be almost as real as actual events. The mind responds to imagery as if something is really happening—especially when the images strongly evoke sensory memories and fantasy. So, for instance, recalling the smell and feel of the air at the start of the first winter snowfall is an image. So is remembering the sound and timbre of Daddy's "I'm pleased with you" voice. Have you ever puckered up at the thought of a lemon? These sensory images are the true language of the body, the only language it understands immediately and without question.

Q: You say that when you do guided imagery, you are in "an altered state." What do you mean by that?

A: By altered state I mean a state of relaxed focus, a kind of calm but energized alertness, a focused reverie. In this state our brain-wave activity and our biochemistry shifts, and our moods change. Attention is concentrated on one thing or on a very narrow band of things. As this happens, we find we have a heightened sensitivity to what we are focused on, and a decreased awareness of the other things going on around us, things we would ordinarily notice. We are all familiar with this state. We're in it when we're so engrossed that we lose track of time or we don't hear people talking to us. When we're in an altered state, we are capable of more rapid and intense healing, growth, learning, and intuitive insight.

Q: One of the benefits of doing meditation or guided imagery is that it helps people to feel that there's a locus of control. What role does that play in a quest for optimal health and well-being?

A: When we have a sense of being in control and can use a simple technique like imagery whenever, wherever, and however we wish, we support our sense of wellness, self-sufficiency, and self-esteem. It has the benign, placebo effect of making us the "locus of control," as they say in social science talk.

Q: Does that mean that guided imagery helps us to have a sense of mastery over what is happening to us?

A: Exactly. We see that beneficial effect all the time with cancer patients who use guided imagery to help overcome the nausea and other side effects of chemotherapy. When we can do something to help overcome a sense of helplessness—the feeling that our lives are out of control—we cope better, feel more optimistic, and have hope for the future. Guided imagery that opens the heart and deliberately evokes feelings of love, gratitude, and compassion is a particularly safe and powerful way to do this—and opening the heart is something the world badly needs.

Q: What are some really good conditions for making imagery as effective as possible?

A: Being relaxed; using all of your senses, especially your kinesthetic or feeling sense; continued practice; going to the same place with the same music or props each time; using touch as a conditioning cue (such as putting your hands over your belly each time, and breathing deeply); not trying too hard or being too exacting about how you do this. You don't even have to believe that it works. You just have to give it a try, putting your analytic mind on hold, and, preferably, try it more than just once. Skill improves with practice. But a lot of skeptics end up doing quite well with imagery.

ticed in the wellness workshop at Omega. It, too, can help you to overcome any resistance to offering forgiveness, and thus end some of the suffering you may feel in your life. Either tape-record the script or have a friend read it to you.

Begin by getting into a sitting position where your back is straight. If it's comfortable, sit on the floor or on a pillow with your legs crossed or on your knees with your buttocks resting on your heels. But if any of those positions are uncomfortable, you can also sit with your legs out in front of you or on a chair with your feet flat on the floor or you can lie down on a mat (try not to fall asleep).

Bring into your heart the image of someone for whom you feel much resentment. Take a moment to feel that person right there in the center of your heart.

And in your heart, say to that person, "For anything you may have done that caused me pain, anything you did either intentionally or unintentionally, through your thoughts, words, or actions, I forgive you."

Slowly allow that person to settle into your heart. No force, just opening to him at your own pace. Say to him, "I forgive you." Gently, gently open to him. If it hurts, let it hurt. Begin to relax the iron grip of your resentment, to let go of that incredible anger. Say to him, "I forgive you," and allow him to be forgiven.

Now bring into your heart the image of someone from whom you would ask for forgiveness. Say to her, "For anything I may have done that caused you pain, my thoughts, my actions, my words, I ask your forgiveness. For all those words that were said out of forgetfulness or fear or confusion, I ask your forgiveness."

Don't allow any resentment you may hold for yourself to block your reception of that forgiveness. Let your heart soften to it. Allow yourself to be forgiven. Open to the possibility of forgiveness. Holding her in your heart, say to her, "For whatever I may have done that caused you pain, I ask your forgiveness."

Now bring an image of yourself into your heart, floating at the center of your chest. Bring yourself into your heart and, using your own first name, say to yourself, "For all that you have done in forgetfulness and fear and confusion, for all the words and thoughts and actions that may have caused pain to anyone, I forgive you."

Open to the possibility of self-forgiveness. Let go of all the bitterness, the hardness, the judgment of yourself.

Make room in your heart for yourself. Say, "I forgive you," to you.

If you felt resistance to doing this exercise, it's helpful to ask yourself why. Might you be having difficulty letting go? Could the resistance you feel be a wake-up call that you should do this exercise regularly to help overcome whatever hinders forgiveness? Sometimes we resist forgiving someone because we believe it means that we are sanctioning his or her negative behavior. However, forgiving someone doesn't necessarily mean we become reconciled *with* that person. We can be reconciled *to* them instead. Many people who told the press that they forgave President William Clinton for both his affair with Monica Lewinsky and not being truthful with the American people said that if he were to run for office again, they wouldn't vote for him. It may be reassuring and helpful to know that forgiving does not mean we condone negative behavior. In fact, we never have to have contact with the forgiven person again.

In Chapter 2, "Stress Awareness," we identified five universal principles of stress reduction that are the basic tenets of the Omega Wellness Program. While all those principles serve as underpinnings of a life that can be filled with vitality and optimal wellness, the first, *As we think so we become,* is a most important reminder of how meditation can help us to unify our minds, bodies, emotions, and spirits.

Two and a half millennia ago, the Buddha, whom many consider one of the greatest psychologists to ever live, put it this way in "Twin Verses" (in Eknath Easwaren's translation):

> *All we are is a result of what we have thought. We are formed and molded by our thoughts. The man whose mind is shaped by selfish thoughts causes misery when he speaks or acts. Sorrows roll over him as the wheels of a cart roll over the tracks of the bullock that draws it. . . . The man whose mind is shaped by selfless thoughts gives joy whenever he speaks or acts. Joy follows him like a shadow that never leaves him.*

Indeed, as the Buddha reminds us, our thoughts shape our inner and outer worlds. If you doubt that, just think for a moment about someone you may have known who was so caught up in a web of resentful thoughts that he or she never seemed to find any peace. Did that individual tend to blame others—friends, relatives, coworkers, and society—for feelings of loneliness, despair, anger, and frustration? In contrast, most of us have also known an angry, resentful individual who seemed to undergo a radical change of heart that helped him to see his life and others' in a new, positive light. Whatever happened caused him to turn around, release his negative and toxic thoughts, and replace them with feelings of love, joy, compassion, and forgiveness.

We don't have to wait for an *extra*ordinary event to change the negative thoughts and feelings that we all harbor at one time or another. By using meditation as a way to acknowledge and then release those thoughts and feelings, we, too, can discover that the happiness that comes from peace, healing, and the joy of being alive in the present moment is, as Joseph Campbell and Jack Kornfield said earlier, our birthright.

BOOKS

Benson, Herbert. *The Relaxation Response.* New York: William Morrow, 1975.

Borysenko, Joan, Ph.D. *The Power of the Mind to Heal.* Carson, CA: Hay House, 1994.

Dass, Ram. *Journey of Awakening.* New York: Bantam Books, 1978.

Davich, Victor N. *The Best Guide to Meditation.* Los Angeles: Renaissance Books, 1998.

Easwaren, Eknath. *God Makes the Rivers Flow.* Petaluma, CA: Nilgiri Press, 1982.

Goleman, Daniel. *The Meditative Mind: The Varieties of Meditative Experience.* New York: Tarcher/Putnam, 1988.

Hanh, Thich Nhat.

   Being Peace. Berkeley: Parallax Press, 1987.

   The Miracle of Mindfulness. Boston: Beacon Press, 1976.

Harp, David. *The Three Minute Meditator.* Oakland: New Harbinger Publications, Inc., 1996.

Kabat-Zinn, Jon. *Wherever You Go, There You Are: Mindfulness Meditation in Everyday Life.* New York: Hyperion, 1994.

Kaplan, Aryeh. *Jewish Meditation: A Practical Guide.* New York: Schocken Books, 1995.

Kornfield, Jack.

   Buddha's Little Instruction Book. New York: Bantam, 1994.

   A Path with Heart. New York: Bantam, 1993.

LeShan, Lawrence. *How to Meditate.* New York: Bantam, 1974.

Levine, Stephen.

   A Gradual Awakening. New York: Doubleday, 1989.

   Guided Meditations, Explorations, and Healings. New York: Doubleday, 1991.

Nisker, Wes. *Buddha's Nature: Evolution as a Practical Guide to Enlightenment.* New York: Bantam, 1998.

Rinpoche, Sogyal. *The Tibetan Book of Living and Dying.* New York: HarperCollins, 1994.

Roche, Lorin, Ph.D. *Meditation Made Easy.* San Francisco: Harper San Francisco, 1998.

Salzberg, Sharon. *Lovingkindness: The Revolutionary Art of Happiness.* Boston: Shambhala, 1995.

Suzuki, Shunryu. *Zen Mind, Beginner's Mind: Informal Talks on Zen Meditation and Practice.* New York: John Weatherhill, 1970.

Tart, Charles T. *Living the Mindful Life: A Handbook for Living in the Present Moment.* Boston: Shambhala, 1994.

Yogananda Paramahansa. *Autobiography of a Yogi.* Los Angeles: Self-Realization Fellowship, 1994.

AUDIOTAPES, VIDEOTAPES, CATALOGS, AND CDS

Academy for Guided Imagery, Inc., for a catalog of audio-/videotapes P.O. Box 2070, Mill Valley, CA 94942. Phone 800-726-2070. www.healthy.net/agi

Dharma Seed Tape Library, Box 66, Wendell Depot, MA 01380 (for information about Insight Meditation audio- and videocassette recordings).

Kabat-Zinn, Jon. "Mindfulness Meditation Practice Tapes." For information about stress-reduction tapes write: Stress Reduction Tapes, P.O. Box 547, Lexington, MA 02171.

Levine, Stephen. For a catalog of tapes of guided meditations and public talks write: Warm Rock Tapes, P.O. Box 108, Chamisal, NM 87521.

New Dimensions Audio Tapes, P.O. Box 569, Ukiah, CA 95482. Phone: 800-935-8273. www.newdimensions.org. Write, call, or go to the Web to get a catalog of New Dimensions tapes. A sampling of tapes by authors in this chapter includes:

+ Kornfield, Jack. *The Power of Meditation and Prayer* and *The Heart of Spiritual Practice*

+ Sogyal Rinpoche. *Living Up to Death: Taming the Mind* and *From Confusion to Clarity: Understanding the Mind*

+ Thich Nhat Hanh. *Basic Buddhist Wisdom*

Parallax Press, P.O. Box 7355, Berkeley, CA 94707. Phone: 510-525-0101. www.parallax.org

Shambhala Publications, Inc., Order Dept., P.O. Box 308, Boston, MA 02117-0308. Phone: 617-424-0030. www.shambhala.com

Siegel, Bernie, M.D. For information about assorted meditation tapes and videos write: ECaP, 1302 Chapel Street, New Haven, CT 06511. Phone: 203-865-8392.

Sounds True, P.O. Box 8010, Boulder, CO 80306. Phone: 800-333-9185. Write or call for a catalog. A sampling of tapes by authors in this chapter includes www.soundstrue.com

- ✦ Borysenko, Joan. *Seventy Times Seven*
- ✦ Hanh, Thich Nhat. *Mindful Moments; Mindful Living*, and *The Present Moment*
- ✦ Levine, Stephen. *A Year to Live*
- ✦ Kabat-Zinn, Jon. *Pebbles and Pearls*
- ✦ Kornfield, Jack. *A Path with Heart* and *Your Buddha Nature*
- ✦ Salzberg, Sharon, and Joseph Goldstein. *Insight Meditation Correspondence Course*

Young, Shinzen. *Five Classic Meditations*. San Francisco: Audio Renaissance, 1989.

INFORMATION ABOUT MEDITATION ORGANIZATIONS, PROGRAMS, AND RETREATS

Academy for Guided Imagery, Inc. (see above) for home study and other programs.

Green Gulch Farm Zen Center, 1601 Shoreline Highway, Sausalito, CA 94965. Phone: 415-383-3134. www.sfzc.com

Insight Meditation Society, 1230 Pleasant Street, Barre, MA 01005. Phone: 978-355-4378.

Kripalu Center for Yoga and Health, Lenox, MA. Phone: 800-741-7353. www.vgemet.net/kali/entrance.html

Lama Foundation, P.O. Box 240, San Cristobal, NM 87564.

The Naropa Institute, 2130 Arapahoe Avenue, Boulder, CO 80302. Phone: 303-546-5295. www.naropa.edu

Omega Institute for Holistic Studies, 260 Lake Drive, Rhinebeck, NY 12572. Phone: 800-944-1001. www.omega-inst.org

San Francisco Zen Center, 300 Page Street, San Francisco, CA 94102. Phone: 415-863-3136. www.zendo.com/~sfzc

Tassajara Zen Mountain Center, 39171 Tassajara Road, Carmel Valley, CA 93924. Phone: 415-431-3771. www.zendo.com/~sfzc

Zen Mountain Monastery, P.O. Box 197PC, South Plank Road, Mt. Tremper, NY 12457. Phone: 914-688-2228. www.zen-mtn.org/zmm

WWW

Calm Centre—www.calmcentre.com—a "calm" think tank involving a number of psychologists, natural therapists, filmmakers, composers, and musicians

Health Journeys—www.healthjourneys.com—homepage for Belleruth Naparstek

Parallax Press—www.parallax.org—click on enter and go to "links"

5.

R, R, & R—
Retreat, Respite,
& Renewal

Throughout history, people wanting to connect with the deepest yearnings of their psyches and souls and/or purify themselves often sought out places where they could retreat from the world. Moses climbed to the top of a mountain; Jesus, driven by a holy spirit, went into a wilderness; and the Buddha sat under a bodhi tree. The Hindu leader Mohandas Gandhi found that place in himself wherever he happened to be on a Monday. His strict practice was to be in solitude and silence throughout the day— even when the king of the British Empire beckoned him to a meeting.

In our world, one that historians actually refer to as "postmodern," it seems that the need and desire to follow in our ancient ancestors' footsteps on a journey of self-discovery is just as great—if not greater. Fortunately, so are our options. One doesn't have to climb to a mountaintop or hike in the desert to get far from the madding crowd. Neither does one have to flee to a monastery or convent to have a time for si-

---

My favorite piece of music is the one we hear all the time if we are quiet.

—JOHN CAGE

---

lence and solitude. That's because today, as in the past, while retreats from daily life may take those traditional forms, they take on many other guises too. Some popular examples that are detailed in guides by travel experts John Benson, Bernard Burt, and Jenifer Miller include:

- A weekend, a week, or a month at places like Omega Institute, Esalen Institute, Mt. Madonna, Feathered Pipe Ranch, Rowe Camp and Conference Center, Kirkridge Retreat and Study Center, and Zen Mountain Monastery, where one's time away includes choosing one of hundreds of hands-on workshops that feed the mind, body, and spirit and spending free time walking in nature, meditating in sacred spaces, drifting in a canoe on a lake, or just being in one's room.

- A trip to health spas such as New Age Health Spa in Neversink, New York, the Greenhouse Spa in Arlington, Texas, and others where one can get pampered with massages, aromatherapy treatments, reflexology, watsu (a water massage), loofah scrubs, seaweed treatments, et cetera, for an hour or around the clock, as well as soak alone in a hot tub, swim, and go for long walks or try yoga, tai chi, nutrition, meditation, biofeedback, breathwork, and other wellness-oriented classes and services.

- A physically, mentally, and emotionally challenging program—such as National Outdoor Leadership School (NOLS), Outward Bound, Breaking Through Adventures, Northwaters Wilderness Programs—that combines hiking, rock climbing, canoeing, and other outdoor activities with a vigil or vision quest experience.

- A self-directed weekend or week alone at a secluded cabin or a friend's vacation home.

- A day or just a few hours that are set aside for relaxation, ritual, rejuvenation, and to care for the soul—be it alone or with a group of others who gather in your house, someone else's house, a park, or a hotel room.

So what calls you? For Henry David Thoreau it was Walden Pond. For Anne Morrow Lindbergh it was the ebb and flow of the sea along the coast of Maine.

For psychoanalyst Carl G. Jung it was a stone tower that he built as a sanctuary for himself.

If you retreat regularly, or have read essays and books by those like Thoreau, Lindbergh, and Jung, who have penned impressions of their retreats, you may already know what kind of respite calls you. However, if you don't, try closing your eyes for a few minutes while you imagine the most wonderful place you could go to replenish your spirit. While there, let yourself experience all the sights, smells, and sounds that you may associate with that real or envisioned place. Spend as long as you want exploring the familiar or foreign surroundings. Take time to "know" how it feels to be there. Then write down a few words or thoughts that help to describe your experience. If words don't come to mind, try using art materials to express your impressions.

To shut our eyes is to travel.

—EMILY DICKINSON

John Benson, author of *Transformative Getaways,* a guide describing hundreds of life-enhancing adventures, vacations, and retreats, says that anyone can enjoy the self-healing benefits of a retreat and return home with life-transforming energy, skills, and wisdom. However, he observes, a getaway may be particularly helpful if you:

+ feel an urge to connect with like-minded souls, explore new paths, and walk down familiar spiritual pathways

+ feel trapped by negative feelings, behaviors, or patterns of thinking

+ suspect you might benefit from practicing or learning a specific healing, centering, or spiritual discipline under the tutelage of an experienced teacher

+ want to delve deeper into recovery or psychological work to which you are already committed

+ feel a need to be with your own gender or sexual-preference group and share their perspectives, griefs, and joys

+ find yourself at a major, life-transforming turning point such as changing careers, getting married, or losing a partner

+ recently experienced severe trauma

If you looked at someone sitting on a beach or hiking the Appalachian Trail or getting a massage at a spa, could you tell whether he or she was on a vacation or a retreat? Probably not, because both come in many guises and that may make it very difficult to know which is which.

The word *vacation* is rooted in the Latin word *vacare,* which means "to empty." Typically, when we go on a vacation, we "empty" ourselves of work, school, and other

In Genesis it says that it is not good for a man to be alone,
but sometimes it's a great relief.
—JOHN BARRYMORE

daily burdens for the sake of pleasure and relaxation. *Retreat* comes from the Latin word *retrahere*, which means "to draw back." It doesn't imply that we get rid of or leave anything behind, only that we move away from a particular place. Either a retreat or a vacation affords the person taking it a respite—a short interval away from our daily world that we commonly call a breather. However, while both are breathers, most retreat leaders would agree that the litmus test for determining whether a foray is a vacation or a retreat is based not upon one's actions, but rather one's intentions.

The driving force behind a retreat is the opportunity to gaze inward and survey one's inner terrain with new eyes. In other words, time spent on a retreat is intentionally dedicated to going below the surface of one's being in the hope of discovering a deeper consciousness—a heightened sense of one's "self." Feminist Deena Metzger, who leads writing retreats for women, puts it this way in her book *Writing for Your Life:* "We withdraw, not only from the concerns of the world and its preoccupations, but from the incessant monologue and concerns within ourselves, in order for something else to come into being."

So what makes a retreat a retreat? The following four steps, according to Jennifer Louden, author of *The Women's Retreat Book:*

+ preparing

+ withdrawing from ordinary life through ceremony and creating a container

+ listening in sacred space

+ reemerging into ordinary space and time

A white explorer in Africa, anxious to press ahead with his journey, paid his porters for a series of forced marches. But they, almost within reach of their destination, set down their bundles and refused to budge. No amount of extra payment would convince them otherwise. They said they had to wait for their souls to catch up.

—BRUCE CHATWIN

During the first step, she explains, one sets an *intention*. It takes the form of a question and is the one step that most distinguishes a retreat from a vacation. *Intention* comes from the word *intendere*, which means "to stretch toward something." Setting one sends a signal that you are turning inward, that you plan to take your time away seriously, and that your retreat is going to be "uncommon, mindful, loving, and intentionally focused on you." Your intention guides you and keeps you focused on what is unfolding during your time away, she notes.

The second step, withdrawal from ordinary life, is not determined by the amount of time you can spend away or by your physical proximity to other people, says Louden. It's about disengaging through symbolic action and by physically and/or emotionally creating a safe space—a container for yourself. Such spaces and places

Intention is the cornerstone of a retreat, according to many retreat leaders. Jennifer Louden suggests doing the following to help form an intention:

+ Set aside time to prepare.

+ Identify the most passionate or persistent longing in your life.

+ Complete the question "On this retreat, I intend to ask myself . . ."

+ Keep the question simple, open, and loving.

+ If you get a statement, reframe it—for example, the statement "I intend to be kind to myself for the next twenty-four hours" might be reframed as "How can I be kinder to myself over the next twenty-four hours?"

don't have to be far away or elaborate. They can be as close and simple as a room in your house, a garden, a park bench, or even a small corner of your office. Your symbolic ceremony of separation doesn't have to be complicated either. It can be as simple as lighting a candle, picking a rune, meditating for a few moments, reading a poem or prayer, doing a visualization, or taking some mindful breaths.

Once you've stepped over the threshold of your daily busyness to withdraw into your own interior, sacred space, Louden says that it's time to listen. For her, this is the heart of a retreat. Yet it is also the hardest part of the retreat to maintain—especially in a world where the silence and solitude are counterculture. This is the time where you go to your center and the work of transformation takes place. It's not a time or place to do the dishes, clean house, read magazines and books, listen to the news, or pay attention to others.

How do you get there? Louden suggests that journaling—about your feelings or why you chose to retreat—is one way. Others include:

- moving to music

- using art materials to express something inside you

- walking

- listening to music

- meditating on a word or metaphor

- listing thought-provoking questions

Finally, there's the last step—reemerging into ordinary space and time. Although reentry may seem to be a straightforward and easy step, says Louden, "it is fraught with the difficulty of leaving sacred space and returning to ordinary space." That's true, she notes, even if your retreat lasted for only a few moments. Therefore, this is the time to acknowledge what you have done, where you have been, and the fact that you have been changed. The acknowledgment can take the form of a vivid memory, a simple memento or talisman, or a note to yourself.

Ultimately, a retreat is a vehicle that steers you to a place of self-discovery, self-expression, and self-healing. There is no "right" or "wrong" way, although in many

> There is nothing in all creation so like God as stillness.
>
> —MEISTER ECKHART

Conversation with Jennifer Louden

Q: After going on all the different types of retreats that you describe in *The Women's Retreat Book,* does one stand out above the others?

A: Back in 1990 I took a month-long women's canoeing trip that was a combined retreat and wilderness experience. It came at a time when everything seemed to be going wrong. I was a screenwriter and had a spec movie script due. But I was horribly blocked and couldn't write it. My primary relationship fell apart and I wrecked my car. It was a dark time.

Q: What kinds of experiences did you have on the trip?

A: A sense of timelessness. The feeling that I was being embraced by a large container that separated me from my outside life. I didn't dream, which is one way that I usually get information about myself. However, I discovered other ways to discover the authentic me. For example, I saw pictures in the rocks and Beatles songs played in my head—incessantly. Back home I would never have paid attention to what they were telling me about myself.

Q: Which was?

A: That I needed to live each day mindfully, be more gentle with myself, and become more aware of my deepest needs and impulses and the inner voice that guides me. I learned that inner voice can come in many guises—sensations, feelings, images, and actual events. Some are familiar; some are not. For example, one powerful image that came to me on another retreat was of a geyser shooting through my body. I realized it was blowing all the stuff that wasn't my true self away. Sometimes that voice is sneaky—like when a bathtub faucet broke off and flooded the house I was renting for a retreat. I couldn't stop the flow and had to get a neighbor to help. I thought, *Okay, now my retreat is over. All bets are off.* I checked into a hotel, got ice cream, and turned on a bad movie. But the retreat had a different idea . . . it kept going until I learned the lesson it had started.

Q: What gifts did you bring back from your first retreat—the canoe trip?

A: I returned home knowing that I could write a book and needed to do that. I trusted that information, and even though I had never written a book I felt driven to do it. Two years later *The Women's Comfort Book* was published. It launched my career.

Q: Are there times when you find retreating to be particularly valuable?

A: When I am angry, exhausted, or stuck. So often in my life I look back at long periods of anguish and see that if I had gotten myself quiet, gotten myself on retreat sooner, I could have received information that could have shortened that anguish. When one of those dark nights of the soul happened not too long ago, I retreated in many different ways. I went to a friend's cabin in Colorado. Back home I got up early in the morning and began the day with a question. "What do I need today?" "How can I have a more balanced day?" I took daily walking retreats, paying attention to my environment instead of my future fantasies. I listened to peacocks screeching in the trees, water running in a nearby creek, and, most importantly, my inner voice.

cultures, including our own, the word *retreat* may muster up visions of mystics and monks sitting and/or meditating for long periods of time in and out of doors. Yet this isn't the way a retreat has to be.

Many of the people who regularly go on retreats find it difficult to spend their time that way and choose more active retreats where experiences in the outer world become metaphors for the way one is living his or her life. Examples include retreats that factor in:

+ hiking, canoeing, sailing, or even rock or mountain climbing

+ expressive arts such as music, writing, painting, drawing, and

+ bodywork such as massage therapy, yoga, qigong, tai chi, and other forms of movement

Rabbi David A. Cooper, author of *Silence, Simplicity, and Solitude*, describes his classical approach to taking a retreat this way: "All of us have a deep reservoir of mystical experience that sustains the part of us some call the soul," he muses. "The soul yearns to be nourished and if the reservoir begins to run low, we can feel ourselves becoming dull, empty, brittle, and arid. If it sinks lower, we enter into states of angst, despair, and depression."

According to Cooper, the path that moves us away from those states is the silence, solitary practice, and simple living that are the cornerstones of what he calls a spiritual retreat. He teaches that living that way for a while replenishes the empty reservoir and brings balance to one's inner and outer worlds.

Thomas Moore agrees. Referring to the stone sanctuary that Carl G. Jung spent years building as his place of personal retreat, Moore says it began as a primitive structure that grew into something more complicated as time passed. In the end this stone turret evolved into a sacred space—a personal temple for Jung's spiritual life. Here Jung would do his soul work, which included painting on the walls, writing about his dreams, thinking his thoughts, recording his visions, and enjoying his memories.

We, too, can follow Jung's example. In *Sharing Silence* Gunilla Norris, who wrote about sacred space, suggested that the act of setting a room apart for silence transforms it into a sanctuary. "When we make a place for silence, we make room for ourselves—a place for breath, for refreshment, for challenge, and for healing." Moreover, like Cooper she advised that "simplicity allows the senses to rest from stimulation." Therefore, it is helpful to keep the space plain and simple with furnishings limited to a few cushions and a rug.

For those not having an extra room, Moore offers other possibilities for daily serving the spiritual needs of the soul by:

+ dedicating a quiet corner of the house for soul work

+ designating a drawer in which you place notes and/or drawings of your dreams and thoughts from the night before

+ purchasing a piece of sacred art that will help to focus your attention on spirituality and then putting it in a place where you will see it

What is important, Moore explains, is that we honor the fact that spirituality demands mindfulness, regularity, attention, and devotion. In a world set up to ignore

One of the greatest necessities in America is to discover creative solitude.

—CARL SANDBURG

soul, it asks for some small measure of withdrawal and that we value soulfulness for its own sake.

While reflecting upon how retreating helps us to value soulfulness, Rabbi Cooper quotes Taoist sage Chuang Tzu. "Men do not mirror themselves in still water. Only what is still can still the stillness of other things."

Whenever Cooper feels the need to make contact with his reservoir of still water he goes on solo retreats that last anywhere from twenty-four hours to forty days. The former is something most of can learn to do through practice, reading books, and/or having someone to guide us. The latter is reminiscent of the monastic type of retreats most of us have only read about in books. In *Silence, Simplicity, and Solitude,* he described one such solitary time during which he spent forty days in an isolated cabin. There wasn't any furniture, Cooper recounted, only the pile of foam cushions upon which he sat in silence most of the day. At night he would sleep upon those same pillows. A wood-burning stove and neatly folded blankets provided warmth—both day and night. In one corner of the room sat a washbasin. The fact that his cooking and eating utensils were minimal mattered not. The fresh fruit and vegetables sitting in a bowl next to a jug of water used for drinking, cooking, and washing sustained him.

During that retreat Cooper discovered that exotic, bizarre, and even dangerous thoughts flooded his imagination. "These inner voyages are not confined by any boundaries. In every corner and at all the edges the map is marked Unknown Territory." Not surprisingly, Cooper also admits that this type of retreat can get boring—indeed so boring that at times even he finds the desire to go to sleep overwhelming.

Why might sleep call so persistently when we're retreating—even when we're in a place like Omega where there are lots of stimulating activities going on? Just think of how many fairy tales or stories you've read where one of the main characters goes to sleep just as something significant is about to happen or be revealed about his or her life. It points to the fact that at certain times, we use sleep to escape from life. However, other times it serves us as a way to retreat. How might we know whether time spent sleeping is one or the other? The answer depends upon why we're doing it and whether we pay attention to our dreams or not. If we go to sleep to keep unpleasant thoughts, memories, and feelings in the dark, then we're choosing to be unconscious like those characters nodding off in fairy tales. If that's the case, then we would do well to look back to all the tales and stories, worldwide, that issue a universal warning that we must be awake to discover our true self and calling. However, if we find ourselves sleeping a lot on a retreat and use it as an opportunity to explore in writing or in the expressive arts what our dreams are telling us about ourselves, it can be a meaningful time.

In her book *The Call of Solitude*, psychoanalyst Ester Schaler Buchholz writes about neurologists who now hypothesize that sleep is not passive but active, a period in which the brain reorganizes itself. We learn and become inspired as we dream, she says. "During sleep the person is on the receiving line, dealing with little or no information from the environment. Dreams can be private riches, the source of poetry and insights."

Heraclitus, a Greek philosopher who lived around 500 B.C.E., said: "We must not act and speak like sleepers. . . . The waking have one world in common, but the sleeping turn aside each into a world of his own." Reflecting on those words, Buchholz concludes that even the earliest scientists understood the alone world of the dream and "the hopes, fears, and memories it houses. We can attempt to share our dreams, but in truth we have only ourselves to confirm these inner flights."

Another way to unearth that which may be calling us to learn and be inspired by a world all our own is to go on a vision quest. The late mythologist Joseph Campbell described this ancient form of retreat as a certain type of myth in which the hero went in quest of a boon, a vision, which has the same form in every mythology. During his interviews with Bill Moyers in the groundbreaking six-part PBS series *The Power of Myth*, Campbell said, "All these different mythologies give us the same essential quest. You leave the world that you're in and go into a depth or into a distance or up to a height. There you come to what was missing in your consciousness in the world you formerly inhabited. Then comes the problem either of staying with that, and letting the world drop off, or returning with that boon and trying to hold on to it as you move back into your social world again. That's not an easy thing to do."

I'd rather wake up in the middle of nowhere than in any city on earth.
—STEVE McQUEEN

Traditionally, Native Americans and other indigenous people worldwide use this ancient means of connecting with one's inner self in a number of ways. For example, many native cultures use quests as a rite of passage during which a male child ritually sheds his childish ways and discerns his calling as an adult. Although each culture may incorporate specific rites that are particular to their spiritual beliefs during the course of the quest, the basics, which reenact the cycle of birth, death, and rebirth, are, as Campbell suggested, universal. Typically, the quest takes on the following format:

- For days, weeks or even longer, the boy goes to a secluded place with clearly defined boundaries. It could be a tipi, a hut, a sacred circle, or a forest.

- He waits patiently, within those boundaries, for a vision to come to him of the direction his life will take in the future.

- Sometimes the boy will fast; other times drugs may be used to distort or heighten his reality.

- When such a vision (there may be more than one) comes, it is usually in the form of animals, other wildlife, guides, signs, and symbols.

- The boy uses all his senses to explore the meaning of the messages he's getting in order to discern his life's calling.

- When he knows what the future holds for him, he returns to his community.

- The trials and tribulations he endured on his quest have transformed him into a man.

For the most part we lack such initiation rites in our culture. Sometimes we call graduation or getting a driver's license a rite of passage, but it's hardly the equivalent of the rebirthing one experiences in the wilderness. Indeed, it seems that the closest we come to a true initiatory experience is that which takes place in some of our religious ceremonies. For instance, on the Sabbath that a Jewish boy celebrates his bar mitzvah or a Jewish girl celebrates her bat mitzvah, he or she leads a part of the religious service. In so doing the child crosses a bridge that separates him or her from adults in that community. Depending upon the ritual and depth of the ceremony, many Christian children experience that sense of passage when they are confirmed.

In her book *Quest* Denise Linn, an internationally known retreat leader of Cherokee descent, offers readers tools that they can use to create a vision quest and experience its transformative and initiatory power. Linn models the different quests described in her book on those that she has facilitated for hundreds of men, women, and teenagers from eighteen different countries. The most popular is her ten-day quest in the Pacific Northwest that's divided into the three essential stages of a retreat that others have described:

+ preparation

+ time away

+ the return

The first stage can last five or six days. When leading a quest, Linn says this is the time during which she addresses the participants' concerns and anxieties. She teaches them how to survive alone in the wilderness and engage in certain rituals such as the creation of their sacred circle. In her book she details similar information.

Next, the seekers spend three days doing a solo quest in the wilderness. Linn advises that "where intention goes, energy flows." Therefore, it's okay to do anything one wants to do within the boundaries of the sacred circle. "Sit. Stand. Lie down. Sleep. Think. Meditate. Stretch. Pray. Sing. Dance. Open your heart. Be still. Talk to God. Nap. Watch the environment around you. Breathe. Write. Cry. Laugh. Forgive. Heal. Love."

This is the time, she says, when the seekers' consciousness and perception of their inner and outer worlds may begin to shift and their self-understanding deepens. They will begin to experience feelings, thoughts, emotions, and memories that may have

I went to the woods because I wished to live deliberately, to front only
the essential facts of life, and see if I could not learn what it had to teach, and not,
when I came to die, discover that I had not lived.
—HENRY DAVID THOREAU

been dormant for a long, long time. Voices, both real and imagined, may speak out of the darkness and/or animals, birds, insects, plants, and even fairies may arrive with life-changing messages.

At the end of their solo phase the seekers return to the base camp and spend two days debriefing. "It's a time of integration," Linn comments, adding there are many ways to adapt these ideas and principles to retreats that can take place at home, in your neighborhood and other locations.

Many programs, such as NOLS and Outward Bound, are not vision quests per se, but build solo time for reflection into a group adventure that challenges participants' minds, bodies, and spirits. For example, the Outward Bound sailing course that is based on Hurricane Island off the rugged Maine coast includes time when "bounders" spend two or more days alone on one of the thousands of tiny islands dotting Penobscot Bay. They are given only a gallon of water, a handful of gorp (good ole raisins and peanuts), two matches, a tin can in which to cook foraged food, and a piece of Visqueen for protection from the elements. Bounders hiking in the desert, canoeing in Minnesota, or rafting in Colorado also go on solos suited to their locations.

Other solos, vision quests, and vigils can be self-directed. Justine Toms, cofounder and producer of New Dimensions Radio, went to the California desert on one such ten-day quest several years ago. Here she shares some thoughts about that solo time:

The contemplative waits in silence and when he is "answered," it is not so much
by a word that bursts into his silence. It is by the silence itself suddenly, inexplicably,
revealing itself to him as a world of great power.
—THOMAS MERTON

I've learned many important lessons. As I sat alone, days passed and nothing happened except some flies kept buzzing around my head. They were a nuisance and their numbers multiplied. They drove me crazy and there was nothing I could do. Endless buzzing, no relief—madness. Suddenly, when I thought I couldn't stand it another moment, I heard a voice. It said, "Maybe the flies are your gift." I was stunned. From that moment on everything changed. I stopped resisting the buzzing and became one with it. I discovered it had tones and overtones—like my life. Each fly sounded different and when all the sounds combined it became a song that shifted my energy. I was no longer agitated. I was calm, peaceful, and attentive. Now the flies were my companions who were teaching me a lot about the way I make choices and the choices I make.

In *Solitude: A Return to the Self* Anthony Storr wrote about Admiral Richard E. Byrd, the first person to fly over the North Pole. Storr describes Byrd's experiences in Antarctica during the winter of 1934 when for five months the navigator conducted meteorological and auroral research and lived alone in a shack. One reason Byrd took this retreat was that he was suffering from bouts of "time sickness" and "time pressure," which were discussed in the previous chapter, and he wanted "to taste peace and quiet and solitude long enough to find out how good they really are." He no longer had time to do things, personally, that he felt were meaningful, said Storr. Indeed, he even questioned whether his life was still purposeful. So he undertook this respite—admitting that he wanted something more than just the privacy the bottom of the earth afforded him. "I wanted to sink roots into some replenishing philosophy," Byrd later reflected.

During his vigil at the weather station Byrd kept a diary, which became the heart of his book *Alone.* In it he wrote that during his time in the tundra he felt "more alive" than he ever had before. On April 14, 1934, he penned the following after his daily walk:

Solitude is the furnace of transformation.

—HENRI NOUWEN

I paused to listen to the silence. . . . The day was dying, the night being born—but with great peace. Here were the imponderable processes and forces of the cosmos, harmonious and soundless. Harmony, that was it! That was what came out of the silence—a gentle rhythm, the strain of a perfect chord, the music of the spheres, perhaps.

It was enough to catch that rhythm, momentarily to be myself a part of it. In that instant I could feel no doubt of man's oneness with the universe. The conviction came that that rhythm was too orderly, too harmonious, too perfect to be a product of blind chance—that, therefore, there must be purpose in the whole and that man was part of that whole and not an accidental off-shoot. It was a feeling that transcended reason; that went to the heart of man's despair and found it groundless. The universe was a cosmos, not a chaos; man was as rightfully a part of that cosmos as were the day and night.

Byrd's words, written a half century before Justine Toms discovered the same sense of awe about the web of life on her vision quest, capture the essence of what a retreat and time for respite and renewal can bring to our lives. Whether we retreat alone or with others; whether we meditate, learn, ponder, wonder, rest, express, and/or pamper ourselves, take on the elements or do all those things, when we gift ourselves with a retreat we return home with something special. Byrd put it this way: "I did take away something that I had not fully possessed before: appreciation of the sheer beauty and miracle of being alive."

⟩ RESOURCES ⟩

BOOKS

Baldwin, Christina. *Calling the Circle.* Newberg, OR: Swan Raven & Company, 1994.

Benson, John. *Transformative Getaways for Spiritual Growth, Self-Discovery, and Holistic Healing.* New York: Henry Holt & Co., 1996.

Boorstein, Sylvia. *Don't Just Do Something, Sit There.* San Francisco: Harper San Francisco, 1996.

Buchholz, Ester Schaler, Ph.D. *The Call of Solitude: Alonetime in a World of Attachment.* New York: Simon & Schuster, 1997.

Burt, Bernard. *Fodor's Healthy Escapes* (6th edition). New York: Fodor's Travel Publications, Inc., 1999.

Campbell, Joseph with Bill Moyers. *The Power of Myth.* New York: Doubleday, 1988.

Cooper, David A.

Renewing Your Soul: A Guided Retreat for the Sabbath and Other Days of Rest. San Francisco: Harper San Francisco, 1995.

Silence, Simplicity, and Solitude: A Guide for Spiritual Retreat. New York: Bell Tower, 1992.

Housden, Roger. *Retreat: Time Apart for Silence and Solitude.* San Francisco: Harper San Francisco, 1995.

Keirsey, David W. *Please Understand Me II: Temperament, Character, Intelligence.* Del Mar, CA: Prometheus Nemesis Book Co., 1998.

Kelly, Jack and Maria. *Sanctuaries: The Complete United States.* New York: Bell Tower, 1996.

Lederman, Ellen. *Vacations That Can Change Your Life: Adventures, Retreats and Workshops for the Mind, Body and Spirit.* Naperville, IL: Sourcebooks, 1996.

Linn, Denise. *Quest: A Guide for Creating Your Own Vision Quest.* New York: Ballantine Books 1997.

Louden, Jennifer. *The Women's Retreat Book.* New York: HarperCollins, 1997.

Miller, Jenifer. *Healing Centers and Retreats.* Santa Fe: John Muir Publications, 1998.

Norris, Gunilla. *Sharing Silence.* New York: Bell Tower, 1993.

Storr, Anthony. *Solitude: A Return to the Self.* New York: Ballantine Books, 1988.

AUDIOTAPES

For catalogs of tapes that discuss silence, simplicity, and solitude write:

Sounds True: P.O. Box 8010, Boulcer, CO 80306-8010 or call 800-333-9185

New Dimensions Audio Tapes, P.O. Box 569, Ukiah, CA 95482-0569, 800-935-8273

WWW

Jennifer Louden's Comfort Channel—www.Jennifer@loudenbooks.com

New Dimensions Audio Tapes—www.newdimensions.org

Omega Institute for Holistic Studies—www.omega-inst.org

RETREAT CENTERS AND PROGRAMS

Because there are over six hundred monasteries, convents, spas, and spiritual and retreat centers in the United States it's helpful to use comprehensive, well-researched guides like John Benson's or Bernard Burt's to become acquainted with them. You can then write, call, or search the World Wide Web for more information. The addresses of a few of the centers and programs mentioned in this chapter are:

Denise Linn Seminars
P.O. Box 75657
Seattle, WA 98125-0657
206-528-2465

Esalen Institute
Highway I
Big Sur, CA 93920
408-644-8476 (for a catalog)
www.esalen.org

Hollyhock
Box 127
Manson's Landing
Cortes Island, B.C.
Canada V0P1K0
800-933-6339

Insight Meditation Society
1230 Pleasant Street
Barre, MA 01005
508-355-4378

Omega Institute for Holistic Studies
260 Lake Drive
Rhinebeck, NY 12572
914-266-4444
www.omega-inst.org

Outward Bound Incorporated
100 Mystery Point Road
Garrison, NY 10524-9757
800-243-8520
www.outwardbound.com

Upaya
1404 Cerrogordo Road
Santa Fe, NM 87501
505-986-8518

6.

The Serious Side of Play and Laughter

Every summer people from all over the globe spend a weekend or a week at hands-on learning centers like Omega. Back home they often describe these places as "overnight camps for adults," because their time away from the pressures of "everyday living" was simultaneously energizing and relaxing, and, most important, fun. While away they discovered that in the process of awakening new possibilities and potentialities, they could also rediscover long-forgotten ways of being in the world. High on that list of how life used to be is the role recreation plays in the process of their *re-creation*.

Because play and laughter are not only fun and games, but important factors that bring balance to an optimal wellness equation, it's important to understand the positive impact they have on our health. In the pages that follow we will explore recent discoveries about the healthful and healing benefits of play and laughter and hear from Omega teachers who can tell us ways to begin experiencing them.

Until recently scientists didn't study why animals play because they couldn't make sense of what seemingly had no purpose, reported a 1997 *U.S. News & World Report*

Life must be lived as play.

—PLATO

---

article. "Courtship has an obvious point," it noted in reference to the frolicsome activities of bighorn sheep. So does fighting, which usually provides the winner with more food or sex. "But play seemed entirely frivolous—and, by extension, so did anybody who studied it."

Sigmund Freud, the father of psychoanalysis, is the one most often blamed for the prevailing attitude that play is a waste of time. His theory was that human beings need sex, love, and work, but not play. What Freud didn't know was what psychobiologist Stephen Siviy found out decades later while conducting experiments with rats at Gettysburg College in Pennsylvania. Here Siviy discovered that when rats play, their brains secrete dopamine, the same chemical that stimulates excitement and elation in people.

Although Siviy was not the first person to begin taking play seriously, he, like scores of other biologists and ethnologists (students of animal behavior) who spend their workdays watching bighorn sheep, bears, wolves, ravens, dolphins, rats, and even some reptiles, cavort, now knows that in certain species play may be as important as eating and sleeping. In fact it's so critical to proper growth and development that today we acknowledge that something once considered "entirely frivolous" is not just fun and games. It's serious business that in certain animals:

- cements social bonds
- acts as a rehearsal for adulthood
- prepares for unexpected situations
- helps them become "cosmopolitan"
- helps restrain aggressive impulses
- teaches negotiation
- develops the ability to gauge the intentions of others

To be playful and serious at the same time is possible,
in fact it defines the ideal mental condition.

—JOHN DEWEY

> All animals, except man, know that the principal
> business of life is to enjoy it.
> —SAMUEL BUTLER

Animal Stories

Many researchers believe that when animals play they're rehearsing for adulthood. Take John Byers, for example. He's an evolutionary biologist at the University of Idaho who has studied young pronghorn antelopes. He says, "If you are a prey species, you practice running away. If you are a predator, you practice pouncing and chomping." He observed that when a young fawn finishes nursing, it will stand there looking dazed.

Suddenly, it will start to jerk around, "as if it has a fly in its brain." Then, like a ballerina, it will begin leaping—vertically—before racing away from the herd. Finally, after running as fast as forty miles an hour, the fawn comes back to rest at its mother's side.

What's the value of that? According to Byers it's "locomotor play" that connects neurons throughout the young antelope's brain—especially in the region controlling and coordinating movement. Other young animals that master skills during play include:

◆ Rhesus monkeys—they learn how to coordinate their muscles so they can race through a tangle of branches without a slip

◆ Kittens—they pounce on rolling balls to master instinctive hunting skills

◆ Chimps and gorillas—they play follow-the-leader, hide-and-seek, and other group games to build social bonds and learn about cooperation

◆ Young hippos—they bite and ram one another during playful bouts that test their strength

◆ Bear cubs—they angle their paws so they don't hurt one another while boxing and learning to defend themselves

> The true object of all human life is play.
> Earth is a task garden; heaven is a playground.
>
> —G. K. CHESTERTON

If those sound like just a few of the reasons that play may also be important for human beings, you're right. Studies of animals and children show, repeatedly, that play is vital to our overall development. Children who don't engage in it may suffer serious consequences. For example, research shows that children who never get to play may grow up to be less socially adept. In her book *For Your Own Good* psychoanalyst Alice Miller tells the story of Jürgen Bartsch, who was imprisoned for murdering four boys. Miller comments that when Bartsch finally confronted his parents about his childhood, one of the questions he asked, tearfully, was "Why didn't you play with me one single time in twenty years?"

O. Fred Donaldson, Ph.D., a play specialist, reports a similar experience he had attending a national play conference.

Case Study

Doug is a young man in his late thirties who was born with cerebral palsy. We were in a ballroom when I asked him if he would like to get out of his wheelchair and play with me. He answered yes with so much enthusiasm that I thought he might leap out of the chair himself. After advising me how I could help him get out of his chair, we got down on the floor. There, like two boys on a lawn, we rolled around, tumbled over and under each other, and finally rested on the carpet—breathing heavily and hugging each other. Later, during dinner, Doug cried while telling me about his parents' fear of touching him. He explained that he had always wanted his father, who had recently died, to play with him. "But he never did," Doug said. "No one ever did."

Donaldson, whose "work" includes playing with street gang members, autistic children, grizzly bears, and wolves, believes that in early childhood we know intuitively that life is there "to be one, not won," and that play is at the heart of that wholeness. Play is *not* about competition, he says, counter to the popular way in which we think of it. "Instead," he adds, "it is a unified heart-body-mind art."

In Sanskrit the word *lila* expresses the essence of that unified art. *Lila* is a "richer" word for play than ours, says author, musician, and computer artist Stephen Nachmanovitch in his book *Free Play: Improvisation in Life and the Arts.* It means divine play— "the play of creation, destruction, and re-creation, the folding and unfolding of the cosmos." It is also play that is free and deep because it is both the delight and enjoyment of this moment and the play of God. Interestingly, he adds, the word *lila* also means love.

So how do those of us who feel that we lost or never had that important and very special love, give ourselves permission to find it again? How do we find our way back to a place in ourselves where we can play freely and deeply enough that the sheer delight and enjoyment of the moment helps to lighten our burdens?

One way to begin is by exploring the various meanings of this universal phenomenon. Doing so may offer some clues as to where and when, during the course of our lifetime, we may have experienced and engaged in it.

One rather bland dictionary definition of play says it's "to occupy oneself in amusement, sport, or other recreation." A similar description appears in *Mosby's Medical, Nursing, & Allied Health Dictionary,* which says active play is "any activity from which one derives amusement, entertainment, enjoyment, or satisfaction by taking a participatory rather than a passive role."

Aristotle's definition, that play is a spontaneous end in itself, is more enlivening and invigorating. So, too, are definitions by Martine Mauriras-Bousquet, a psychobiologist who works for UNESCO's Education Sector and applies play theory to communication and training. Hers include:

+ An activity which is its own justification and exists in its own right

+ An oasis of happiness in the desert of the so-called serious life

+ A moment in time in which we don't ask life to be anything but what it is or to have any purpose other than itself

- A desire for that which one plays, not desire for something which one lacks and feels one must obtain

- A desire for the here and now, for the passing and the coming moment

In other words, she says, "Play is pure appetite for living, not for this or that type of life made desirable by fashion or habit, but for things as they are, for life as it is." Yet, as idyllic as that sounds, Mauriras-Bousquet is also quick to put a damper on things by pointing out a truth too many of us learned while growing up: that for our civilization play is a waste of time because it is associated with words that imply it is not serious. Donaldson says, in our society children are given manifestos that define play in terms of who, what, where, when, why, and how it's acceptable. He then goes on to list the following phrases—all of which, he says, "de-mean" children's play and lead to our eventual disenchantment with it.

As you look over his list, see how many of these "don'ts" sound like echoes from

---

Try this with one or more people— family members, friends, coworkers

- Quickly list all the sights, sounds, smells, tastes, feelings, and other sensory images from your childhood play that you can recall.

- Look over your list and share it with a partner or others in your group.

- Note similarities and differences in the way people who are approximately your age played.

- Make the same observations about the ways in which those older and younger than you played.

- Discuss how play has changed over the years.

your past. Check those that apply—and, if you hear others not listed, don't hesitate to name them aloud and/or write them in:

+ Don't play on the grass!
+ Don't play in the house!
+ Don't play with your food!
+ Don't play with yourself!
+ I don't have time to play now.
+ I'm too busy/old/tired/big to play.
+ Go outside and play!
+ Don't play in those clothes!
+ Play quietly.
+ Don't play so roughly.
+ Don't play on your bed.
+ Don't play in the rain.
+ Don't play around.
+ You shouldn't play with them.

Play, as viewed by the World Health Organization, is a mirror of society that reflects its basic values and transmits them to the child. Therefore, the de-meaning of the spirit of play that's reflected in the above list alters the context of children's lives, observes Donaldson. It transforms how we view ourselves and act with children, and ultimately that view causes both children and adults to see the big, wide, wonderful world around them getting whittled down to black-and-white choices such as safe versus unsafe, "us" versus "them."

It's never too late to have a happy childhood.

—TOM ROBBINS

Blake once led the painter Samuel Palmer to his window and,
pointing to a group of children at play, said, "That is heaven."

—STEPHEN MITCHELL

Listen to the mustn'ts child,
listen to the don'ts
listen to the shouldn'ts,
the impossibles, the won'ts
listen to the never haves
then listen close to me—
anything can happen child,
ANYTHING can be.
                                    —Shel Silverstein

It's no wonder that by the time we grow up we are *afraid* to play. We've listened to so many reasons not to that we fear being embarrassed, says Howard Moody, a play-meister who is a member of Omega's core faculty, director of LifePlay, and a trainer and consultant for Professional Play Leaders Association of America.

Moody, who believes that play puts you in touch with the grace of the universe, explains, "Play is such a dynamic, joyful response to being alive—even under the most dire circumstances. It's a time when children and/or adults can have positive, sponta-neous, enjoyable and meaningful experiences with each other." The main reason we, as adults, fail to reap those benefits, Moody adds, is that we begin to think play is frivolous and actually lose our ability to do it.

One reason that play gets categorized as a senseless waste of time is that in our culture we mistakenly equate silliness and stupidity, says Moody. In fact, they are two very different things, he adds. The word *silly* is rooted in *silli*, a Middle English word for "blessed," "fortunate," "kind," "cheerful," and "innocent." That means being silly is a very healthy thing. However, *stupid*, which means "uninformed," "uneducated," and "pointless," is not.

During his workshops at Omega, Moody helps teenagers and adults regain the

According to Howard Moody, the language of play among children and wildlife is spoken through:

+ eye contact

+ a sense of touch

+ a certain kindness

+ a lack of contest

Understanding this language gives us the ability to give and receive:

+ kindness

+ trust

+ love

+ belonging

+ touch

+ compassion for any being with whom we share the earth

spirit of play, laughter, and silliness that they may have lost years earlier. It's about awareness of self and others, he says. "If you notice people playing, you probably have a yearning to do that too. Play is a way for us to feel an important sense of belonging. But very quickly in our goal-oriented society, it gets turned into a contest in which we must learn to compete in order to survive instead of being accepted as a way to be in the world and a joyful response to being alive."

Moody recommends doing the following to help recover our natural ability and instinct to play. Doing them with a partner will help you to overcome any feelings of awkwardness or embarrassment:

+ Go to a park and watch children.
+ Play with a child and let him or her lead you.

- Touch flowers and nature in a way that gives and receives love.

- Tell or write fantasy stories.

- Try skipping.

- Talk in gibberish.

- Make faces at yourself in the mirror.

There's a Buddhist saying that Fred Donaldson quotes when he guides adults back into the childlike world of play. It goes like this: "The mind simply becomes as it was in the beginning when we knew nothing and had yet to be taught anything at all."

To that he adds, "Beside every adult there is a little child who can continually remind us with a tug on our clothes and spirits, prompting us in the very midst of our 'busyness,' to an awareness of something that stirs in the basements of our memories. It matters not if it seems foreign, because it comes from a part of us that remembers a yearning for a great belonging and reminds us that we do belong to the human community; that we are of infinite value like every human being."

If you've lost your characteristics of childlikeness and hope to recover them, try incorporating into your life these six basic play principles that Donaldson teaches:

- Be not afraid of life.

- All life is of one kind.

- Touch is our primary language.

- Be a beginner.

- Smooth moves follow a clear heart.

- Expect nothing, be ready for anything.

Laugh and the world laughs with you.

—ELLA WHEELER WILCOX

Turning again to the Sanskrit word *lila*, Nachmanovitch reminds us that this all-encompassing word for play may be the simplest thing there is—spontaneous, child-ish, disarming. "But as we grow and experience the complexities of life, it may also be the most difficult achievement imaginable." Is it worth it? "Yes," he answers, because "its coming to fruition is a kind of homecoming to our true selves."

Wherever, whenever, children play, the universal sound of laughter fills the air and anyone within earshot is apt to laugh along, or at least smile. If that suggests that laughter—our vocal response to joy, happiness, and humor—is contagious, you're right. However, unlike viruses and colds that cause *dis*-ease, laughter does just the op-posite by promoting health and healing.

Perhaps no one directed the various medical communities' attention to these ben-efits more than the late Norman Cousins, who was editor of the *Saturday Review* and the author of several books on emotions and healing. The story of how he coupled positive emotions with Marx Brothers movies and *Candid Camera* videos to help his medical team heal him of a debilitating, painful, and life-threatening disease is now legendary. "I discovered that ten minutes of solid belly laughter would give me two

---

There are three things which are real: God, human folly, and laughter. The first two are beyond our comprehensions. So we must do what we can with the third.

—JOHN F. KENNEDY

> Nobody ever died of laughter.
>
> —MAX BEERBOHM

hours of pain-free sleep," he often said when asked for examples of how laughter helped him deal with a condition called ankylosing spondylitis.

In the years following his recovery, Cousins began writing and lecturing about the benefits of incorporating into one's life the biblical axiom "A merry heart doeth good like a medicine." Like a pebble cast in the water his preachings and teachings about the value of laughter had a ripple effect. Now, two decades after the publication of his best-seller *Anatomy of an Illness*, medical schools, research centers, hospitals, and, most important, people suffering from chronic and life-threatening illnesses are taking seriously the joys of laughter that Cousins took seriously. If laughter isn't *the* best medicine, it's one of the best, they acknowledge.

Back then Cousins suspected that laughter quelled pain because it stimulated the production of endorphins—the hormones that serve as the body's own morphine and help produce a "runner's high." Today we know he was running his theory on the right track.

The first study to probe Cousins's anecdotal evidence about the healing power of

Norman Cousins believed that the following positive emotions and attitudes played as vital a role in healing his body, mind, and spirit as humor did:

+ love

+ hope

+ faith

+ will to live

+ purpose

+ determination

Ever wonder where we get the phrase *He's in a bad humor?*

The root of the word is *umor,* which means "fluid" or "liquid." In the Middle Ages, medical practitioners thought *humor* referred to an energy related to a specific body fluid or emotional state that determined one's health and disposition. For example:

◆ sanguine humor—blood and cheerfulness

◆ choleric humor—bile and anger

◆ phlegmatic humor—mucus and apathy

◆ melancholic humor—black bile and depression

humor and positive emotions appeared in the *Journal of the American Medical Association* (*JAMA*). In that article the prestigious journal reported, "The research shows that laughter helps the body to provide its own medications."

More recent studies show that laughter stimulates the production of catecholamines, hormones that may cause the brain to release the body's natural opiates—endorphins. But that's not all that happens. A growing body of physiological, sociological, psychological, and even anthropological studies now show that even small doses of humor benefit our minds, bodies, and spirits in healthful and surprising ways.

How does a good chuckle, chortle, or "cracking up" over something we perceive as funny do that? Think about times when you've laughed hard and heartily. While laughing you took deep breaths, you sighed, and, finally, you relaxed—sometimes for just moments before laughing again. Each time, whatever was making you laugh encouraged your cardiovascular and respiratory systems to function better and boosted your hormonal, nervous, and immune systems.

If you can laugh at it you can survive it.

—BILL COSBY

Robert Provine, Ph.D., an anthropologist at the University of Maryland, hangs out in the natural habitats of humans—city streets, shopping malls, classrooms, bars, et cetera—in order to "appreciate laughter as a social vocalization of the human animal." In more than a decade of doing this, Provine has managed to nail down the fact that laughter is a universal instinct that serves some primitive social function.

What he does know is that laughter is to us what calls are to birds and barks are to dogs. While most laughter is set off by auditory cues, jokes are not the main instigation. More often the hilarity is provoked by such innocuous questions as "Where have you been?" or "You're doing what?"

Some of Provine's other findings include:

- People are thirty times more likely to laugh in groups than alone.

- Women laugh far more than men, except when they are listening to other women.

- Bland phrases trigger laughter four times more than formal jokes.

- When a person is talking, he/she chuckles 46 percent more than the listener(s).

- Humans aren't the only animals that laugh. Apes do also.

- Laughs have the structure of "ha-ha-ha" or "ho-ho-ho" but not "ha-ho-ha-ho."

"Mirth is a total body experience," reported William F. Fry, Jr., M.D., a psychiatrist at Stanford Medical School, in *Health & Humor Journal*. "We have scientific laboratory evidence, not speculatory ideas, that the skeletal muscular system and the central nervous, respiratory, cardiovascular, immune, and endocrine systems are responsive and active during the response of mirthful laughter."

Fry began exploring the therapeutic value of humor back in the 1950s. In one of his studies now considered a classic, he set out to determine the ventilating and heart-strengthening impact of laughter. It was no joke when after ten minutes of strenuously rowing he discovered that just ten seconds of belly laughter yielded the same aerobic results.

Studies by other researchers reach similar conclusions. For example, they show that some good side-slapping guffaws can help to increase blood oxygen levels, clear mucus, make us more alert, and give our memory a boost. In other words, a laugh a day may keep the doctor away. Here are some other findings that may give you reasons to do something that tickles your funny bone today:

- Even though your blood pressure actually rises when you laugh heartily, afterward it gets lower.
- Laughter lowers levels of epinephrine (which is also called adrenaline), a hormone that responds to physical or mental stress. Lower levels of epinephrine can reduce blood pressure and help alleviate other cardiovascular problems.
- A good laugh lowers secretions of the stress hormone cortisol. Reduced cortisol level helps the immune system to produce greater numbers of beneficial white blood cells and to function more normally.
- There are eighteen different smiles. The most revealing is the smile of enjoyment.
- When we look forward to going somewhere or doing something that makes us laugh, we have a physical phenomenon called "an anticipatory response." This is considered positive stress that results in healthier hormonal response.
- Laughter expands the capillaries in our face. That's why we get such a cheery glow when we're having a real good time.
- The brain activity that stimulates laughter takes place in different lobes and it enhances alertness and memory.
- The term *fits of laughter* is appropriate because we actually lose muscle control when we laugh long and hard.
- When it comes to stress-busting, fifteen minutes of hees and haws offer benefits similar to six to eight hours of Buddhist meditation.

Although Freud discounted the value of play to the human condition, he was reputed to have an extensive collection of jokes. He was also one of the first people to probe the therapeutic role of humor and laughter. In fact, many of the current discoveries about the psychological benefits of humor and laughter echo early observations that Freud made in his book *Wit and Its Relation to the Unconscious*. For example, the famed psychoanalyst noted that:

+ Jokes are one of the ways that humans defend against disturbing emotions such as fear, anxiety, and anger.

+ Humor helps to relieve the pain people suffer as a result of misfortune. This, in turn, allows them to deal with their life's situations in an intelligent, mature, and constructive fashion.

+ Laughter and humor foster social relationships and mutual feelings of pleasure.

Comedian Steve Allen puts it this way: "Humor serves as a social lubricant." It also helps us to make light of what are essentially serious matters such as death and disease. "We cannot spend all our time feeling pain and weeping, so laughter has been an evolutionary development which helps us get around these otherwise apparently hopeless obstructions," he said in an interview in *Health & Humor Journal*.

Medical professionals agree. For example Bernie Siegel, M.D., author of *Love, Medicine and Miracles* and other books on how to live positively with chronic and life-

Comedian Steve Allen is often a keynote speaker at conventions that explore the healing power of humor. He suggests doing the following to enhance your sense of humor:

+ Read great literary humorists such as James Thurber, Robert Benchley, S. J. Perelman, and others.

+ Read funny newspaper columnists such as Dave Barry and the late Erma Bombeck.

+ Watch professional comedians in an analytical way to see why they're funny.

+ Take Norman Cousins's advice and watch Laurel and Hardy, the Marx Brothers, Charlie Chaplin, and other great oldies.

> It better befits a man to laugh at life than to lament over it.
>
> —SENECA

threatening illness, says that you don't have to be a genius or rocket scientist to see that laughter helps people and that it can help you. All you have to do is look at their happy faces.

Back in the seventeenth century a physician named Thomas Sydenham said, "The arrival of a good clown exercises more beneficial influence upon the health of a town than of twenty asses laden with drugs." Patch Adams, M.D., founder of the Gesundheit Institute in West Virginia and a clown who sports a bulbous red nose while making mirth in hospitals worldwide, puts it this way: "Laughter is the white noise of happiness. People crave it as if it were an essential amino acid. When the woes of existence beset us, we urgently seek comic relief. The more emotions we invest in a subject, the greater its potential for guffaws.... Humor and fun (which is humor in action) are equal partners with love as key ingredients for a healthy life."

Perhaps Adams takes his cue from another of his predecessors, Henri de Mondeville, a fourteenth-century professor of surgery, who wrote, "Let the surgeon take care to regulate the whole regimen of the patient's life for joy and happiness, allowing his relatives and special friends to cheer him, and by having someone tell him jokes." Today, medical professionals put it this way: "He who laughs, lasts."

RESOURCES

BOOKS

Adams, Patch, M.D. *Gesundheit!* Rochester, VT: Healing Arts Press, 1993.

Allen, Steve. *Make 'Em Laugh.* Buffalo, NY: Prometheus Books, 1993.

Cousins, Norman.

   Anatomy of an Illness. New York: Bantam Books, 1981.

Head First: The Biology of Hope and the Healing Power of the Human Spirit. New York: Penguin Books, 1990.

Donaldson, O. Fred, Ph.D. *Playing by Heart: The Vision and Practice of Belonging.* Deerfield Beach, FL: Health Communications, Inc., 1993.

Nachmanovitch, Stephan. *Free Play: Improvisation in Life and the Arts.* Los Angeles: Jeremy P. Tarcher, 1990.

Wooten, Patty, R.N. *Compassionate Laughter: Jest for Your Health!* Salt Lake City: Commune-A-Key, 1996.

WWW

Adventure Game Theater—http://www.agt.org

American Association for Therapeutic Humor—http://www.aath.org

Funny Times—www.funnytimes.com/ft

Humor Archives (from around the Web)—alabanza.com/kabacoff/inter-links/humor.html

Humor and Health Institute and Journal—http://www.intop.net/~jrdunn/index.html

Humor Matters—http://www.humormatters.com

(The) Humor Project—http://www.humorproject.com

Jest for the Health of It!—http://www.mother.com/JestHome

The Laughter Remedy for Stressed-out People & Organizations—http://www.laughterremedy.com

ORGANIZATIONS, CATALOGS, AND MISCELLANEOUS PUBLICATIONS

Adventure Game Theater and/or LifePlay
P.O. Box 416
Lee, MA 01238
Phone: 1-888-792-PLAY
E-mail: info@agt.org

American Association for Therapeutic Humor (AATH)
222 Meramec, Suite 303
St. Louis, MO 63105
Phone: 314-863-6232

Clown Supplies, Inc.
The Castles
Route 101, Suite C7
Brentwood, NH 03833
603-679-3311
Catalog sales of a wide variety of clown supplies, props, and gags.

Funny Times
P.O. Box 18530
Cleveland Heights, OH 44118
216-371-8600
Monthly newspaper with cartoons and funny articles.

Humor and Health Letter
P.O. Box 16814
Jackson, MS 39236
601-957-0075
Newsletter about laughter research and applications.

Humor Project
110 Spring Street
Saratoga Springs, NY 12866
518-587-8770
www.humorproject.com
Sponsors biannual "Humor and Creativity" conference and publishes *Laughing Matters*,
    a quarterly journal.

Laughter Therapy
P.O. Box 827
Monterey, CA 93942
Candid Camera video films for free rental to use for stimulating laughter for recovery
    from illness. Send letter explaining plans for use.

National Association for the Humor Impaired
400 South 15th Street
Suite 201
La Crosse, WI 54601

Whole Mirth Catalog
1034 Page Street
San Francisco, CA 94117
Catalog with many humorous items, toys, gags, and books.

7.

A Discussion of
Fitness That Fits

Take a few moments to close your eyes and imagine a colorful sunrise over a calm, beautiful lake surrounded by pine, spruce, maple, and other trees. As the sun comes up on the eastern end of the lake, quiet, peaceful-looking people of all ages, dressed in sweats, pajamas, skirts, shorts, bathing suits, and jeans are gathered on a beach. Slowly, they are mimicking an instructor's dancelike movements. Dreamily, they watch the horizon through soft eyes as dawn becomes day. Deep mindful breaths accompany their movements—they take in the fresh morning air as if it were a fluffy white cloud, then push out an expired gray one. No one seems concerned about whether their movements are perfect.

Now look a little more closely at their faces. You see their relaxed expressions. No one looks tense, frustrated, or fearful that they're doing the "dance" steps wrong. Many wear smiles—half smiles, broad smiles, serene smiles. No one is straining. Now

---

Your body is the harp of your soul,
And it is yours to bring forth sweet music from it or confused sounds.

—KAHLIL GIBRAN

---

see yourself among them. You, too, look calm. You, too, wear a smile. You, too, are breathing mindfully. Though you're not quite sure what to do, it feels okay to be in whatever place you're in. You go with the flow. There's no pressure to do anything else. You, too, are celebrating the dawn and it feels wonderful.

Those of you who have been to Omega and joined in the lakefront early-morning tai chi sessions or the yoga and movement classes held elsewhere on the campus may feel right at home with this imagery. So might those of you who haven't visited Omega but have participated in some physical activity that engaged not only your body and muscles, but your spirit too. Spend a few moments thinking about that activity. Is it something you do now or have done in the past? What was it that unified your mind, body, spirit, and emotions and suspended ordinary time? Did it happen while practicing yoga, tai chi, or qigong? Or was it during a round of basketball, tennis, racquetball, or golf? Perhaps that sense came over you while you were running, swimming, sailing, or even raking leaves. Where was it? How did it feel? Wouldn't you like those movements and motions we call exercise to always feel that way?

For many Americans finding a way to factor exercise into an optimal health equation can be difficult, if not impossible. After long hours on the job or meeting the demands of an endless "to-do" list, just the idea of making time to "work out" can seem absurd. Call it an attitude problem, if you will, but just the mention of the word *work* can be enough to make couch potatoes of all shapes and sizes exclaim, "I don't need or want *more* work to do. I need and want more time, energy, relaxation, fun, and peace in my life."

As we learned in the previous chapters, most of us crave more fun and relaxation, but we find it hard to believe that exercise can be a means to time-shift, get in the

---

Each morning in Africa a lion awakens and knows it must run faster than the slowest gazelle to survive. Each morning in Africa a gazelle awakens and knows it must run faster than the fastest lion to survive. Which are you—a lion or a gazelle? It makes no difference as long as each morning you run.

—ANONYMOUS

"zone," and expand the present moment. Conditioned by the "no pain, no gain" mantra of the seventies and eighties, many of us tend to equate exercise with joyless activities. Spurred on by Madison Avenue's prompting to look picture perfect, we're told to trim tummies, build bulk, or do whatever it takes to look lank if we want to be accepted by our peers. Rarely do ads exclaiming that benefit point out that doing aerobic and weight-bearing activities purposefully might have a greater benefit in our lives.

In the pages ahead we will explore the greater contribution that regular exercise can make to the quality and, possibly, the quantity of the days of our lives. We will also learn that while exercise and sports can be important paths to take on our journey to overall fitness and optimal health, they are not ends in themselves. As we learned in other chapters, it is only when exercise and sports are balanced with rest, good nutrition, stress-reduction techniques, and emotional intelligence that we can begin to understand how powerfully and holistically they can revitalize and sustain us on this road we call our life.

According to cardiologist Dean Ornish, M.D., the first clinician to offer documented proof that heart disease can be reversed, there's no doubt that exercise will make you fit. However, he adds, "exercise alone is not enough to make you healthy"— fitness and health are not the same thing. For example, in his best-selling book *Dr. Dean Ornish's Program for Reversing Heart Disease,* he writes that in recent years several outstanding athletes who really looked fit either died from heart disease or were severely disabled by it. Among them was Jim Fixx, the man who ignited the running revolution and died while exercising. Others include basketball player Peter Maravich, who

We should conduct ourselves not as if we ought to live for the body,
but as if we could not live without it.

—SENECA THE YOUNGER

died while playing the sport to which he dedicated his life, and Tony Conigliaro, a star player for the Boston Red Sox, whose heart attack permanently disabled him before he died in 1990.

Zeroing in on Conigliaro's story, Ornish recalls that he first met this champion when he was an intern at Massachusetts General Hospital in Boston. As the paramedics wheeled the thirty-seven-year-old athlete into the cardiac arrest room, Ornish remembers being struck by the contrast between Conigliaro's athletic physique and the fact that he was suffering from a massive heart attack. Despite the fact that he looked so strapping on the outside, Conagliaro had major coronary blockages inside. Later Ornish learned that Conigliaro never fully recovered because his heart had stopped beating for five minutes before he arrived in the emergency room.

The indelible lesson Ornish learned that night was that exercise and fitness are not synonymous. From his perspective as a cardiologist he discovered that someone whose body looked toned and in "perfect" shape on the outside wasn't necessarily in similar health on the inside. *Fitness* refers to the "training effect"—a person's level of conditioning, he explains. "The simplest measurement of fitness is how long it takes for your heart rate to return to normal after vigorous exercise. The sooner your pulse returns to its usual resting rate, the more fit you are. Another measurement of fitness is your resting pulse rate—the slower it is, the more fit you are (assuming you are not taking cardiac medications). A third measurement of fitness is how far and long you can exercise."

Other factors that medical professionals and fitness experts look at in relation to these physiological benchmarks include:

+ strength—the amount of force exerted by muscles when someone lifts weights or does chin-ups

+ flexibility—the range of motion of a person's joints and muscles

+ body fat—the percentage of lean muscle tissue compared to body fat

+ coordination—the harmonious functioning of muscles or groups of muscles in the execution of movements, and

+ speed and reaction time

> If it weren't for the fact that the TV set and the refrigerator are so far apart,
> some of us wouldn't get any exercise at all.
>
> —JOEY ADAMS

Fitness is even more than all those measurements and parameters, however. A complete picture of fitness is more the sum of its physiological parts. Viewed from a systems perspective it includes elements related to the psyche and soul as well as the body. Here are a few ways in which other experts define it:

◆ Growing evidence in psychoneuroimmunology, which acknowledges the influence of the brain-mind on the neuromuscular, hormonal, endocrine, and immune systems, leads us to redefine fitness not just as the ability to do work or even as longevity but as a state of serenity, plenitude, and expansiveness (inner peace).

   —Dan Millman, Hall of Fame gymnast and author of *The Inner Athlete*

◆ It's the ability to stay calm in the midst of physical, emotional, and mental stress. It is analogous to the eye in the hurricane that, though peaceful, supports all of the dynamic activity about it.

   —John Douillard, author of *Body, Mind, and Sport* and a former triathlete

◆ Fitness is something that can be physiologically and psychologically transformative because it improves the hours of your day and adds years to your life. It increases your creative ability and your capacity to handle stress, and it helps stabilize your emotional state.

   —running guru George Sheehan, author of *Running and Being*

> Those who think they have not time for bodily exercise will
> sooner or later have to find time for illness.
>
> —EDWARD STANLEY

Cardiologist James Rippe, M.D., writes that early in his career he discovered that the patients who triumphed over life-threatening cardiovascular disease were those who got involved in their health care, believed in themselves, cultivated optimism and hope, and paid attention to their daily habits. "They helped me understand the power of the human spirit and that good health is a partnership between doctor and patient with the patient playing the deciding role," he noted.

Reflecting upon that early lesson, Rippe says his patients' cardiac rehabilitation program really opened his eyes to the positive effects exercise, nutrition, and stress reduction could have on people with heart disease. Eventually, the evidence that daily habits impacted long-term health led him to establish the Center for Clinical and Lifestyle Research at Tufts University School of Medicine.

When asked to describe what being fit means to him, Rippe goes back to 1975 when he was a twenty-seven-year-old first-year student at Harvard Medical School. At the time he was a running fanatic who chalked up forty to fifty miles per week. "I thought I had a terrific fitness program, but I was wrong. Sure my level of cardiovascular endurance was high, but my program was way out of balance."

Rippe comments that he was sore all the time. Moreover, his upper body wasn't strong enough to take part in certain sports without risking significant injury; his nutritional habits were "lousy," and he was a stressed-out medical student most of the time. He also admits he had a terrible attitude problem. "I viewed people who didn't exercise at the level I did as lazy and unfit." Although he recognizes that his take on exercise was prevalent in the 1970s and 1980s, he now sees how his attitude discouraged many people from thinking that their own efforts could impact their fitness and their life. Describing the way the myth he and others helped to perpetuate discounted others' efforts, Rippe adds, "Many people came to believe the misconception that if you weren't training for a marathon or a triathlon or performing high-intensity aerobics, you couldn't possibly be fit."

Today, he bases his key concepts of fitness on the definition put forth by the World Health Organization: Fitness is maintaining or developing the capacity to meet the challenges of daily life. "We now know that having the physical health and spiritual well-being

> to meet these challenges requires fitness, endurance, flexibility, functional fitness (balance, mobility, physical activity), mind-body interactions, the ability to manage stress, good nutrition, and weight management. We also now know that these fitness factors are highly modifiable."

According to the 1996 Surgeon General's report on physical activity, one in four Americans (40–50 million people) refuse to exercise even when it's disguised as a "leisure activity." Of course, the flip side of that negative statistic is that three quarters of the population *is* motivated to move in one way or another and that number includes 47 million Americans who didn't *just* exercise, but exercised "frequently" in 1996. According to a 1998 report by the Sporting Goods Manufacturers' Association, that figure is up from 39.5 million less than a decade earlier. Additionally, a majority of the frequent exercisers forty-five and over reported to the SGMA that the main reason they work out is not to improve their appearance but to maintain their health and vitality.

Studies indicate that if those surveyed by the SGMA keep up their exercise regimen it will serve them well. Of course, the same applies to the rest of us, no matter how young or old we happen to be. Exercise can be a panacea for many of the problems we encounter as we age, says Andrew Weil, M.D., director of the integrative medicine program at the University of Arizona at Tuscon. For example, exercise can:

- improve circulation, which makes the heart a more efficient pump and maintains the elasticity of the arteries

- help tone the respiratory system by increasing the exchange of oxygen and carbon dioxide, which, in turn, helps the body eliminate metabolic wastes

- further aid elimination by promoting the flow of perspiration and movement of the intestines

- stimulate the release of endorphins in the brain that help to fight depression and to boost moods

- help regulate metabolism and the body's economy of energy

+ neutralize stress, which promotes greater relaxation and sounder sleep

+ enhance immune function

Additional benefits of exercise reported by recent studies include:

+ a decreased risk of osteoporosis and diabetes

+ a possible protection against cancer of the colon, breast, ovaries, and cervix

+ an increase in HDL, the "good" form of cholesterol (see Chapter 8)

+ a decrease in LDL, the "bad" form of cholesterol (see Chapter 8)

If you are among those who shy away from or resist doing exercise, spend a few moments thinking about why. Is it because you feel you don't have time, or are there other reasons? Now think back to your childhood. Unless you had a disability, movement and stretching came naturally. Around one year of age and certainly by the time you were two, your biological clock set off something that motivated you to stand up and get going. And that you did despite all the ups and downs, stumbling and bumbling,

Are we an exercise-resistant nation? You be the judge.

+ In the 1990s we expended an average of 800 *fewer* calories a day than we did in the 1960s, reported a study in the *International Journal of Obesity*.

+ Only half of the youth in our country regularly participate in vigorous physical activities for 20 minutes three to five times a week

+ In the 1990s attendance in physical education classes dropped from 42 to 25 percent.

+ Over the past thirty years children six to eleven years of age have shown a 54 percent increase in the prevalance of obesity. Children twelve to seventeen have shown a 39 percent increase, according to *American Family Physician*.

+ In 1995, 62 percent of men and women over the age of fifty-five years were living sedentary lives.

More Studies

In a 1998 article in *Lancet,* researchers from the Royal Free Hospital School of Medicine in London reported that in 1,031 men with coronary artery disease or a prior stroke, physical activity led to a 56 percent reduction in overall mortality risk and a 44 percent decrease in risk of death from cardiovascular disease compared to sedentary men with similar histories. Altogether, 5,567 men participated in the study in which they filled out two questionnaires about their exercise habits—first in the late 1970s when they were fifty-two years old and then in 1992 when they were seventy-two. Researchers then followed the men for an additional four years. They concluded the reduction in mortality was most dramatic for 796 men who started doing moderate exercise between the two surveys. Their exercise took the form of walking, gardening, or light housework done several times a week or cycling, running, or swimming at least once a week.

In an article in the *Journal of the American Medical Association* (*JAMA*), researchers at the Institute for Aerobic Research reported that in an eight-year study of over 13,000 men and women who were apparently healthy, the sedentary or least fit group had a death rate more than three times greater than the most fit, a very active group. The subjects took treadmill tests and were placed in one of five groups based on heart and respiratory fitness. Ultimately, the study showed that even walking just thirty minutes daily (moderate exercise) reduced premature death almost as much as running thirty to forty miles a week. Furthermore, when compared to the sedentary group, deaths from *all* causes were lower in the remaining four groups.

The April 1998 issue of *American Family Physician* reported that 70 percent of all cancer patients undergoing radiation and chemotherapy suffer from fatigue and impaired physical performance. In a study to determine whether exercise could have a positive effect on patients with solid cancerous tumors, researchers found that patients in the control group had a higher loss of physical function than those in a training group who followed an exercise regimen for thirty minutes a day. An aerobic exercise program immediately after high-dose chemotherapy is safe and may prevent severe loss of physical performance, they concluded. Furthermore, exercise may also decrease some of the toxic side effects associated with chemotherapy.

bruises and bumps it took to overcome 14.7 pounds per square inch of gravity you mastered the skills needed to put one foot in front of the other while keeping your balance. Furthermore, once you got those motions down pat, you didn't stop. You didn't say you liked the view from the floor better and regress back to crawling. Instead, you began to expand your repertoire to include toddling, running, hopping, skipping, and jumping with an unequaled sense of joy, spontaneity, and freedom.

So what stopped you? What, for you, put a damper on moving spontaneously, joyfully, and exuberantly? Was it always being picked last for kickball? Getting a message from a parent or teacher that you weren't good enough? Not making the team? Was it that no matter what, you *had* to win at any cost and therefore wouldn't risk playing anything you weren't the best at? If so, you weren't alone. A poll by Louis Harris showed that as many as half of all Americans experienced their first major failure in life in sports.

What are some other reasons? Was it because you had a poor body image and found it traumatic to put on a swimsuit or dance leotard? Or perhaps you suffered an injury while exercising and feared the same thing would happen again? Maybe, as we discovered in the chapter on play, it was because you often got the message to "slow down" or "grow up" and in so doing outgrew sports and other big-muscle activities and moved into a more sedentary lifestyle.

If you are a woman, it could also be that society sent you a message that you

A sound mind in a sound body.

—JUVENAL

weren't supposed to be athletic. Gynecologist Christiane Northrup, M.D., points out that many girls don't excel in sports because no one ever taught them the skills they would need. "One of my friends who was a pro baseball player told me that when boys are first learning to throw, they also throw 'just like a girl,' " notes Northrup. Boys, she adds, learn to "throw like a boy" from practicing over and over again with those who are more skilled than they. It's part of their cultural heritage.

All told, the reasons above suggest that many people identify with the emotional and physical suffering that comes when we're picked last, told not to bother, or viewed as someone who is not "good enough" or clumsy, slow, and unathletic. As Northrup and others remind us, however, the negative and painful feelings generated by those thoughtless comments can be counterbalanced by regular exercise and feeling fit. The late Rudolf Laban, a choreographer, dancer, and teacher from Czechoslovakia who developed a system of movement called Labananalysis, summed it up this way: "Children and primate man have both a natural gift for bodily movement and a natural love for it. In later periods . . . man becomes cautious, suspicious, and sometimes even hostile to movement. He forgets that it is the basic experience of existence."

Research on the psychological benefits of exercise focuses on stress reduction, antianxiety effects, and antidepressant effects, according to psychiatrist Michael H. Sacks, M.D., a marathoner, swimmer, and cyclist. After reviewing several studies that looked at the psychological and physiological impact of emotional stress upon exercisers and nonexercisers in varied circumstances, Sacks concluded that although the jury is still out, studies suggest that regular exercisers exhibit healthier responses to stress than their sedentary counterparts.

In an article he wrote for the book *Mind/Body Medicine: How to Use Your Mind for Better Health,* Sacks explains that data accumulated since the 1970s shows that regular exercise has a "tranquilizer effect" that can decrease anxiety. In other words, even though your anxiety level may increase at the beginning of a workout, it will then stabilize enough that by the time you finish there's less anxiety than when you started. After-

The saying "fit for life" certainly applies to Mexico's Tarahumara Indians. For this indigenous tribe living in Copper Canyon, one of North America's deepest chasms (deeper than the Grand Canyon), running is both a way of life and a sport. According to the worldview held by the tribe's seventy thousand members, people peak physically when they are in their sixties—not when they're teenagers or young adults. Tests of the Tarahumaras' cardiovascular fitness, lung capacity, and endurance confirm their beliefs.

In 1998 David Roberts, a reporter for *Smithsonian* magazine, spent time with the Tarahumaras. Later he wrote:

At one o'clock in the valley below Samachique, the women's race began. Representing rival settlements in the neighborhood, two teams of eight, including girls, lined up at the starting line. Each team had a pair of interlinked hoops made of bent vines wrapped in cloth. As we watched, a woman on each team snagged her team's hoop with the curved tip of a peeled stick and flung it some ten yards along the path. Then she and her teammates ran after it, repeating the process. In a kind of endless relay, the members took turns advancing the hoop while their teammates tagged along, more or less together. The teams dwindled in the distance; through binoculars I saw them round a far post and head back.

The women vanished from view and reappeared thirty-five minutes later. A local explained that each lap was about four miles in length and that the race would end after ten laps had been run, or one team threw in the towel. Wearing sweaters, skirts, and plastic shoes or tire-sole sandals, these women were running a course longer than an Olympic marathon and a half, up and down a trail alternately rocky and marshy, jumping streams, crawling through fences, all the while flinging cloth hoops ahead of them!

Later, two teams of men and boys lined up on the same course. They propelled a sphere, about the size of a softball, carved of wood, not kicking it soccer-style, but deftly rolling it onto their bare toes and flinging it into the air with swings of their legs. The men's lap was twice as long as the women's: each finisher would have run eighty miles!

ward, a postexercise period of relaxation can set in that may last up to four hours. Within twenty-four hours the original level of anxiety returns, and although that

> You have to stay in shape. My grandmother, she started walking five miles a day when she was sixty. She's ninety-seven today and we don't know where the hell she is.
>
> —ELLEN DEGENERES

means exercise is hardly a cure for anxiety, it does suggest that if you exercise in the morning you might feel less stressed at work during the day. Then again, if you exercise in the afternoon, it may make it easier to fall asleep and catch some needed *zzzz's* at night.

Does it matter what kind of exercise we do to mitigate anxiety? No, says Sacks. Light exercise such as walking or swimming can reduce stress levels just as effectively as vigorous jogging. He also points out that people who exercise tend to be less depressed than people who don't. Although the reason why presents a chicken-or-the-egg conundrum—do people stave off depression by exercising or do less depressed, more energetic people exercise?—the fact is that studies show that exercise can be as good as or better than standard medical treatment for moderate depression.

In conclusion, Sacks finds that both our psychology and physiology contribute to the beneficial effects exercise can have on our moods. The factors that play into those effects include:

- the decision to take up exercise
- the symbolic meaning of the activity (are you running in a park because you're outdoors and love it or are you running from a mugger?)
- the distraction from worries
- the acquisition of mastery of a sport
- the effects of self-image
- the biochemical and physiological changes that accompany the activity

When we approach exercise as just another task—maybe even a burden—it represents the antithesis of what Thich Nhat Hanh and others taught us earlier about being awake, aware, and ever mindful. It's a hazard that even Henry David Thoreau

> An early morning walk is a blessing for the whole day.
>
> —HENRY DAVID THOREAU

encountered while at Walden. In a June 1862 article, "Walking," that appeared in the *Atlantic Monthly,* he confessed:

> *I am alarmed when it happens that I have walked a mile into the woods bodily, without getting there in spirit. The thought of some work will run in my head, and I am not where my body is,—I am out of my senses. In my walks I would fain return to my senses.*

Like other athletes who know the experience of "flow" or being in "the zone," master racewalker and journalist Carolyn Scott Kortge recognizes that there is a joyous connection that "returns us to our senses," when our minds and bodies fall into step together and we use two eyes instead of one to focus on a goal. We regain a perspective that might have been otherwise lost. Our everyday fitness programs become retreats of renewal and realignment that guide us safely along a path of well-being for body, mind, and soul.

During the course of a summer over twelve thousand people come to Omega to help renew and realign themselves. Many take the Wellness Program or other workshops that incorporate walking, specific sports, or different forms of body movement to help concentrate and fine-tune their focus and reacquaint their minds with the fact that they are intricately connected to their bodies and souls.

The names of some of the Omega workshops held over the years suggest ways to crack the armoring effect of the "shell" that can separate the mind and body. "The Dance of Tennis," "The Tao of Boxing," "Beyond Basketball," "Movement as a Spiritual Practice," "Spirit in Motion," "Life Dancing," and "Swing Dance Ecstasy." With few exceptions these workshops are designed to meet participants at their particular level of fitness and competency and introduce them to a "practice"—a process—that leads not to perfection but to a deepening awareness that their body, mind, emotions, and spirit are one and long to be whole.

Among the most popular workshops are those that teach different forms of yoga,

According to Carolyn Scott Kortge, author of *The Spirited Walker,* the steps that transform exercise walking into a spirited, whole-body workout begin right where you are. Here are four "steps" that Kortge advises her students and readers to take. Clearly, they apply to other forms of physical activity as well:

+ *Make a Move:* Spirited walking begins with the simple act of walking and with the recognition that walking has many parallels to life and offers a fresh point of view. When you walk you move forward, go toward something, and take steps. Additionally, you get from one place to another by changing your position and the action changes your perspective.

+ *Take a Chance:* Spirited walking feeds on curiosity and challenge and thereby pushes you out of your comfort zone. By stepping out of your comfort zone you move beyond well-known patterns and paths and venture into brand-new territory. The experience heightens your senses and the trail leads you toward self-awareness that can take exercise beyond calorie burning and heart rates.

+ *Get an Attitude:* Spirited walking is about awareness. Your self-talk reflects an attitude that you carry with you wherever you go. That makes it more important than where you walk, when you walk, how often you walk, how fast you walk, or how you go the distance.

+ *Go for More:* Spirited walkers reflect a willingness to seek more from exercise. If you are a spirited walker, you ask more than the usual from yourself and try different things such as speeding up your pace slightly or extending your route. In return for your spirit of adventure you get benefits. You discover your workout provides a metaphor and your energetic movement opens doors in other parts of your lives as well.

tai chi, and qigong. Known collectively as Eastern healing arts, these mind-, body-, and spirit-oriented practices can help balance the opposing forces and tensions in our lives. Take, for example, the workshop called "Natural Yoga: The Science of Happiness, the Secret of the Self" that is taught by Dinabandhu Sarley, coauthor of *The Essentials of Yoga.* He describes the workshop as an eclectic mix of meditation, Hatha yoga, mantra chanting, prayer, self-reflection, lecture, and group discussion. Sarley teaches that yoga is much more than a workout, and when it becomes a way of life—

> Whatever is flexible and flowing will tend to grow,
> whatever is rigid and blocked will wither and die.
>
> —TAO TE CHING

a path to spiritual awakening—it can "enhance one's vitality, health, peace of mind, effectiveness in work and relationships, and result in a more settled sense of one's place in the universe."

When Chungliang Al Huang, a tai chi master and dancer-choreographer, describes his popular Omega workshop, "Living Tao, Cultivating Te: The Way of Power and Integrity," his words resonate with Sarley's. During his five-day course Taoist philosophy, Neo-Confucian pragmatism, Western positivism, and the vitalizing disciplines of tai chi practice get woven together in a way that strengthens his students' abilities to sustain personal health and well-being, enhance dynamic human relationships, and balance work and enjoyment of living.

People throughout the Eastern Hemisphere consider yoga, tai chi, and other systems of movement and exercise to be health tonics because they can make us both physically and mentally sound. Tai chi "lubricates" every part of the body and relaxes the mind, says William C. C. Chen, an Omega tai chi teacher who is considered one of the most renowned in the West. Speaking specifically about just a few of the benefits of tai chi (which can also apply to yoga and qigong), he adds, "This ancient system renders our thinking lucid, turns our temper gentle, and brings us peace of mind that helps us to function well in our hectic world. It enables a person to attain what the ancient Chinese sages called 'the golden mean,' in which human desires and frustrations are harnessed and transformed to benefit the individual." In other words, yoga, tai chi, and qigong are proven ways to empty the mind and the body at the same time and make them more alert and effective.

The ever-growing popularity of Eastern healing arts such as yoga, tai chi, and

> "I Sing the Body Electric."
>
> —WALT WHITMAN

> There is but one temple in the universe and that is the body of man.
> —NOVALIS

qigong in this country is not surprising. As Americans have become better educated as to the benefits of integrating complementary modalities into their health-care regime, the number of places offering them has risen in response. No longer are healthful approaches to movement, breath awareness, and mindfulness from India, China, Japan, and neighboring countries relegated to centers like Omega or considered the bailiwick of pretzellike yogis or "new age" aficionados. The fact is that today a growing number of physicians and hospitals throughout the country are incorporating these disciplines into rehabilitation, pain reduction, and stress-management programs.

Such acceptance within the traditional medical community suggests that the Eastern healing arts discussed here offer serious benefits to practitioners who take both the movements and theories behind them seriously. For example, although the word *yoga* comes from sacred Hindu scriptures called the Vedas, it is not a religious practice, but is understood to be a unitive discipline. A unitive discipline, explains Georg Feuerstein, Ph.D., author of *The Shambhala Guide to Yoga* and *Living Yoga*, is one which simplifies one's consciousness and energy to the point where one is free of inner conflict and lives in harmony with the world.

In Sanskrit *yoga* can mean "union," "team," "constellation," and "conjunction." "It is derived from the verbal root *yuj*, meaning "to harness, yoke, prepare, equip, fasten," Feuerstein adds. And even though each branch differs in its methods and techniques, the differences can be regarded as creative variations on the same fundamental theme. Students studying yoga learn to perform *asana*, a sequence of postures, and to focus on *pranayama*, breathing awareness. Many report that they sweat more during a yoga workout than any other form of exercise they've tried. Yet, they add, no other form of exercise leaves them feeling as relaxed, limber, vitalized, and comfortable with their body.

Hatha yoga, raja yoga, karma yoga, bhakti yoga, jnana yoga, and tantra yoga com-

In *Discovering the Body's Wisdom* massage therapist Mirka Knaster says that Indian, Chinese, and Japanese movement arts are useful in attaining or regaining physical health at any age because they can:

- loosen and free muscles and joints to improve posture, joint mobility, and flexibility
- strengthen bones as weight-bearing exercises
- tone internal organs
- deepen respiration
- stimulate circulation
- reduce tension in the sympathetic branch of the autonomic nervous system and enhance the parasympathetic aspect
- develop balance, coordination, and a sense of centeredness

Additionally, these practices can:

- quiet the mind
- cultivate consciousness and moral character
- serve as a way of being as well as a way of doing
- foster self-knowledge
- strengthen your connection to your own body wisdom

prise the six major branches, which like all branches divide into other forms that are taught worldwide. In the United States hatha yoga is the most popular form. That's no surprise since, according to Feuerstein, "hatha yoga was invented by masters who felt that most people are too distracted to devote themselves wholeheartedly to the spiritual side of yoga."

One of the smaller branches taught at Omega is astanga yoga. According to

Try This

Here are some easy yoga exercises to relax your shoulders, neck, and eyes. You can do them anytime you are reading or working at your desk. They are just a few of the many exercises that appear in another Omega Institute Mind Body Spirit title, *The Essentials of Yoga.*

NECK AND SHOULDERS
TURKEY STRETCH
Sit with your spine straight, both feet flat on the floor. Imagine there is a cord attached to the top of your head, and it is gently pulling you to sit up just a little bit taller. Direct your gaze in front of your nose and bring your hand to your chin. Now inhale deeply, resting your hand on your chin. Exhale slowly, gently pressing your chin toward your neck. You should feel this stretch lengthening the back of your neck. Do this three times.

SHOULDER RELEASE
Sit with your spine straight, both feet flat on the floor. Keep your arms by your sides, palms turned inward. As you inhale, roll your shoulders up to your earlobes, and then exhale, rolling them back down. Go slowly with your breath and movements. Feel your spine lengthen. Repeat this five times.

EYES
EYE CALISTHENICS
Begin by taking in deep inhalations and letting your breath out slowly. Relax your shoulders. Now, keeping your head and shoulders still, inhale slowly and look to the far left. Follow this with a slow exhalation and a look to the far right. Do three full sets, and then blink your eyes for several seconds. Top this off by closing your eyes and taking three long breaths.

STRETCH DOWN TO UP
Again, begin with a relaxed, deep breath. Relax your shoulders and rest your hands on your thighs. Keep your shoulders and head still. Slowly inhale, stretching your eyeballs up toward the ceiling—or even better, toward the sky. Now exhale, looking down. Do this for three full sets, then close your eyes for three long, gentle breaths.

instructor Beryl Bender Birch, astanga is the original, classical style of hatha yoga. K dalini maha yoga, acu-yoga, and Iyengar yoga are just a few of the other variations on hatha and other styles of yoga.

Simply stated, qigong means "working with the energy of life, learning how to control the flow and distribution of qi [see box on page 186] to improve the health and harmony of mind and body," according to qigong master Kenneth S. Cohen. There is not just one but thousands of styles and schools of this holistic system of self-healing, exercise, and meditation. Today it remains an evolving practice that dates back thousands of years and includes healing postures, movement, self-massage, breathing techniques, and meditation.

Qigong is at the root of self-care in the Chinese health-care system, adds Roger Jahnke, ODM. "It is the essence of how 'Physician, heal thyself' operates in China. It is the current link to the ancient source of Asian shamanism and magic. And yet, with all these qualities of the unusual and the esoteric, qigong has a very practical role in the maintenance of health and the healing of disease." Jahnke, who has been practicing acupuncture and traditional Chinese medicine for over two decades, adds that there may be thousands of systems and traditions of qigong. These range from simple calisthenic-type movements with breath coordination to complex autoregulatory-type exercises where heart rate, brain-wave frequency, and other organ functions are altered, intentionally, by the practitioner.

As a practice, explains Cohen, qigong techniques are divided into two general categories: dynamic or active qigong (*dong gong*) and tranquil or passive qigong (*jing gong*). The former includes obvious movement. The entire body either moves from one posture to another, as though performing a dance, or the practitioner holds a posture while his or her arms move through various positions. "Dong gong is the most popular kind of qigong in both China and the West. It is *yang*, active, yet it conceals the *yin*, passive. Externally there is movement, but internally, the mind is quiet, peaceful, and at rest."

If anything is sacred, the human body is sacred.

—WALT WHITMAN

Ever hear the words *qi, chi, ki,* and *prana* and wonder what they mean? Essentially, they all refer to "life energy," a "vital force."

In China, *qi* or *chi* is the animating power that flows through all living things. In Japan this bioenergy is called *ki.* "A living person is filled with it. A dead person has no more *qi*— the warmth, the life energy, is gone," says Kenneth S. Cohen, a qigong master.

In the living, *qi* exists in every part of the body. It flows through more than fifty meridians, which form invisible channels. The Chinese believe that *qi* causes our blood to circulate, activates our organs, transforms the food we eat, and releases other bodily fluids when necessary and causes wastes to be excreted as sweat and urine.

In India and other places in the world where yoga is practiced, *prana* animates every aspect of life. *"Prana* manifests materially in five primary states or forces known as the *pancha maha bhutas:* earth, water, fire, air, and ether," writes Mirka Knaster in *Discovering the Body's Wisdom.* These are similar to *qi* in that they are not literal, but metaphorical, elements, she says. "Water, or the liquid condition, is associated with bodily fluids, the kidneys and genitals; air or gas energy enables the body to move and is connected to the nervous system; earth, or the solid state, is related to the body's waste materials, and so on. Each element also creates the senses and oversees their functions. For example, ether with hearing and the ear, and fire with the eyes and seeing."

Historically, *tai chi* (also called tai chi chuan and/or spelled taiji and pronounced "tie-jee") means "supreme ultimate fist" or "highest reach." It also means "stillness in motion/movement in stillness," according to Chungliang Al Huang. Although Westerners have only recently embraced this "soft" martial art (as opposed to "hard" martial arts like kung fu, karate, or judo), which has its roots in qigong, in the East it's the way millions of people greet the dawn.

Like those studying qigong, tai chi students focus their efforts on learning a sequence of movements and poses that flow into one another and look like a very slow choreographed dance. The long form has 108 different movements and poses. Shorter forms practiced in the United States incorporate 20 to 40 different poses, the most popular of which is the "yang" style, which has 37 poses. As in yoga and qigong, tai chi poses are based upon what can be learned from nature. Hence, in tai

How good are yoga, tai chi, and qigong for your health? A growing international database of thousands of scientific studies indicates that all three can affect, positively, the mind, body, and spirit.

For example, several studies show that elderly people who practice tai chi can improve their blood pressure and balance. Improving their balance makes them less susceptible to falls. One often cited study took place at Emory University School of Medicine in Atlanta. There researchers looked at whether activity could improve the balance and alleviate the mobility problems faced by older people. Tai chi was compared to other forms of exercise. Of 215 seniors aged seventy to ninety-six, one third performed balance exercises, one third took a tai chi class, and the final third, who were a control group, met weekly for a discussion. After fifteen weeks the researchers found that the tai chi group not only enjoyed greater improvement in balance and mobility, they actually reduced their risk of multiple falls by 47 percent. Additionally, their blood pressure fell and they reported that the quality of their life improved because of a reduced fear of falling.

In another clinical study conducted by the Northern Colorado Allergy Asthma Clinic, university students with asthma, ranging in age from nineteen to fifty-two years, were taught yoga—specifically breath-slowing exercises, postures, and meditation—three times a week for sixteen weeks. A control group used only medication. Both groups kept daily symptom and medication diaries and completed weekly questionnaires. The yoga group reported significantly enhanced relaxation, positive attitude, and better yoga exercise tolerance with a tendency toward decreased use of their prescribed inhalers. Researchers concluded that yoga techniques proved to be a beneficial adjunct to the medical management of asthma.

chi, many of the poses mimic real and mythological animals and go by names such as "Retreat to Ride Tiger," "White Crane Spreads Its Wings," "Grasp Sparrow's Tail," and "Golden Pheasant Stands on One Leg."

The real beauty of all these movement arts is that people of all ages and abilities can do them, especially because they are nonimpact forms of exercise. Yoga and qigong, in particular, have been adapted to meet the needs of the disabled. Studies show that tai chi is a particularly good way for people with brittle bones or weakened hearts to exercise without placing too much stress on the body.

Forget the Adage "Practice Makes Perfect"

In their book *Working Out, Working Within: The Tao of Inner Fitness Through Sports and Exercise,* sports psychologist Jerry Lynch, Ph.D., and tai chi master Chungliang Al Huang emphasize the fact that striving for perfection is in itself an act of imperfection because it is an attempt to achieve the unachievable.

> *Tao wisdom encourages you to yield to your tendency to be perfect; when you do, the anxiety, stress and tension caused by your futile attempts at the impossible will be reduced, you will feel better, and your performance will improve. Also, you will recapture the joy, fulfillment, and passion of sports and exercise as you enter this magical arena with the pure spirit of play, without having to be what you can't be—perfect. Yielding to the unachievable in sports and exercise trains you to develop a deeper inner sense of compassion as you begin to understand that you live in a world where even the greatest of athletes are imperfect. . . . Paradoxically, when you become spiritually fortified with compassion for your shortcomings, you begin to get closer to perfection.*

Lynch and Chungliang point out that there's a difference between perfection and excellence. The former is not a goal or a place to reach. Perfection is simply a guide that can keep you on track, heading in the direction of self-improvement. So if the pursuit of perfection keeps derailing your efforts to exercise, they suggest you try the following:

✦ Remind yourself that seeking perfection is futile folly—an attempt to achieve the unachievable.

✦ Be kind to yourself and try to do the best with what you've got.

✦ Imagine yourself performing with excellence, a process-based concept, instead of perfection, an outcome-oriented concept.

✦ Shoot for perfection, knowing, at all times, that you will fall short.

- Recognize that even when you shoot for perfection and fall short, you're still farther along than you were prior to that effort.

- Remember when you fall short to exhibit self-compassion and not measure your self-worth by the outcome.

- See mistakes as your physical life presenting you an opportunity to further your inner fitness.

- Tell yourself that your self-worth should always be gauged by the process of how you "play the game" on *and* off the court.

As you might expect, in this melting pot of a country, yoga, tai chi, and qigong instructors teach many forms besides those touched upon here. Some hold rigidly to classical theories and practices; others adapt the physical movements to meet the needs of specific American populations. For example, over the course of a summer, the fifteen or more classes offered at Omega take different approaches to Eastern movement and martial arts. Yet each is consistent with the center's mission and vision for holistic studies.

As with any other kinds of exercise, training, or sports, the way in which you learn yoga, tai chi, or qigong is important. The books and tapes listed in the resources section can be good sources of information and ways to get started in the privacy of your home. However, taking a class or working privately with an instructor is the best way to learn the movements and get answers to your questions. Since there are no official organizations in the United States that regulate and/or license yoga, tai chi, and qigong teachers, here are some tips for finding an instructor:

- Before beginning your search keep in mind what has encouraged/discouraged you to exercise in the past.

The key to all life experience is movement.

—IDA ROLF

- When gathering recommendations from friends, relatives, coworkers, et cetera, ask:

  —how they came to choose this class and how long they've taken it

  —what they enjoy most about the class/instructor

  —what they enjoy least about the class/instructor

  —what the instructor focuses on—movement, breathing, meditation, philosophy

- Call for any brochures or literature and make an appointment to observe a class, attend an introductory session, and talk to the instructor.

- Write down your questions and/or concerns and share them with the instructor.

- Ask specifically about the instructor's experience/credentials and the form and/or school he or she teaches.

- Ask the instructor what he or she expects of you as a student both in and outside of class.

- If the program seems to fit, decide whether you can make a forthright commitment to attending classes and practicing at home for a trial period of time.

- Reflect upon the cost and promise of taking on this program and following through with what the instructor expects.

- If you decide to get started, write down your commitment and an affirmation that reflects what you believe is the promise of taking this class.

Ultimately, when it comes to exercise, there's good news and bad news. The bad news is that our national "epidemic of inactivity" results in 250,000 deaths a year, according to the Centers for Disease Control and Prevention. The good news is that the American College of Sports Medicine reports that twenty to thirty minutes of exercise most days of the week are all that it takes to avoid contagion.

What kind of exercise? That's the real bonus. Any kind of physical activity that gets you up and moving and, most important, that you find enjoyable. In other words,

FYI

If you really want to enhance your health and fitness, consider emulating the lifestyle of our Stone Age ancestors. According to studies conducted at Colorado State University, the *Homo sapiens* who wandered this planet 750,000 years ago expended much, much more energy than we do today.

According to researcher Loren Cordain, a sports-science professor who studied the "exercise regimens" of our Paleolithic ancestors, "the closer we can reproduce the environment in which we evolved, the closer we can come to optimizing health and fitness. Hopefully, this means freedom from the common degenerative diseases, heart disease, mental problems, and stress. Obviously, you can't go back and be hunter-gatherers. But by emulating what we can of their worlds and leaving out the worst of it, we can get a better shot at optimizing our own health."

Cordain, reported a 1996 article in *Insight in the News,* came to that conclusion after comparing the remains of prehistoric humans with those of contemporary hunter-gatherers such as the !Kung in Africa, the Ache in South America, and the Intuit in the Arctic. He discovered that we are predisposed, genetically, to a lifestyle that is much more active than the one most of us pursue. Cavemen spent their days running, lifting, and working, which is something many modern laborers do. However, only some blue-collar workers do that kind of exercise and white-collar workers don't.

Cordain's recommendations for achieving the best health possible include:

+ exercising *much* more than we do

+ making daily activities more demanding—for example, take stairs instead of elevators

+ including both aerobic and weight training in any fitness regimen

exercise doesn't have to be relegated to a particular form, class, or kind. If you can't take a "formal" approach to moving your body, you can "cross-train" by making variety the spice of your exercise life. You can walk one day, bike another, dance on another, join friends for a weekly pickup game of basketball or round of golf on yet another.

Conversation with Elston Hubbard, Octogenarian, Walker, Resident of "the Old West End" in Toledo, Ohio, and Retired University Professor

Q: You don't just get out and take a daily stroll around your historic neighborhood, you seem to have other agendas. What are they?

A: More than two decades ago my late wife, Marietta, and I decided that we could do more than just walk when we went out for exercise. As long as we were spending that time walking we felt we should also be doing something for our neighborhood. So we started taking bags with us and filling them with the litter we found along the way.

Q: How far did the two of you go? How long would it take?

A: That would depend. Sometimes there was lots of litter to pick up; other times there were lots of people to talk to. Most of the time Marietta and I would be out for an hour or so and walk two or three miles.

Q: Was your goal to get a certain amount of exercise?

A: That was just part of it. Occasionally we would find money. Over the years we each found twenty-dollar bills. As a matter of fact, we found all kinds of bills and coins but never a fifty-cent piece. One of my goals was to save up enough money to buy a grandfather clock.

Q: After Marietta passed away, you continued walking and picking up litter.

A: I felt it was important to continue—as important as talking to the neighbors and doing my bit for the neighborhood. In the last few years I've had a couple of small strokes. I believe the walking has helped me to keep going. The last stroke affected my balance a bit, but it hasn't stopped me from walking, except now I have to use a cane.

Q: Have you gotten enough money for your grandfather clock yet?

A: Not yet, but I will.

A man's health can be judged by which he takes
two at a time—pills or stairs.
—JOAN WELSH

If that mix still doesn't fit your need for fitness, another way of looking at exercise is to approach everyday activities with a new attitude. Gardening, housecleaning, walking the dog, and mowing the lawn can all be done more mindfully. Amazingly, all can effectively meet recommendations that we exercise enough to burn 150 to 200 calories a day.

Take gardening as an example of a task turned into "exercise" that can yield a bounty of benefits. According to Jeffrey Restuccio, author of *Fitness the* Dynamic *Gardening Way,* "Gardening can serve as an alternative to competitive sports for those who prefer to compete against themselves and the vagaries of nature. It's ideal for those who seek more qualitative and spiritual rewards from their lifestyle. Gardening is truly an activity for everyone, in which young and old, rich and poor, quick and slow, big and small, can be on the same playing field."

Weeding, pruning, watering, mulching, and harvesting one or two small flower and/or vegetable patches are just a few of the gardening activities that, when done mindfully for several hours a week, can improve your flexibility, muscle tone, and aerobic fitness, reports Restuccio. For example, spending twenty minutes weeding, mulching, and digging into and turning over a compost pile will increase your flexibility by stretching your arms and legs and raise your metabolism and pulse rate enough to burn 140 calories. If before you get started you take a brisk five-minute walk around the yard or block and then take another five- or ten-minute walk when you finish to cool down, you will have burned over 150 calories and done both aerobic and weight-bearing exercise in the process. When you get tired of doing those things, there are always others to be done. Use your imagination and ingenuity. Try trading your gas-powered mower for a people-powered one. It will strengthen your muscles in your arms, legs, and chest and burn between 350 and 450 calories an hour—25 percent more than you would burn guiding the self-propelled type.

Get the picture? There are lots of ways to work physical activity into your schedule and have it be productive and fun. Live in the city where you don't have a garden to tend? Be imaginative. Instead of raking your lawn, sweep the sidewalk. You might even try wearing headphones and listening to music while you do it. And if you feel the urge to make the broom your dance partner, go for it! You just might become so entrained to the music and sweeping motion that as you go with the flow you'll never give a second thought to what the neighbors think.

And so it goes. Thinking about driving your car to the car wash? Soap it up yourself instead. You'll spend the same amount of time you would driving somewhere, waiting in line, and then driving home. And by doing it yourself you will help tone your arm muscles and save money too. Don't have an urge to walk alone? Go with a friend who's similarly inclined. No such animal? Adopt a dog—at least twice a day it

The following list of activities shows you approximately how many calories you burn per thirty minutes of a specific activity. Of course, the actual number will depend upon how vigorously you do the activity and how much you weigh.

Activity	Calories
Hoeing	180
Dancing	187
House painting	150
Gardening	150
Making beds	135
Scrubbing	135
Walking the dog for two miles	120
Sweeping/mopping	115
Raking leaves	105
Vacuuming	85
Washing dishes	66
Watching TV (sitting)	45
Watching TV (reclining)	30

will urge you to go out for a walk. And when it comes to walking, remember, if you park your car as far from the mall or work as possible, you'll be tallying up extra exercise and probably saving time you would have spent circling the lot too. The same is true of taking stairs instead of elevators and escalators. And even though you might not save time, you might be buying some in terms of the measure of your days by getting off a bus a stop or two early and walking the rest of the way to your destination.

Remember, exercise is about a process that when coupled with good nutrition and stress reduction can guide you toward optimal health, vitality, and even a longer life. If, after trying scheduled and purposeful activities such as walking, yoga, tai chi, jogging, swimming, weight training, et cetera, you still find yourself intimidated by the idea of doing thirty minutes at a time, try breaking up your exercise into more manageable segments. If you work at a desk, get up every hour or so and take a five- or ten-minute walk. Turn coffee breaks into opportunities to venture up and down a flight or two of stairs; turn a lunch hour into fifteen or twenty minutes of walking and errand running before eating. Other ways to transform everyday tasks into healthful exercise include walking to the post office instead of sticking letters in your mailbox; turning the curb at the gas pump into a place to do step aerobics while you fill 'er up; or standing up to do some stretches while a commercial fills the airwaves.

Wonder how much good just a few minutes of exercise here and there can really do? Recent studies of runners compared those going for thirty minutes at a stretch with those who broke their runs into ten-minute segments. Both groups reaped similar benefits, but surprisingly, those who ran for ten minutes at a time actually showed greater improvements in their cholesterol levels.

Henry David Thoreau wrote, "We are all sculptors and painters, and our material is our own flesh and blood and bones." As such, the decisions we make about how to use the artist's tools we have on hand will determine how we create and re-create ourselves now and in the future.

Exercise is one of those tools. How we choose to use it to help paint or sculpt the picture of optimal health and fitness that we see for ourselves is entirely up to us. And, quite frankly, no matter how much effort we put into it, there's no guarantee the final product will be the masterpiece we may have envisioned. However, one thing can be assured—that by choosing to pick up this tool we call exercise and using it, the work in progress that we call our lives will be better, happier, and more fit for it.

✍   RESOURCES   ✍

BOOKS

Birch, Beryl Bender. *Power Yoga: The Total Strength and Flexibility Workout.* New York: Fireside, 1995.

Bodian, Stephan, and Georg Feuerstein (ed.). *Living Yoga: A Comprehensive Guide for Daily Life.* New York: Tarcher/Perigree, 1993.

Christensen, Alice. *The American Yoga Association Beginner's Manual.* New York: Simon & Schuster, 1987.

Christensen, Alice, and David Rankin. *Easy Does It: Yoga for Older People.* New York: Harper and Row, 1979.

Cohen, Kenneth S. *The Way of Qigong: The Art and Science of Chinese Energy Healing.* New York: Ballantine Books, 1997.

Douillard, John. *Body, Mind, and Sport: The Mind-Body Guide to Lifelong Fitness and Your Personal Best.* New York: Harmony Books, 1994.

Feuerstein, Georg.

The Shambhala Guide to Yoga. Boston: Shambhala, 1996.

Yoga: The Technology of Ecstasy. Los Angeles: Jeremy P. Tarcher, 1986.

Huang, Chungliang Al, and Jerry Lynch. *Working Out, Working Within: The Tao of Inner Fitness Through Sports and Exercise.* New York: Tarcher/Putnam, 1998.

Iyengar, B.K.S. *Light on Yoga.* New York: Schocken Books, 1995.

Jackson, Phil. *Sacred Hoops: Spiritual Lessons of a Hardwood Warrior.* New York: Hyperion, 1995.

Jahnke, Roger, O.D.M. *The Healer Within: The Four Essential Self-Care Methods for Creating Optimal Health.* San Francisco: Harper San Francisco, 1997.

Kabat-Zinn, Jon. *Wherever You Go, There You Are.* New York: Hyperion, 1994.

Knaster, Mirka. *Discovering the Body's Wisdom.* New York: Bantam Books, 1996.

Kortge, Carolyn Scott. *The Spirited Walker: Fitness Walking for Clarity, Balance, and Spiritual Connection*. San Francisco: HarperCollins, 1998.

Millman, Dan. *The Inner Athlete: Realizing Your Fullest Potential*. Walpole, NH: Stillpoint Publishing, 1994.

Restuccio, Jeffrey P. *Fitness the Dynamic Gardening Way*. Cordova, TN: Balance of Nature Publishing, 1992.

Rippe, James M., M.D. *Fit Over Forty: A Revolutionary Plan to Achieve Lifelong Physical and Spiritual Health and Well-Being*. New York: William Morrow, 1996.

Sarley, Dinabundhu, and Ila Sarley. *The Essentials of Yoga*. New York: Dell, 1999.

Sun, Wei Yue, M.D., and William Chen, Ph.D. *Tai Chi Ch'uan: The Gentle Workout for Mind & Body*. New York: Sterling Publishing Company, Inc., 1995.

MAGAZINES

T'ai Chi, Wayfarer Publications, P.O. Box 26156, Los Angeles, CA 90026. Phone: 213-665-7773.

Yoga International, RR1, Box 407, Honesdale, PA 18431.

Yoga Journal, P.O. Box 12008, Berkeley, CA 94712.

AUDIOTAPES AND VIDEOTAPES

Most video stores can order these tapes by title and/or title and distributor.

Carradine, David. *David Carradine's Tai Chi Workout*. PMN Distribution.

Chen, Dr. Ji Liang. *Ba Duan Jin Qi Gong*, Omega Wellness Series. Phone: 800-878-8270.

Dunn, Terry. *T'ai Chi for Health*, Yang Short Form. Interart.

Folan, Lilias. *Lilias! Alive with Yoga*. Rudra Press. Phone: 800-876-7798.

Freeman, Richard. *Yoga: Ashtanga Yoga*. The Primary Series. Delphi Productions. Phone: 303-443-2100.

Livingarts, P.O. Box 2939, Venice, CA 90291. Phone: 800-254-8464. www.livingarts.com

   ✦ *Living Yoga's* A.M. *and* P.M. *Yoga for Beginners*
   ✦ *Living Yoga's Abs Yoga for Beginners*
   ✦ *Yoga Journal's Yoga Practice for Beginners*

Mystic Fire Video, P.O. Box 442, New York, NY 10012. Phone: 800-999-1319. www.mysticfire.com

+ *Asana: Sacred Dance of the Yogis*
+ *Autobiography of a Yogi* (read by Ben Kingsley)—Audio
+ *Ei Ei Yoga* (twenty-five yoga postures for children)
+ Leonard, George. *The Tao of Practice*
+ *What Is Yoga?*

New Dimensions Audio Tapes, P.O. Box 569, Ukiah, CA 95482-0569. Phone: 800-935-8273. www.newdimensions.org

+ Huang, Chungliang Al. *Being in the Zone*
+ Stamford, Bryant. *Seeing Through the Exercise Myth*

Sounds True, P.O. Box 8010, Dept. HS98, Boulder, CO 80306-8010. Phone: 800-333-9185.

+ Cohen, Ken. *Qigong*
+ Wyoma. *African Healing Dance*

Tai Chi for Elders. Terra Nova Films.

Wellspring Media, 65 Bleeker Street, Fifth Floor, New York, NY 10012. Phone: 212-674-4912. www.videocollection.com

+ *Discovering Chi*
+ Folan, Lilias. *Lilias Yoga*
+ Singh, Ravi. *Instyle Yoga*
+ *Tai Chi Workout*

WWW

Doing a search on the World Wide Web for the words *fitness, exercise, yoga, tai chi, qigong,* et cetera, will produce thousands of sites. Some even offer animated on-line classes. Begin by going to the home pages of health-related sites that appear in other chapters. You can also find and get to interesting links by going to any of the encyclopedia sites, such as www.encarta.com or www.britannica.com. The sites for newspapers such as *USA Today* (www.usatoday.com) or *The New York Times* (www.nytimes.com) can also link you to lots of information about exercise and exercise-related sites. All the search engines on the Web will also turn up an endless number of places to go. The search engine at Starting Point brings up an excellent list—www.stpt.com. Here are a few others:

Fitness Online is a Web site for several mass market fitness and exercise consumer magazines—www.fitnessonline.com

The Internet's Fitness Resource—*Web Magazine* calls this "the grandmother of all fitness links"—www.netsweat.com

Qi Journal—Web site for the quarterly magazine—www.qi-journal.com

Power Yoga—the site for Omega teachers Thom and Beryl Bender Birch—www.power-yoga.com

Prevention magazine's site—www.healthyideas.com

Qigong and Tai Chi Internet Resources—numerous links to other sites—www.holisticmed.com

Yoga Central—an on-line yoga class with live audio—www.yogaclass.com

The Yoga Site—an eclectic collection of yogic connections—www.yogasite.com

8.

Nutrition for Health and Healing

On November 30, 1998, the cover of *Newsweek* didn't feature the face of a president, pope, pariah, or popular actor. In fact, it didn't spotlight anyone famous or infamous. In their stead, against a stark white linen backdrop, stood a glistening silver fork piercing a stalk of broccoli. At last, the food that one U.S. president loved to publicly hate had made it to the big time under a bold black-and-red banner headline proclaiming: CANCER & DIET: EATING TO BEAT THE ODDS.

In the story that followed, numerous cancer experts stated why the nutrients in certain foods might be lethal weapons in the fight against this insidious, fear-provoking disease. One of them, Mitchell Gaynor, M.D., head of medical oncology at Strang Cancer Prevention Center in New York, summarized the benefits of eating a low-fat diet starring broccoli, its cruciferous relatives, and a long list of multi-colored veggies and fruits from other families this way:

We've seen the future, and the future is food.

—MITCHELL GAYNOR, M.D.

Eating the right foods is as specific to stopping cancer before it starts as wearing a seat belt is to lowering your risk of a fatal automobile accident.

To the delight of vegetarians, the adherents of certain religious beliefs, and a growing number of medical professionals, the article celebrated the veracity of the adage "An apple a day (along with most of the foods you'll find in your supermarket's produce department) keeps the doctor away." It then went on to describe how preliminary evidence suggests that plant foods and their constituents (*phytonutrients*) may disrupt the formation of malignancies—particularly those in the prostate gland, breast, colon, and lungs.

Cancerous tumors grow slowly over a long period of time, a team of reporters explained. The growth process involves three steps:

- ✦ initiation of potentially cancerous changes in a cell's DNA

- ✦ promotion of uncontrolled growth in a damaged cell

- ✦ progression of a cancerous lesion into a mass that can invade other tissues

Based on facts and figures from the American Cancer Society, the American Institute for Cancer Research, and other sources, diets filled with healthful phytonutrients (instead of fats, refined sugar, and simple carbohydrates) combined with exercise and weight control could someday retard or prevent any or all of the stages of growth of tumors, the *Newsweek* article asserted. In so doing, it concluded, the incidence of cancer could be reduced by 30 to 40 percent. Worldwide, that translates into 3 to 4 million fewer cases a year.

Recent research reported in scores of medical and professional journals makes it clear that other life-threatening and chronic conditions also may be prevented and even reversed by eating a low-fat diet that contains lots of fruits, vegetables, and complex carbohydrates. Those conditions include coronary artery disease, strokes, adult-onset diabetes, high blood pressure, autoimmune diseases, asthma, and allergies. For example, an experimental group of patients committed to making lifelong lifestyle changes by following cardiologist Dean Ornish's program for reversing—not just temporarily halting—heart disease actually succeeded. Their artery-blocking plaque was reabsorbed from their coronary arteries and their heart disease regressed, Ornish reported in leading medical journals and the popular press.

By now the components of the holistic "Life Choice" program for reversing heart disease that Ornish and his colleagues orchestrated may sound like a familiar refrain. They include:

+ eating a nutrient-laden diet that has 10 percent of calories from fat
+ practicing specific stress-management techniques that include meditation and yoga
+ moderate aerobic exercise, and
+ meeting regularly in small groups to talk with other patients

Recently, newer and updated studies by Ornish and others show that the original reversals he reported weren't anomalies. Not only did the health of those who continued to follow his program remain stable, in many cases the course of the heart disease and side effects continued to reverse itself five years later. In a December 1998 article in the *Journal of the American Medical Association* (*JAMA*), a research team led by Ornish reported that the experimental group in the study of atherosclerosis patients showed a 91 percent reduction in frequency of angina after one year and a 72 percent reduction after five years. Control patients, who received standard care and followed the diet recommended by the American Heart Association, had a 186 percent increase in angina frequency after one year. They did show a 36 percent decrease after five years, which Ornish attributed to the drug regimen that patients in this group followed as part of their "standard" care. Ultimately, what the indisputable results of this study tell us is that when we're responsible for and proactive about our health and well-being, our bodies will reward us.

Andrew Weil, M.D., an expert in the healing qualities of medicinal plants, tells similar success stories about the ways in which dietary and lifestyle changes positively impacted the debilitating effects of his patients' chronic and life-threatening illnesses. Many of the basic components of the program Weil describes in his best-selling

---

Most illnesses which befall men arise either from bad food,
or from immoderate indulgence in food, even of the wholesome kind.
—MOSES MAIMONIDES

> Let food be your medicine and medicine be your food.
>
> —HIPPOCRATES

book *8 Weeks to Optimum Health* match those in Ornish's. However, Weil's dietary recommendations include several foods—for example, fish—that Ornish factors out of his recommendations for people who already have cardiovascular disease.

In *8 Weeks to Optimum Health* Weil emphasizes the holistic mind-set that's the underpinning of the Omega Wellness Program and this book: "Health is wholeness and balance, an inner resilience that allows you to meet the demands of living without being overwhelmed." In other words, people with inner resilience can encounter and interact with germs, allergens, and carcinogens and successfully resist infections, allergies, and cancer.

Could that mean that on any given day—all things considered—whatever we funnel through our mouth and into our bodies either helps to build up our inner resilience or contributes to its demise? Indeed, as a nation we now know *that* familiar fact of life better than at any other time in our history. Unlike the people in the famed Framingham, Massachussetts, heart study (see box) who discovered years after they volunteered for the ongoing research that their high-fat diets and a smoking habit might be killing them, we no longer live in the dark. With information from the Framingham and scores of other scientific studies in tow, we now know the healthful benefits of:

- ◆ eating a low-fat diet plus all those fruits and vegetables that your mother said were good for you
- ◆ using herbs, vitamins, and other supplements that are proven to be effective ways to help prevent, treat, and control several health-related conditions and overcome the effects of toxicities in the environment, and
- ◆ controlling your weight through diet and exercise

The week before *Newsweek* ran the article on food and cancer, *Time* carried a similar one. This time a pharmacist's bottle graced the cover. But instead of Viagra or a

Framingham Facts

In 1998, after $43 million, fifty years, and a thousand research papers, the Framingham Heart Study continues to be a benchmark report on how Americans live and die.

The long-term study, which has been called one of the great ones of the century, began in 1948 when researchers looked to the town of Framingham, Massachusetts, to show them why one in four men over the age of fifty-five developed heart disease. The researchers originally recruited 2,336 men and 2,873 women. In 1971 they initiated a second stage of the study and recruited 5,135 sons, daughters, and sons- and daughters-in-law of the first participants.

Several key findings of the study have affected the way doctors treat their patients—when it comes not only to heart disease, but to cancer, arthritis, osteoporosis, and other disorders too. They include:

+ Smoking is bad for the heart.

+ High blood pressure is not a normal consequence of aging.

+ High cholesterol leads to heart disease.

+ High cholesterol comes from eating too much saturated fat.

+ High levels of high-density lipoprotein (HDL, "good" cholesterol) actually protect against heart disease.

+ Fluctuations in weight from yo-yo dieting pose a risk of heart disease.

Although many health professionals say that the study continues to make a major contribution to the falling rate of heart disease over the last half century, it has yet to produce significant results showing the benefits of weight loss and exercise. In other words, despite the 1967 statistics from the Framingham study that showed that obesity increases the risk of heart disease, we remain a nation of couch potatoes. Today one third of the nation is obese, which is up from one quarter in 1980.

Dos, Don'ts, Maybes

Would you be surprised to learn you already know a lot about which foods contribute to your health and which don't? The following exercise is a group participation project in the Omega Wellness Week Program. It will give you an overview of the information about nutrition and healthy eating that you already have stored away.

Spend a few minutes thinking about food—all kinds of food. Then list foods, additives, and beverages that you believe enhance your health under a *Do* column. List those you believe can be harmful to your health under a *Don't* column. If you are not sure about a food, list it under *Maybe*. If you believe a food can be "good" for you under certain circumstances and "bad" under others, list that under *Maybe* also. After you write your list, set it aside. We'll come back to it later.

Niagara Falls of other pills, the bottle from "XYZ Pharmacy" contained a bouquet of herbs—ginkgo, echinacea, St. John's wort, and others. The number of refills was "unlimited" and the boldfaced headline, appropriately typed in a plant-colored green, invited readers to learn about: "The Herbal Medicine Boom."

This article pointed out that Americans, who spent more than $12 billion on natural supplements in 1997, were rediscovering the healing power of "an ancient form of medicine that *was* medicine for thousands of years—and that remains so for 80 percent of the world's people." Appropriately, the article warned readers about the hazards of the indiscriminate use of medicinal herbs before concluding, "...these flowering gifts from the past can be powerful medicine—but handle with care."

In the pages ahead we will show you ways to "handle" your diet and any medicinal herbs, vitamins, and other supplements you may choose to take "with care." Additionally, we recognize that many of your choices concerning nutrition and supplementation may be ones that you made years ago or that someone else made for

Food is an important part of a balanced diet.
—METROPOLITAN LIFE INSURANCE CO., 1978

Herbal Healing

It is estimated that 25 percent of all modern pharmaceutical drugs are a form of plant medicine. Aspirin comes from white willow bark. Digitalis, a heart medication, comes from foxglove, and the yew tree gives us Taxol, which is used in the treatment of ovarian cancer. And, as *U.S. News & World Report* pointed out in an article, "The Herbal Medicine Boom," "There might have been no sexual revolution without the birth-control pill, derived from a Mexican yam."

Because government agencies don't oversee the regulation of herbs sold in health food stores, through the mail, over the Internet, and on your supermarket and convenience-store shelves, it is up to you, the consumer, to get as much education as you can before taking these remedies. Some have been popular "folk" medicine for generations. Ginger quells motion sickness. Cayenne pepper used externally can help relieve the pain of arthritis. Aloe soothes burns. Cranberries help cure urinary tract infections. In some people echinacea acts like chicken soup and does wonders for colds, flu, and bronchitis. For constipation and regularity, flaxseed, plantain, and senna seem to move things along.

Excellent sources of information are the resources listed at the end of this chapter. Here are some suggestions for ways to safely incorporate herbs into your diet and get the healing benefits many herbs and medicinal foods offer.

✦ Remember, a primary use of herbal supplements is to help us heal when we're ill. Taking them at other times may or may not be in the best interest of your health. It's also important never to use them as a way to self-medicate a serious condition. So if you're interested in taking herbal supplements, first ask yourself why. Is it because everyone is doing it? Or is it because you have a condition you believe they can help? Certain herbs can be safely used preventatively—as a booster tonic—to help underlying weaknesses or deficiencies and to make the immune system stronger.

✦ Read some of the latest literature on the herb. Make sure the claims made for herbs are substantiated. Many claims aren't. Look to the scientific sector for evidence of an herb's efficacy. Ginkgo is a good example. Researchers have found that extracts made from the leaves of ginkgo trees can increase blood flow to the brain and enhance memory for some people—especially Alzheimer's patients. The results of those studies are available at your local library, on the Internet, and elsewhere. Although ginkgo is not toxic, reading about it will help you make an informed choice about taking such a widely available herb.

+ Make sure to buy herbs that contain standardized extracts. Next best are tinctures followed by freeze-dried preparations. Most important is that any vitamins, minerals, herbs, or other supplements you buy come from a reputable source and have an expiration date. Herbs in a bin will not have an expiration date, so inquire about their freshness.

+ Incorporate familiar foods being sold as herbs into your diet naturally. Instead of buying garlic supplements, cook with the real thing to flavor foods. The same goes for rosemary, curry, ginger, and other foods and spices. Use herbal teas to reap some of the benefits of herbs sold in bottles.

+ According to James A. Duke, Ph.D., author of *The Green Pharmacy* and a leading authority on healing herbs, these common, all-natural herbs are safe: bay leaf, parsley, mint, ginkgo, peppermint, fenugreek, dill, sage, garlic, spearmint, chives, skullcap, chervil, oregano, comfrey, and milk thistle. However, many others cannot be used in combination with certain treatments. It's important to check with your health-care provider if you are taking herbs and pharmaceutical medications simultaneously.

+ When you take herbal supplements, monitor your reaction. Even herbal teas can cause side effects if they contain caffeine or if you are hypersensitive to certain ingredients.

+ Remember, the suggested doses on bottles are there for a reason. You can overdose on certain herbs.

you. As a result, you may be eating certain foods purely out of habit with little or no conscious awareness of either the positive or negative effects they may have upon your health.

A good example of habituated eating is the typical American diet, which consists of a variety of red meats and potatoes swimming in gravy instead of a garden variety of fruits, vegetables, and complex carbohydrates. Rationales that people give for continuing to adhere to this and similar fat-laden diets include "I've always eaten that way" or "It's too late to change now."

Other habituated food choices that we make may, in fact, be the result of choosing not to make a choice. In other words, the laissez-faire or "so far so good" attitudes described in the introduction may be a driving force behind the fatty-foods pileups on the plates of people still in a healthy sector of a health/disease continuum. And finally, we also understand that all of the professional jargon and lingo related to diet may be confusing. Not one wellness workshop goes by without one or more students admitting that they suffer from the paralysis of analysis: "Even with all the information that's available, I still can't sort out what I'm supposed to be doing," they say.

Throughout this book we have shown you a middle path leading to optimal health, not one that goes off in a fanatical or radical direction. The same is true of our discussion of nutrition and supplementation during the Omega Wellness Program. In fact, upon arrival, many participants are surprised to learn that we're not militant and that the vegetarian menu we serve to guests is considered "gourmet" throughout the world.

Additionally, we don't insist that you become a vegetarian. Instead, we recommend that if you eat meat you limit it to lean cuts and eat them no more than two to three times a week. If you eat fish, our recommendation is that you limit your intake to salmon and other cold-water varieties. These are high in omega-3 essential fatty acids (good fats) and less likely to harbor parasites and toxic chemicals. But more about that

82: Percentage of people who know that a poor diet can increase their risk of cancer
15: Percentage who have changed their diet to lower that risk.

—*HIPPOCRATES* MAGAZINE 1/89

later. For now, why not take a few moments to ponder these questions and statements about the foods you choose to eat:

- My favorite/least favorite foods are . . .
- The last time I ate a food I really loved was . . .
- How was that delicious food prepared? Who prepared it? What did you like about it (flavor, texture, smell, preparation)? Where were you while you were eating it?
- When was the first time you can remember eating that food?
- How was it prepared at that time? Who prepared it? Where were you?
- The last time I ate a food I really didn't like or hated was . . .
- How was it prepared? Who prepared it? What didn't you like about it (flavor, texture, smell, preparation)? Where were you when you were eating it?
- Have you tried and/or do you like other foods belonging to the same food group as the one you don't like?
- What memories do you associate with specific foods you like?
- What memories do you associate with foods you hate?

Former President George Bush once said, "My mother made me eat broccoli. I hate broccoli. I am the President of the United States. I will not eat any more broccoli." If you don't eat broccoli, what's your excuse?

Today, more than a decade after pioneer cardiologist Dean Ornish published his first studies on reversing heart disease, he professes a skeptic's response to the words *bypass surgery.* Increasingly, he says, scientific studies show that patients having bypass surgery will need more. Within five years of their operation, he explains, the arteries of half the patients are clogged again. "So for me bypass surgery is now a metaphor—bypassing the problem rather than dealing with the underlying causes. It's like mopping up the floor around an overflowing sink without also turning off the faucet."

Like all physicians who view health holistically, Ornish believes that the body's capacity to heal itself is significant, and he prefers that patients take a noninvasive route to that destination when feasible. However, he doesn't advise patients and the hundreds of thousands of people who have read his books *not* to take cholesterol-lowering drugs or have surgery when faced with an acute care situation.

"If someone came into the emergency room complaining of crushing chest pain, I would use whatever invasive procedures and drugs might be necessary to help him survive a life-threatening situation," Ornish says. Only later, when the patient became stable and ready for rehabilitation, would he discuss his program for reversing heart disease and how to use it as an alternative to commonly prescribed drugs.

Central to Ornish's program is a therapeutic low-fat meatless diet. Daily, no more than 10 percent (20 grams) of the calories in the diet can come from fat. That's two-thirds less fat than the 30 percent daily recommendation from the American Heart Association. Not surprisingly, many people consider it to be "really radical." Whether or not Ornish's recommendations are really radical is a matter of interpretation. Probably red-meat eaters would call it that. However, someone eating a very low-fat diet that occasionally included some poultry or fish might not consider Ornish's diet radical at all. In the wellness program we view Ornish's and other low-fat, meatless diets as one end of a sweeping spectrum of nutritious diets that you can follow precisely or merely use as guidelines for designing your own.

The buffet-style meals that we serve to thousands of guests each summer at Omega reflect that spectrum. The menu is very nutritious and vegetarian, yet once a week we serve fish as a dinner choice along with other main courses like pasta and a vegetarian stew. At breakfast, scrambled and/or boiled eggs appear next to an eggless tofu scramble, oatmeal, whole-grain cereals, miso soup, homemade muffins, yogurt, and fresh fruit. Salad dressings made with polyunsaturated oils, fat-free dressings, vinegars, and condiments are available to complement the greens, other fresh veggies, soups, and a variety of cooked beans and grains served at lunch. The whole-grain, locally baked breads served at every meal can be eaten plain or with butter, a soy spread, organic peanut butter, or jam. Beverages include juices, skim milk, and soy milk. You get the idea. When you come to Omega there's enough variety to meet the particularities of almost every vegetarian diet—whether it's Ornish's, someone else's, or your own.

Omega's menu and the healthy diets explained below are designed to help you to set a course. No one diet is the main course or *the* answer unless you are following it

What does it mean when Ornish, the American Heart Association, and others tell us to limit our intake to a certain percentage? The Vegetarian Resource Group, a nonprofit organization that educates the public about vegetarianism and the interrelated issues of health, nutrition, ecology, ethics, and world hunger, explains that for most adults, 30 percent or less means between 55 and 66 grams of fat a day for men. For most women it means between 40 and 50 grams of fat daily. The higher amount is for extremely active individuals and the lower amount by sedentary people or those who are trying to lose weight. This group also warns that such low amounts of fat are not normally encouraged for small children. The USDA says all children under the age of two need more fat and that by the age of five they should be eating no more than 30 percent.

To help you get a better idea of what that means the Vegetarian Resource Group publishes the following table showing the amounts of fat in many foods vegetarians eat. They compare these foods to an average-size hamburger (no quarter-pounders here) on a bun that has 20 grams of fat and is the equivalent of the total fat allowance in Ornish's diet.

Butter, 1 pat	4 grams of fat
Vegetable oil, 1 Tbsp	14
Nuts and seeds, 1 oz.	14
Tofu, 4 oz.	5
Cooked dried beans, 1 cup	1
Eggs, 1 large	6
Whole milk, 1 cup	8
Skim milk, 1 cup	Trace
Cheese, 3 ounces	27
Fruit, 1 medium	0
Avocado, half	15
Grains, 1 cup cooked	1
Vegetables, 1 cup	0–1
Peanut butter, 1 Tbsp	8

for religious, ethical, strict medical, or weight-related reasons. We recommend that you be wary of any diet that promises "perfect" health and look instead for one that will help balance your intake of healthful foods and do its role in promoting "optimal" health.

The primary foods that registered dietitians and nutritionists recommend that we eat, abundantly, are the complex carbohydrates—grains, vegetables, and most fruits. They are the body's basic source of energy because they get converted into the body's chief form of fuel—glucose. They are also the same foods that form both the foundation (bread, cereal, rice, and pasta) and first layer (vegetables and fruits) of the four-story Pyramid Food Guide published by the U.S. Department of Agriculture (USDA). Together, these two layers are excellent sources of the dietary fiber we need to cleanse our colon of waste products and help control blood cholesterol. The third level of the pyramid is divided into dairy products and the meats and beans groups. Topping it off are high-fat (oils) and sugary foods.

Long before this consumer guide to healthy eating came along, people in other

It is nearly fifty years since I was assured by a conclave of doctors
that if I did not eat meat, I should die of starvation.
—GEORGE BERNARD SHAW, VEGETARIAN

Sorting Out Some of the Diets

When the editors of *Delicious!*, a monthly magazine available on the Internet and in health-food stores, discovered that they were as confused about the different diets as their readers, they decided it was time to get things sorted out. Findings from two of the many diets that they analyzed are summarized below. We have also added our own recommendations. They all serve as examples of how those eating healthy diets can go in slightly different directions while still traveling the same road.

In summarizing the *Delicious!* diets, nutrition expert Melissa Diane Smith wrote, "All emphasize nutrient-dense, whole foods and avoid or limit the processed foods most often associated with disease—refined and partially hydrogenated oils, sugar, concentrated sweets, white flour products, and processed meats. But none of these diets works for everyone. Our biochemistries are as individual as our fingerprints, and our bodies respond differently to combinations of foods." We agree.

LOW-FAT VEGETARIAN DIET such as Dean Ornish's

+ 75–85 percent carbohydrates, which include vegetables, fruits, legumes, and grains

+ 10–15 percent protein from legumes and grains

+ 5–10 percent fat that comes from plant foods in small amounts

MACROBIOTIC DIET created by Michio and Aveline Kushi

+ 70–80 percent carbohydrates that include whole grains, vegetables, seaweed, and legumes

+ 10–15 percent protein from tofu and other soy products, whole grains, legumes, and small amounts of seafood

+ 10–15 percent fat from fish, sesame oils, and small amounts of plant and animal foods

cultures, worldwide, used the three food groups on the bottom plus dry beans as energizing, protein-rich mainstays of meatless diets. Despite the popular belief in our culture that diets that eliminate meat and fish don't provide enough protein, plant-eating people in the Middle East, Far East, South America, and elsewhere have historically proven otherwise. Whether their diets remained meatless

+ because they were gatherers who never became hunters

+ because of circumstances such as poverty, or

+ because they chose not to eat meat for religious or ethical reasons,

studies show that people outside the Western world who eat foods high in complex carbohydrates have not, as a rule, been protein deficient except during times of famine.

In the following passage from the best-selling book *Diet for a Small Planet,* author Frances Moore Lappé describes some traditional staples of people in foreign cultures that have recently become tasteful foreign fare in restaurants nationwide. Although she originally felt that combining different food groups in a meal ensured the maximum usable protein, Lappé later concluded this was not necessary. Her rationale—one

A man of my spiritual intensity does not eat corpses.

—GEORGE BERNARD SHAW

You put a baby in a crib with an apple and a rabbit. If it eats the rabbit and plays with the apple, I'll buy you a new car.

—HARVEY DIAMOND

proven to be sound—was that in the course of a day any well-rounded vegetarian diet easily supplied all of a person's protein needs.

Virtually all traditional societies used grain and legume combinations as their main source of protein and energy. In Latin America it was corn tortillas with beans, or rice with beans. In the Middle East it was bulgur wheat with chickpeas or pita bread falafel with hummus sauce (whole wheat, chickpeas, and sesame seeds). In India it was rice or chapatis with dal (lentils, often served with yogurt). In Asia it was soy foods with rice. In each case the balance was typically 70–80 percent whole grains and 20–30 percent legumes, the very balance that nutritionists have found maximizes protein usability.

You don't need to be a rocket scientist or biochemist to understand the food pyramid. It was designed so that even young children can make some sense of it. Now is a good time to compare the "Do, Don't, or Maybe" exercise that you did earlier to the food pyramid. What does it tell you about the dietary information you have accumulated either intentionally or passively? Were heavy concentrations of the foods, such as animal products and fats, that are in the top half of the pyramid on your list of "Don'ts" or "Maybes"? Were those on the bottom three quarters of the pyramid on your list of "Dos"? Which were missing? Which hadn't you thought about?

If you stick to pleasing your palate with foods on the bottom half of the pyramid (with the addition of dried beans, peas, and lentils, which can be counted as servings of vegetables) and take only occasional forays into the remaining areas, you not only promote optimal health but reduce your risk of getting the leading chronic and life-threatening diseases. Indeed, you may even help to prevent the onset of genetic and environmentally caused illnesses you have never heard of.

We recommend the following daily servings of the foods in each section of the food pyramid as follows. If you consume about 1,600 calories a day, you would eat

Studies Support Sound Eating

A combined analysis of thirteen studies on cancer and fiber showed that the risk of colon and rectal cancer could be reduced by approximately 31 percent if people increased their daily fiber consumption by about 13 grams daily. That represents an average increase of 70 percent over current consumption levels in the United States.

A number of studies conclude that adding soy to your diet can reduce your LDL ("bad") cholesterol. In a review of those studies published in the *New England Journal of Medicine*, editors found that study participants with high cholesterol reduced their cholesterol by about 10 percent when they substituted soy for animal protein. Typically, the participants ate 47 grams of soy products daily. Although the reason(s) why soy may lower cholesterol is unclear, researchers suggest that the proteins in soy may change levels of certain hormones. This in turn may cause the liver to manufacture less cholesterol.

A study of blood-plasma levels of vitamin C, vitamin E, and carotenoids of 112 people aged forty to seventy included seventy-seven patients with cataracts. According to the *American Journal of Clinical Nutrition,* persons in the study who consumed fewer than 3.5 servings of fruit or vegetables daily had an increased risk of two different types of cataracts.

The *American Journal of Public Health* reported that over a period of twenty-one years, the risk of diabetes as an underlying cause of death among 25,600 Caucasian Seventh-Day Adventists was half of the risk for all American Caucasians. Within this population the male vegetarians (those who rarely ate fish and had meat or poultry *less* than once a week) had a substantially lower risk than did nonvegetarians of diabetes as an underlying or contributing cause of death. Furthermore, the prevalence of diabetes was lower for both vegetarian men and women.

In a 1985 study of thirty-two patients over the course of 6.7 months, their diastolic blood pressure was significantly reduced when they ingested an average of 62 percent of their calories in the form of uncooked food. Additionally, many of the patients experienced a significant weight loss, and 80 percent of those who smoked or drank abstained spontaneously.

the smaller number of servings. If you consume 2,800 calories more or less, the number of daily servings would gravitate toward the larger number. You can eat as many servings of fruits and vegetables as you'd like:

Bread, cereal, rice, and pasta	6–11
Vegetables	3–5—use very generously
Fruits	2–4—use very generously
Dairy products	2–3—use very sparingly if at all
Meat, poultry, fish, dried beans, eggs, and nuts	2–3 times a *week* if at all
Fats, oils, and sweets	use very sparingly

But, you may wonder, what counts as a serving? The labels required by the USDA on almost all packaged foods should give you exact amounts. If you buy your food in bulk you can follow these USDA guidelines:

Bread, Cereal, Rice, and Pasta
1 slice of bread
1 ounce of ready-to-eat cereal
$^1/_2$ cup of cooked cereal, rice, and pasta

Vegetables
1 cup of raw leafy vegetables
$^1/_2$ cup of other vegetables—cooked or chopped raw
$^3/_4$ cup of vegetable juice

Fruit
1 medium apple, banana, orange
$^1/_2$ cup of chopped, cooked, or canned fruit
$^3/_4$ cup of fruit juice

Milk, Yogurt, Cheese
1 cup of milk or yogurt
1.5 ounces of natural cheese
2 ounces of processed cheese

Meat, Poultry, Fish, Dry Beans, Eggs, and Nuts

2–3 ounces of cooked lean meat, poultry, or fish

$^1/_2$ cup of cooked dried beans, 1 egg, or 2 tablespoons of peanut butter

Try This

You see pictures of variations on the theme of the food pyramids everywhere—on packages of food, in advertisements, and in stories in the media. Yet how many times have you really *seen* one and related it to your diet? Why not try doing that for one or more days this week? Here's how:

+ Number the food groups in the pyramid from the bottom up: 1 = grains; 2 = vegetables; 3 = fruits; 4 = dairy; 5 = meat, poultry, fish, dried beans, eggs, and nuts; and 6 = fats, oils, and sweets.

+ Divide a piece of paper into columns that represent the meals and/or snacks you eat on a typical weekday. If you eat three meals and don't snack in between, you'll have three columns. If you snack between meals and after dinner, you may have six columns. If you only graze, you may have ten or more columns.

+ Each time you eat something, note the food group or groups that it came from by number in the appropriate column. Be sure to include all the groups that you are aware of—especially those represented by the top of the pyramid. You may want to indicate a ballpark number of servings too. You can put those in parentheses next to the number for the food group.

For example, if you eat a bowl of oatmeal and slice of cantaloupe for breakfast, you would put the numbers 1 for grains and 3 for fruits in the appropriate column. If you prepared the oatmeal with milk you would add the number 4. If you prepared it with water, you wouldn't add anything else. If you put any kind of sweetener (including honey) or a pat of butter on it, you would add a 6. If it was a small bowl of oatmeal you might place a 1 for one serving alongside each of the food groups represented. If it was a large bowl you might write in a 2 or 3. The same would apply if you used both honey and butter, 12.

◆ Before going to bed, tally up the number of times a day you eat foods from particular groups and reflect upon what those numbers tell you.

◆ Take a few moments to write down a few thoughts about the foods you choose to eat, when you choose to eat them, and whether or not you believe they are contributing to your health and well-being.

If you are satisfied with the balance of food in your diet, congratulations. If you are not satisfied, do you feel caught in the tension of opposites when you look at what you know about a good diet and then see a list of what you are eating? What might that tension be saying? Where do you feel it? Ask yourself if there is just one thing in your diet you might want to change. If there is, and even if it seems minor, reflect upon the cost and promise of making that change. Should you decide to make it, write down your commitment to do so.

Fat

In the pages ahead we will be looking at the roles specific foods, vitamins, minerals, and other supplements play in our diet and overall health. We begin with one food that has captured more than a fair share of the press during the last decade—FAT.

Sometimes, just mere mention of the word can spark a debate hot enough to fry a lot of temperaments. Which fats are good? Which are bad? Should you use butter or margarine, or neither? What about oils?

If you've been confused by all the debates and discussions around our national fixation with fat, you're not alone. Especially since fats that were supposed to be good less than a decade ago are now considered bad and vice versa. So what gives? What does it take to get straightened out? Hang in there. Read on to get the skinny on fat.

The question at the heart of the debate over fats is not whether we need them.

Making the Move

Wonder how to get from here to there if you are thinking about cutting back on the amount of meat in your diet or becoming a vegetarian? The following tips may help to make the transition easier:

✦ Don't jump right in "cold turkey."

✦ Ponder the reason(s) you want to make a change. Are they religious, ethical, health related, guilt related, all of the above? Then state the reason(s) in writing.

✦ Decide what kind of changes you want to make to your diet. Ask yourself if you want to give up all meat, cut back on all meat, just eliminate red meat, et cetera. Note your thoughts and decision in a journal.

✦ Think about how the dietary changes you will be making will fill your nutritional bill. Will you be getting the nutrients you need? Consider using the information about nutrition and supplementation in this chapter as a starting point. Books that are listed at the end of this chapter are excellent sources of additional information. Consider making an appointment with a nutritionist to discuss your thoughts and concerns.

✦ Scan or read several vegetarian cookbooks with low-fat recipes. Note recipes that tempt or tantalize your taste buds and consider substituting one, once a week, for a high-fat meal with or without meat. Then move toward substituting a low-fat vegetarian meal for more than one meal.

✦ Have a spirit of adventure. Remember that variety is the spice of life and that great vegetarian cooking includes lots of interesting condiments and spices that may seem mysterious at first.

✦ Try using meat as a side dish, garnish, or flavoring rather than as the centerpiece of your meal. If you eat well-marbled steaks you can reduce fat significantly by switching to lean cuts such as flank steak. If you eat chicken legs, try breasts. If you eat any poultry try removing the skin, which is loaded with saturated fat.

- Experiment with soy products as substitutes for meat and dairy products. Soy is an excellent source of protein and comes in many shapes, flavors, and textures that resemble meats, cheeses, and other foods. You can substitute soy milk for cow's milk in most recipes. If you're not ready to give up milk, try switching from whole milk to low-fat or no-fat milk.

- Introduce additional high-fiber grains, vegetables, and fruit very slowly. They can leave you feeling bloated and gassy if you incorporate them into your diet with too much gusto.

- Don't sabotage your diet by substituting the foods you miss with sweets. Sweets contain empty calories from lots of sugar and tend to be high in saturated fat.

- Shop the perimeters of your supermarket first. Begin in the fresh fruits and vegetable department and fill your cart up knowing that you can eat most of what you find there to your heart's content (literally). Try adding at least one new vegetable or fruit every week.

- Make an extra effort to buy certified organic foods, which are free of pesticides, whenever you can. Today, very little of our produce is grown locally by organic farmers. Instead it comes from all over the world laden with pesticides. Studies show that certain pesticides can be carcinogenic. Since you don't know which pesticides remain on your food when it comes to market, wash all produce you buy thoroughly.

- Be patient. This is about a lifelong process, not a quick fix. It might take you longer to prepare a meal because the recipes are new. It might take you longer to shop because you don't know where to find certain ingredients in your supermarket. If you try to do everything right way, you may feel overwhelmed and discouraged.

We do. Along with protein and carbohydrates, fat is a macronutrient that provides us with "fatty acids" such as linoleic acid, which we need to survive. Fats also transport the fat-soluble vitamins A, D, E, and K to our intestines for absorption and they are integral to the overall growth and development of infants and young children. Fats beneath the skin insulate us from the cold and fats around organs serve as protective barriers. Without enough fats containing "essential fatty acids" (EFAs) our skin becomes dry because it loses moisture. Recognizing that, even Dean Ornish makes an allowance for up to 10 percent (20 grams) of his patients' daily diets to be from "good" fat. The American Heart Association raises its recommendation to 30 percent. We suggest that a range of 15 to 25 percent of the "good" fat is appropriate.

What is a good fat? One way to answer that question is to say what it's not. First, it's definitely not a *saturated* fat. Unlike unsaturated and polyunsaturated fats, which are liquid, these artery-clogging fats are generally solid at room temperature. They are found in meat and dairy products and tend to be high in cholesterol. Typically, commercially prepared fried foods are filled with saturated fats and supermarket breads and bakery products harbor a good dose too. Saturated fats can also be highly concentrated in seeds and nuts. Coconuts and coconut oil are good examples.

Additionally, good fats are definitely not margarine or most other substitutes for butter. During the manufacturing process the oil in margarine and solid shortenings is hydrogenated. That means hydrogen gets pumped into the oils, which makes them hard enough to feel and taste like butter and extend their shelf life. While that's appealing to both consumers and manufacturers, it's important to know that during this process, unsaturated oils become a saturated fat called a hydrogenated trans fatty acid. In its new form it no longer behaves like a good fat once it is ingested. According to Harvard epidemiologist Walter C. Willett, M.D., "these fats do everything wrong," because they raise risk factors for cardiovascular disease by lowering good cholesterol, increasing bad cholesterol, raising triglycerides and lipoprotein. In other words, margarine is not good for you—even when it's made from one of the healthy oils.

From Willett's comment you can see that fats can behave badly. But which are the bad fats? According to author Jack Challem, a nutrition specialist, the following are principal types of fats, both good and bad:

+ saturated fats

+ omega-9 monosaturated fats (olive and canola oils)

+ omega-6 polyunsaturated fats (other vegetable oils, nuts, and seeds)—an essential fatty acid (EFA)

+ omega-3 polyunsaturated fats (fish, flaxseed, and flaxseed oil)—an EFA

✻   ✻   ✻

> We are what we eat.
>
> —ADELLE DAVIS

Each of these fats has different building blocks, he explains. As a result they turn into different fatty acids in the body. When the balance of those containing the EFAs gets skewed, they can wreak havoc. For example, small amounts of omega-9's are considered heart healthy. But the typical American diet tends to overdose on omega-6's, which can have just the opposite effect and actually crowd out the beneficial effects of the omega-9 fat. Omega-6's behave the same way around the health-promoting omega-3's. It's not that we don't need omega-6's, we do. They can make a significant contribution to the way our immune system functions and they have antiinflammatory properties. However, when we get the wrong amounts, it becomes a clear case of too much of a good thing, reports Challem. Scientific evidence shows that too much omega-6 increases our susceptibility to inflammatory disorders such as asthma, arthritis, and allergies. Furthermore, laboratory animals fed omega-6 EFAs are more likely to gain weight than are those fed omega-3 EFAs.

There are other problems too. Ornish reminds us that *all* oils are 100 percent liquid fat. Fat calories don't get used up as quickly as calories from other sources. It takes more energy to burn fat than it does to burn complex carbohydrates such as grains. That means that fat is lower in the pecking order and our bodies store excess amounts—not only around our waists, but on the arterial walls as well. If too much gets put away for future use, we eventually look and/or feel "fat." As we said before, being overweight is linked to an increased risk of heart disease, cancer, adult-onset diabetes, and other conditions.

According to a report from the famed Mayo Clinic, cancer may be promoted by dietary fats because they stimulate abnormal cell division. Some fats are susceptible to

> No diet will remove all the fat from your body because the brain is entirely fat. Without a brain you might look good, but all you could do is run for public office.
>
> —COVERT BAILEY

production of the infamous substances called free radicals. These are toxic molecules that damage cells. If they damage your body's immune system, they can affect the aging process and your susceptibility to certain diseases. "In most studies the specific food most strongly associated with increased risk of colon cancer was red meat," the report concluded.

Lest you think there's really not much good news about fat out there, remember we need them. Even Ornish has been known to comment, "Cholesterol isn't all bad either," because it is an essential fat and an important component of cell membranes. Additionally, it forms the building blocks of some important hormones such as estrogen and testosterone.

Three fourths of the cholesterol that we need is actually manufactured by our bodies, even when we reduce our intake of saturated fat, Ornish explains. Therefore, it's not the cholesterol that's the problem. It's the excess cholesterol in our systems from outside sources such as meat that leads to heart and other diseases.

With rare exceptions, he tells us, our bodies will make exactly the right amount of cholesterol to meet our needs. "You have exquisitely sensitive feedback mechanisms that tell your liver to increase or decrease the amount of cholesterol it manufactures." That means under normal circumstances when you eat more cholesterol your body manufactures less of it. However, as with other fats, eating too much of it can overwhelm the ability of the body to regulate its production.

The two sets of initials associated with cholesterol can be a source of confusion too. HDL stands for "high-density lipoproteins" and LDL stands for "low-density lipoproteins." The former moves cholesterol away from the artery walls and back to the liver. That makes it "good." The latter keeps the cholesterol circulating in the blood. That makes it "bad" because it forms deposits that clog arteries. Although studies show that fats such as olive oil may help to "lower" cholesterol, Ornish states:

Although many people believe that adding olive oil or safflower oils to the food will lower their cholesterol levels, this is simply not true. Adding any oil to your food will raise your cholesterol. While some oils are higher in saturated fat than others, all oils contain some saturated fat. So the more oil you eat the more saturated fat you consume. Canola oil is the oil lowest in saturated fat. If you use any oil, canola oil should be your choice.

Not surprisingly, not everyone agrees with Ornish's oil of choice. First on Andrew Weil's shopping list is olive oil, which contains oleic acid, a fatty acid that we process faster than other fats. Canola oil comes in a distant second. Mainly, Weil says, because it lacks the oleic acid, but also because manufacturers use chemical solvents or high heat to extract it. Both processes alter the chemistry of fatty acids in ways Weil calls "undesirable." Like Ornish he, too, reminds readers that even the best fats are still fat and will raise cholesterol. We recommend that you use either oil sparingly and that you:

+ buy it in a dark container, which helps preserve freshness

+ keep your oil in a cool place or the refrigerator to retard oxidation and prevent it from going rancid, and

+ *never* add other ingredients such as garlic, vegetables, or spices to the bottle

In *8 Weeks to Optimum Health*, Weil outlines a lifetime wellness program that begins by helping readers to tune up their bodies with an oil change:

+ Go through your pantry and refrigerator and remove all oils other than olive oil.

+ Get rid of any margarine, solid vegetable shortenings, and products made with them.

+ Read labels of all good products so that you can dispose of any containing partially hydrogenated oils.

+ If you do not have any extra-virgin olive oil on hand, buy a bottle and start using it.

+ If you want a neutral-tasting oil, buy a small bottle of organic canola oil from the health food store.

The final skinny when it comes to fat is that once you ingest it you have to use it to lose it. We believe that exercise—even a half-hour walk—is the best way to do that because it helps your body to burn excess carbohydrates and fats. Over time, this not only prevents weight gain but helps you to lose weight as well. It's not that you burn fat just while you exercise, explains Jeffrey Bland, Ph.D., a leading researcher in the field of diet and nutrition. Instead, regular activity contributes to the overall metabolic control of your body. This, then, allows your body to respond efficiently to any additional calories you consume. "Medical scientists call this the *thermogenic response*, the ability to burn extra calories as heat without storing them as fat." That response can be enhanced only when you're not sedentary and are engaged in regular physical activity.

In some circles, discussions of whether dairy products should be a part of a wholesome diet can be as impassioned as those about fats. While there's no doubt that milk, yogurt, cheese, and even ice cream can be rich sources of the calcium needed to build bones, we doubt the value and health benefits of getting it from cows. Plain and simple, here are some reasons why:

+ Human beings are the only species on earth to intentionally ingest the mammary secretion of another species. In their natural habitats other mammals drink only mother's milk.

+ Dairy products are one of the leading causes of allergies in infants, children, and adults.

+ Dairy products contain lots of saturated fat. Cheese is the major source of fat in the American diet.

+ Fewer cases of certain types of cancer are reported in countries where people get their calcium from sources other than dairy products.

+ People throughout Asia, who don't drink milk but rather get their calcium from seaweed, bok choy, and other greens, tend to have less osteoporosis than Americans.

+ Only organic dairy products are certified to be free of bovine growth and other hormones that can result in growth or overgrowth of cells that respond to them.

We maintain that whether you include dairy products in your diet is a matter of choice. The joy of eating extends way beyond feeling satisfied that you've swallowed enough nutrients. Nutrition expert Bland agrees. Although he advises his readers to eliminate dairy products from their diets, he also believes that there is nothing wrong with having a bit of ice cream. It becomes harmful only when it displaces health-promoting foods in the diet. There are people who have attached themselves to an extreme position that can create additional stress or cause related stress to be carried into an overfocus on their diet, he observes. In either case their expectation levels are so high that they are setting the stage for discontent and disillusionment.

If you feel dairy products are important additions to your diet, consider using organic low-fat or no-fat varieties that are free of hormones and other additives. If such a switch feels dramatic, make the changes in stages. Don't jump from whole milk to skim milk unless you thrive on doing things cold turkey. Instead, first switch to milk that contains 1 or 2 percent fat. Then try 1-percent and then no-fat milk. Studies show that when we reduce the amount of fat in our diets our craving for it disappears. Within weeks of giving up saturated fat we literally lose our taste for it, and fatty foods that once tasted "normal" can now taste overpowering and even cause indigestion.

Supplements

According to Bland, in the early years of our nutritional knowledge there was considerable confusion about the role of nutrients in human physiology. All we really knew was that they could help prevent vitamin-deficiency diseases like scurvy, beriberi, pellagra, and rickets. During that time we didn't have a clear idea of which food constituents influenced health and by what means they did it. Because of that confusion numerous theories were advanced to explain how food and nutrients interact with the body's physiological machinery and genetic messages.

These theories separated into two basic schools of thought that for the last twenty years have stimulated discussion among individuals interested in nutrition and health. The first, which Bland calls the "vitalist" perspective, assumed food contained something beyond rational understanding that played a major role in determining health.

Testing for Food Hypersensitivities and Allergies

Many people are hypersensitive to dairy products and other foods and don't even know it because they never make the connection between low-grade symptoms and something they've eaten. Some reactions to foods can be so peculiar that the association is made only by accident. For example, one participant in an Omega wellness workshop said it was only by chance—and a long shot at that—that he discovered that an undiagnosed allergy to eggs was affecting an underlying allergy to grass and weeds. As he explained it, once the allergy to eggs was uncovered, the allergy to grass and weeds was easier to control. Furthermore, it was found that what seemed to be a random pain in a toe on his left foot was actually related to eating eggs in the winter.

If you notice some stuffiness, aches and pains, mild indigestion, skin rash, diarrhea, rapid pulse rate, sleeplessness, or some other symptom after eating a particular food, you may want to try this simple "test" to see if you are sensitive to it. Foods that commonly cause hypersensitivities include wheat, milk, corn, yeast, soy, citrus, shellfish, beef, potatoes, and coffee, tea, or chocolate.

- Eliminate the food or ingredient from your diet for seven days. Note how you feel.

- It's common to feel *worse* on the third and fourth days. If you do, note it.

- If you felt worse on the third and fourth days, note whether you feel better on days five through seven.

- Intentionally reintroduce the food on the eighth day. Do not eat it with other foods, and wait three or more hours before eating other foods.

- If you react to it again, you know it's an irritant and should eliminate it from your diet.

The only way it could be understood was by faith, anecdote, and intuition. The second theory was the "mechanistic" perspective. It was based on the premise that proper science and clinically controlled studies could rationally determine the role of nutrients in physiological function, he explains.

"Through this discussion, a consensus has emerged that says questions about nutrients, nutrition, and health can best be answered by rational scientific investigation. Such investigation allows us to confirm observation, anecdote, and clinical experience and reject myths that interfere with the successful delivery of nutritional medicine." He concludes that the mechanistic approach, which relies on science to answer questions about the mechanism of the action of nutrients, is more appropriate if the objective is to improve long-term health outcome.

It is precisely this perspective that teaches us about the value of adding certain nutritional supplements to our diets. Although at one time it was believed that well-balanced diets such as those described in this chapter would provide us with all the nutrients we need (except vitamin B_{12}, which mostly comes from animals), today we know that may not be true. For the most part we don't eat locally grown or homegrown foods. Our produce comes from around the world. As we mentioned before, unless the fruits and vegetables abundantly filling supermarket bins are certified organic they may contain pesticides and other additives that can affect the quality and quantities of nutrients in our food and the way in which our bodies absorb and use them.

We also live in a polluted world that assaults our bodies from toxic quarters. It's a world our ancestors never imagined. Irritants causing all kinds of symptoms find their way into our bodies via an arsenal of products that take the form of everything from household cleaners and hair sprays to copy-machine fluids, lawn fertilizers, and industrial wastes. They do it with such vengeance that some people whose sensitivity is heightened then suffer from a twentieth-century phenomenon called "environmental illness."

While you can't always escape your environment and chemicals, you can take steps to mitigate their effects, Bland told readers of *Delicious!* magazine. Here are the steps he suggests:

+ eating a nutritious diet
+ boosting your overall health with vitamin/mineral supplements
+ drinking lots of pure water
+ avoiding stress, and
+ periodically cleansing your system with a detoxification program under the guidance of a health professional

Boosting your overall health with vitamins and supplements may seem like an easy thing to do until you actually go to buy them. It used to be that unless you went to a health-food store, all you could find were rather low-dose multivitamins. Today, you may be overwhelmed by the array of vitamins, minerals, and herbs that line the shelves along the pharmaceutical aisle in your supermarket. Looking around, the message that it may be necessary to take more than a multiple vitamin is clear. But how much more?

If you ask your physician, he or she may find the question as baffling as you do. One reason is that traditionally, medical schools didn't require prospective doctors to take nutrition courses. Few even offered them. That situation is changing—however, the change is coming a lot more slowly than nutritionally oriented physicians and health-care professionals hoped it would. As recently as 1993 a survey of medical schools revealed that only thirty-eight had nutrition programs. Typically, those that did focused the course on dietary recommendations and not the therapeutic role vitamins could play in the prevention of life-threatening and chronic illnesses. Indeed, most doctors who did their training just twenty-five or thirty years ago recall that as students they never learned anything about vitamin C except that it prevented scurvy. When asked if a quarter of a century later they've ever seen a case of scurvy, these same doctors typically answer no.

Although they haven't seen scurvy and a long list of once common diseases that they learned about in medical school, many doctors are now beginning to see vitamins, minerals, and herbs in a new light. Thanks to the growing body of scientific evidence supporting the therapeutic use and effectiveness of these nutrients in the prevention and treatment of cancer, heart disease, and other conditions, physicians are becoming ever more mindful of the idea that their patients can benefit from taking them.

At Omega we recommend taking a multivitamin/mineral supplement that includes antioxidant vitamins. One reason is that multivitamins contain the dosages that prevent one nutrient from interfering with the absorption of another. Another is that the proper dosage allows the vitamins and minerals to work synergistically. Shari Lieberman, Ph.D., C.N.S., author of *The Real Vitamin & Mineral Book*, says that interaction is important because it replicates the way in which nature packages nutrients together in foods.

The following information is not meant to be a comprehensive guide to supplementation or medical advice. View it instead as an introduction to a holistic health maintenance regimen that includes B vitamins, antioxidants, and minerals that is proven to be safe while helping to promote optimal health for almost everyone. Furthermore, remember that your biochemistry is unique. If you are taking any drugs or are on a special diet for medical reasons, you should check with your doctor to see if he or she believes adding certain vitamins can be harmful.

Additionally, we don't suggest using any supplements in doses larger than those we recommend without getting sound medical and/or nutritional advice. When it comes to supplements, more isn't necessarily better. Finally, we suggest you introduce supplements slowly, one at a time. It's important to stop taking them if you experience any side effects. A good example would be niacin. Although scientific studies show that niacin may help lower cholesterol levels, it can cause your face to flush and perspire.

Begin exploring what vitamins may offer by thinking about these questions. If you don't take vitamins, why not? If you take vitamins and minerals, why do you take them? Is it because you believe you are supposed to take them? Is it because you believe they can bring a quality to your life that's missing? Are you taking them as a substitute for food? Are they a form of health insurance? Do you know how they work? Why they work? If they work? Do you feel they are worth all the money you may be paying for them?

Vitamins contribute to the manufacture of hormones, blood cells, and chemicals used by the nervous system. In the overall picture of our health another way to see them is as coenzymes—catalysts that facilitate the body's ability to make efficient use of the energy that is stored in food. They fall into two categories: fat soluble (A, D, E, and K) and water soluble (C plus eight B vitamins).

The only vitamins that we manufacture on our own are vitamins D and K. Therefore, we, like all other animals, must obtain all the other vitamins that our bodies require from outside sources. Each species has its own profile of what substances it needs as substrates (basic building blocks that include vitamins) that help it function optimally. For example, most animals except primates, guinea pigs, fruit bats, and a handful of others produce all the vitamin C they'll ever need. Because we're incapable of doing what species we consider to be "lower" can do, however, we must get vitamin C from citrus fruits and other sources.

We need minerals too. Overall, they help to build strong bones, maintain our immune cells, and carry oxygen in the blood. Minerals get divided into two categories: those that we need in large amounts, such as calcium, magnesium, and phosphorus, and a group of those needed in very small amounts which we call *trace* minerals. Trace minerals include, but are not limited to, zinc, iron, copper, iodine, selenium, and fluoride.

Which ones do we need? Most important, all those we can get naturally from a healthy, balanced diet. No matter what manufacturers put into bottles, they can't duplicate all the phytonutrients found in food. For example, scientists estimate there are about six hundred carotenoids, which are an integral part of the vitamin A family. Beta-carotene, which is packaged both as a component of multivitamins and on its own, is just one carotenoid.

But what about all the others? Again, for the time being, the best source still remains a good diet. Researchers still haven't identified every one of the thousands of phytochemicals in produce. Only recently they discovered that ten or more servings a week of tomatoes can help protect men from prostate cancer. Tomatoes contain the carotenoid lycopene. Similarly, they found that the carotenoids lutein and zeaxanthin, present in spinach, can help protect against macular degeneration, the most common source of vision loss in older adults.

Given everything we've learned about diets, the environments, and our individual biochemistries, what kinds of supplements can and should we take? To begin, we recommend taking vitamins A (as beta-carotene), B, C, D, E, and K, as well as calcium, chromium, iodine, iron, magnesium, manganese, potassium, selenium, zinc, and other minerals.

Instead of talking about the first vitamin on the list—**vitamin A**—think instead about a water-soluble precursor to it called beta-carotene. The reason is that vitamin A is fat soluble, which means it must be taken with food to be absorbed. Moreover, it can accumulate in the body and reach toxic levels. But those problems are not true of beta-carotene, which the body can turn into vitamin A whenever it needs to.

As an antioxidant (see vitamin C), **beta-carotene** helps prevent heart disease and lung, prostate, and cervical cancers. Good sources of carotenes include colorful vegetables and fruits—especially those carrots your mother always told you to eat so you would see better at night. Others include tomatoes, papayas, melons, mangoes, sweet potatoes, oranges, and dark green vegetables such as turnip greens, collards, and broccoli. To get an adequate supply of beta-carotene we should eat about 15 milligrams a day (the equivalent of five large carrots) or take a daily supplement that has at least 25,000 IU (international units).

The **B vitamins,** B_1 (thiamin), B_2 (riboflavin), B_3 (niacin), B_6 (pyridoxine), B_{12} (cobalamin), folic acid, and pantothenic acid, serve us in many ways. They're important to energy production. They're essential to the metabolism of carbohydrates, protein, and fat. They're involved in healthy cell division and growth. They're necessary for the formation of red blood cells and the protective coating surrounding our nerves. They support the immune system and help prevent iron-deficiency anemia. They are used in the treatment of PMS and carpal tunnel syndrome. And the list goes on. B_{12} is the only B vitamin that is not found in many vegetables. It is available from sea vegetables such as kelp, kombu, and nori. Many people use that fact as a reason to keep eating red meat and fish. Of the latter, mackerel, herring, sardines, salmon, and oysters are all good sources of B_{12}. Those who eat dairy products can get B_{12} (along with vitamin D) from a glass of milk or cup of yogurt. With the amount of fortified food available today, it's not hard to get adequate amounts in fortified soy milk, enriched soy products, and enriched cereals or by taking vitamins. We recommend the following doses. Vitamins in the B family should always be taken together.

B_1—50 mg
B_2—25 mg
B_3—25 mg
Niacinamide—100 mg (conjugated form of B_3)
B_6—50 mg
B_{12}—100 mcg
Biotin—150 mcg
Choline—75 mg
Folic acid—800 mcg
Inositol—25 mg

PABA (para-aminobenzoic acid)—25 mg

Pantothenic acid (B₅)—250 mg

Of all the vitamins, you've probably heard more and know more about **vitamin C** than any other. Some people believe it's a cure for everything—especially the common cold. "I do not believe that vitamin C is a panacea that will cure everything from AIDS to cancer, but I do believe that we have yet to discover and appreciate all of its protective effects," says Weil. According to the *Journal of the American Dietetic Association*, this popular vitamin helps us to build strong connective tissue and it allows the healing system to repair wounds. Additionally, almost every proponent of higher doses of vitamin C follows the lead of the late Nobel Prize laureate Linus Pauling, M.D., who believed that megadoses can encourage healing on all levels, especially when it comes to helping the body protect itself from oxidative damage by the highly reactive molecules known as free radicals. Although free radicals get lots of bad press because they are generated by exposure to chemicals and energetic toxins, it's important to know they are also a by-product of normal metabolism. Pauling, who took 18,000 mg of vitamin C daily, presented his pioneering work on vitamin C and cancer at Omega. He believed that taking vitamin C ensures the body's own biochemical mechanisms will scavenge free radicals and destroy them before they do harm. That's because vitamin C functions as a powerful *antioxidant.*

What exactly does that mean and what does an antioxidant do? According to Alan Gaby, M.D., an expert in nutritional therapies and former member of the advisory panel of the National Institutes of Health Office of Alternative Medicine, antioxidants work in several ways. For example, they:

+ may reduce the energy of the free radicals

+ stop the free radical from forming in the first place, and/or

+ interrupt an oxidizing chain reaction to minimize the damage of free radicals

Like Pauling, advocates of doses of vitamin C higher than those found in most multivitamins usually recommend that you take it throughout the day. Current research shows that taking 500 mg three times a day may be ideal for optimizing the ability of white blood cells to fight infections and toxins. What happens if you take too much vitamin C? Because it is water soluble, your body will eliminate excess amounts through sweat and urine. Are there any side effects? Generally, diarrhea and flatulence are the only reactions people have to taking too much. Gaby recommends that people with a history of kidney stones, surgery to the small intestines, iron overload, kidney failure, or glucose-6 phosphate dehydrogenase check with their doctors before supplementing with vitamin C.

Interestingly, even though megadoses of vitamin C are considered safe, for years the U.S. recommended daily allowance (RDA) for this important vitamin was just 60 mg. That's enough to prevent scurvy, but it does little else. Since 1994 the Food and Drug Administration has required that the nutrition information on all processed foods be in terms of Daily Values, not RDAs. However, when it comes to vitamins, RDAs still appear in many of the charts and literature. In the Omega Wellness Program, we recommend taking 1,000 to 1,800 mg daily.

Vitamin D plays a key role in the absorption of calcium. Good sources include egg yolks and sea bass, tuna, cod, herring, and halibut. However, even if you never eat any of those products, you still get vitamin D because whenever you're exposed to sunlight, the body manufactures it from a cholesterol derivative in the skin. For that reason, unless you live in a cave, you will probably get enough vitamin D. If you need a dose for insurance, remember, you'll get it in just about every multivitamin on the market.

Vitamin E is another powerful antioxidant that's been the subject of numerous studies. In 1997 *Health* magazine listed it as one of the year's ten top medical advances, saying, "In the never-ending quest for an antiaging pill, vitamin E emerged as a leading candidate." That same year the American Heart Association cited this vitamin as one of the "top ten heart and stroke research advances" for the previous year. Researchers now hypothesize that because vitamin E is an anticoagulant it plays a significant role in the prevention of cardiovascular disease. Numerous studies are under way to prove the hypothesis. The same is true of the role that vitamin E may play in the prevention of cancer. *Health* magazine noted several studies linking vitamin E and aging. A study at Columbia University found that high doses of vitamin E administered over a two-year period slowed the progression of Alzheimer's disease in patients. In a study at Tufts University elderly men and women taking 200 mg of vitamin E daily showed dramatic improvements in their ability to resist infections such as pneumonia and other illnesses. Their bodies produced disease-fighting antibodies in levels two to six times greater than those in people who got a placebo. Vitamin E is fat soluble, so it must be taken with food. Vitamin E has also been shown to be a useful treatment for several female disorders, including fibrocystic breast disease, painful or excessive menstruation, and PMS. For example, in a controlled study reported in *JAMA*, women with breast lumps experienced a complete regression after using 600 IU of vitamin E daily for four weeks. In another study cystic lesions and tenderness disappeared in twenty-two out of twenty-six women who over the course of eight weeks took 600 IU of vitamin E.

Vitamin E is found in many foods high in saturated fats. These include vegetable oils, salad dressings, margarine, seeds, nuts, and peanut butter. It also is found in wheat germ and whole-wheat products. Since it is not proven to be toxic, supplements may be the best way of getting it into your diet. D-alpha tocopherol is natural vitamin E. D*i*-alpha tocopherol is synthetic vitamin E. We recommend 400 to 800 mg of mixed tocopherols daily.

Vitamin K is crucial to blood clotting. Some believe that it may help to prevent osteoporosis and cancer. It's abundant enough in the foods we eat. Natural sources include everything from spinach and broccoli to whole wheat, ham, beef, cheese, and egg yolks. There's no reason to take any extra vitamin K unless prescribed by a doctor.

Of all the minerals, **calcium** has gotten the most press in recent years because of the role it can play in the prevention of osteoporosis. Interestingly, whenever we ask

---

Gluttony is an emotional escape, a sign that something is eating us.

—PETER DE VRIES

---

participants in the Wellness Program whether or not they are concerned about osteoporosis, only the women raise their hands. Perhaps the media is to blame, because it seems to favor the distaff side when it discusses the pitfalls of not having enough calcium in your diet. However, it's equally important for men to know that they, too, are at risk for osteoporosis. They just get it later in life than their counterparts.

Recent studies show that besides bone-building benefits, calcium also helps normalize blood pressure and it may lower the risk of eclampsia in pregnant women. As we mentioned before, in dairy-free diets good sources of calcium are cooked dark, leafy greens such as kale and chard. Also, the key to calcium is not just taking it in, but making sure that we metabolize it well by following the dietary recommendations we make in this chapter. Taking in too much protein leads to a loss of calcium through the urine. Additionally, there are problems associated with taking calcium. One is that it can be constipating. If calcium affects you that way, consider taking it with magnesium, which acts as a laxative. Another is that calcium can be a problem for people with certain conditions. If you are under a doctor's care for any illnesses, check with him or her before taking calcium or any other supplements. Calcium carbonate is the cheapest calcium supplement available. Calcium citrate is absorbed better. We recommend calcium citrate or ascorbate—500 to 1000 mg.

Magnesium complements calcium and together they help to properly conduct electrical impulses in nerves and muscles. When taken at bedtime, calcium and magnesium can promote sleep because the combination acts as a mild neuromuscular relaxant. If you take a calcium supplement we recommend looking for one that's already combined with magnesium in a ratio of one to one, or two parts calcium to one part magnesium. Good sources of magnesium include halibut, buckwheat, nuts, seeds, and leafy green vegetables.

Remember the trace minerals mentioned earlier? Until recently we didn't hear much about them. In fact, we weren't even aware of the important role they play in our diet until the 1930s when people living in certain areas of the country developed

> Man does not live by bread alone.
>
> —MOSES

serious health problems resulting from low thyroid activity. The condition known as hypothyroidism caused people to have enlarged thyroid glands. When public health officials studied people in a region of the country that became known as the "Goiter Belt," they discovered those with hypothyroidism suffered from a deficiency of the trace mineral iodine. Later, says Bland, the discovery of the iodine deficiency in the Goiter Belt led to the discovery of other trace mineral deficiencies such as iron deficiency anemia. Today we know many of the consequences of not having needed amounts of not just iodine, but iron, zinc, copper, chromium, selenium, manganese, and molybdenum too. Other trace minerals include vanadium, boron, and nickel.

"Two factors influence the level of trace minerals in the diet," Bland wrote in *Delicious!* magazine. "The first is the quality of the soil in which food is grown, and the second is the degree of processing these foods." Soil treated with fertilizers leaches trace minerals. Since these minerals aren't needed for the plant to grow and they are tasteless, consumers have no way of knowing whether their food contains any of the trace minerals that their bodies need.

One of the most important trace minerals is **selenium**. It activates an antioxidant enzyme called glutathione peroxidase, which may protect our body from cancer. For example, in 1996, *JAMA* reported a double-blind seven-year study following over thirteen hundred people. Those given 200 mcg of selenium daily had a 50 percent drop in the cancer death rate compared with the placebo group. Earlier, the *British Medical Journal* reported that in a four-year case-control study investigating the relationship between serum concentrations of selenium and vitamin A, inadequate vitamin A or beta-carotene intake was associated with an increased incidence of lung cancer among smoking men with low serum selenium. Selenium activates thyroid hormones and may also reduce the risk of macular degeneration, atherosclerosis, and abnormal pap smears (cervical dysplasia). Since it can facilitate the absorption of vitamin E and vice versa, it's wise to take them together. We recommend taking 200 mcg of selenium daily.

Here are some examples of the roles several of the trace minerals play in optimizing our health:

- Chromium—helps stabilize blood sugar
- Copper—helps regulate the utilization of iron and the building of hemoglobin and red blood cells
- Iron—helps prevent anemia
- Manganese—helps to activate an important oxidative stress-protective enzyme
- Molybdenum—activates enzymes that are responsible for detoxifying foreign chemicals and other toxic materials
- Selenium—helps activate an enzyme that works with vitamin E to quench free radicals and other toxicities in the body
- Zinc—helps regulate protein synthesis in the body and assists in muscle development and wound healing

At this point you may also be wondering about other ancillary supplements (often called "other nutritional factors") that you may be hearing or reading about. As we mentioned earlier, it's important to ask yourself the questions on pages 209–210 before deciding whether to take them. Many that don't get classified as either vitamins or herbs have been proven to be of some benefit to people with coronary heart disease, arthritis, diabetes, cancer, and other chronic and life-threatening conditions.

For example, in an experimental study of **coenzyme Q_{10} (CoQ_{10})**, a powerful antioxidant that protects the body from free radicals and aids metabolic reactions, nearly two thirds of a group of forty patients in severe heart failure showed objective and subjective improvement following treatment with 100 mg of CoQ_{10} daily. In another study, after three months, fifteen diabetics who received 60 mg of CoQ_{10} daily showed greater blood sugar control. The CoQ_{10} also promoted their insulin synthesis and secretion.

Acidophilus, a beneficial bacterium scientifically known as a *probiotic,* is another example of a secondary supplement. Its correct name is *Lactobacillus acidophilus.* Like its counterpart, *Bifidobacterium bifidum*, acidophilus favorably alters the intestinal microflora balance, promotes good digestion, boosts immune function, inhibits the growth of harmful bacteria, and increases our resistance to infection. A 1993 study found that probiotic supplements used to recolonize the intestines of patients taking antibiotics prevented up to 50 percent of the infections that usually occur after antibiotic use.

Again, our recommendation is to find out all you can about the potential benefits and/or side effects and interactions related to taking *any* supplement. This will help you to make informed decisions about how each may help to optimize your health. And remember, these are supplements and should never be used as a substitute for a healthy diet.

In conclusion, it's important to remember that a true sense of happiness can never simply come from what we eat. Frequently, people who feel uplifted by a particularly satisfying and tasty meal say that they feel happy. However, that happiness is transient at best. While there's no doubt that good nutrition makes an important contribution to our sense of wellness and inner balance, from a holistic perspective it's only a piece of the picture, puzzle, or pie (sans saturated fat, refined sugar, and whipped cream topping). Consistent happiness can only be attained when we can accept things as they are, experience a sense of awe and wonder at the marvel of creation, and have an evolving love of life.

RESOURCES

BOOKS

Bland, Jeffrey, Ph.D. *The 20-Day Rejuvenation Diet Program.* New Canaan, CT: Keats Publishing, 1997.

Blumenthal, Mark. *The Complete German Commission & Monographs: Therapeutic Guide to Herbal Medicines.* Integrative Medicine Communication, 1998.

Duke, James, Ph.D. *The Green Pharmacy.* Emmaus, PA: St. Martin's Paperbacks, 1997.

Lininger, Skye, D.C.; Jonathan Wright, M.D.; Steve Austin, N.D.; Donald Brown, N.D.; and Donald Gaby, M.D. *The Natural Pharmacy.* Rocklin, CA: Prima Publishing, 1998.

Ornish, Dean, M.D.

    Dr. Dean Ornish's Program for Reversing Heart Disease. New York: Ballantine, 1996.

    Eat More, Weigh Less. New York: HarperCollins, 1993.

Robbins, John. *Diet for a New America.* Tiburon, CA: H. J. Kramer, 1987.

Robertson, Laurel, Carol Flinders, and Brian Ruppenthal. *The New Laurel's Kitchen.* Berkeley: Ten Speed Press, 1986.

Weil, Andrew, M.D.

    8 Weeks to Optimum Health. New York: Fawcett, 1997.

    Natural Health, Natural Medicine. Boston: Houghton Mifflin, 1990.

Werbach, Melvyn R., M.D. *Nutritional Influences on Illness* (2nd ed.). Tarzana, CA: Third Line Press, 1996.

Yeager, Selene, and the editors of *Prevention. New Foods for Healing.* Emmaus, PA: Rodale Press, 1998.

MAGAZINES

Delicious! magazine, New Hope Natural Media, 1301 Spruce Street, Boulder, CO 80302. Phone: 303-939-8440.

Dr. Andrew Weil's Self Healing (newsletter) 800-523-3296

New Age Journal, 42 Pleasant Street, Watertown, MA 02172. Phone: 815-734-5808. www.newage.com

Vegetarian Journal, The Vegetarian Resource Group, P.O. Box 1463, Baltimore, MD, 21203. Phone: 410-366-8343.

Vegetarian Times, P.O. Box 420235, Palm Coast, FL 32142-0235. Phone: 800-829-3340.

WWW

American Botanical Council—information about the use of herbs and phytomedicinals—www.herbalgram.org

American Dietetic Association—www.eatright.org

Ask Dr. Weil—www.drweil.com

Blonz Guide to Nutrition, Food & Health Resources—probably one of the only sites you'll ever need to visit; the links will take you to the best sites for nutrition and related subjects—www.blonz.com/blonz/nfindex2htm

Delicious! magazine—www.delicious-online.com

Fast Food Finder—get lots of info about more than a thousand fast-food items—www.olen.com/food

Father Nature's Farmacy—James Duke's homepage, which is the Agricultural Research Service—www.ars-grin.gov/duke

Fitnesslink—www.fitnesslink.com

Food Guide Pyramid—www.ganesa.com/food/index/html

HealthComm International, Inc.—homepage for Jeffrey Bland, Ph.D.—www.healthcomm.com

Healthnotes—huge on-line database of nutritional supplements and other health matters—www.healthnotes.com

Mayo Clinic—go to Mayo Clinic's nutrition information index—www.mayohealth.org

Preventive Medicine Research Institute—Dean Ornish's homepage—www.ornish.com

Virtual Vegetarian—on-line version of *Vegetarian Times* magazine with excellent links—www.vegetariantimes.com

Epilogue

One evening an ailing elderly sheikh called his three sons to his bedside to tell them about their inheritance. He said that after he died he wanted the eldest son to have half of his camels. The middle son would get one third. The youngest son would get one ninth. Later that night the sheikh passed away. After their father's funeral the sons ordered their servants to bring them the camels so each could claim his inheritance. To their surprise the servants returned from the stable with seventeen camels. "What are we to do?" the middle son asked. "I don't know how we can divide up these camels according to our father's wishes." Neither did the other sons.

The eldest son pondered the question for a while. Finally, he told his brothers, "I don't know what to do, but I know where to go for an answer. I will be back soon." He then traveled to the home of the village wise one and explained his predicament. The wise man listened and then said he would return home with the eldest son and see what he could do to help. With that the wise man got his camel and they set off together.

Choose life so that you and your descendants may live.

—DEUTERONOMY 30:19

When they arrived, the wise man immediately walked up to the herd of seventeen camels and added his own to it. He then proceeded to divide the camels according to the late sheikh's wishes. The eldest son got nine camels. The middle son got six. The youngest son got two. That made seventeen camels. The wise man then took back his own camel and went home.

We often tell this story during the Omega Wellness Program as an example of how vitamins act as catalysts. As the story points out, without such a stimulator, certain things just don't come together, work out, or change. However, with the right catalyst they do. Yet, as vital a role as the catalyst can play in such situations, it disappears after it does its job.

Many of the students who come to Omega are like the sheikh's eldest son. In their hometowns and everyday lives they are in search of new perspectives, new paradigms that can help them discover answers to the questions that they've had about their health and happiness. When they travel to Omega, most arrive hoping to connect with a wise person—a catalyst—who can affect their desire to make some positive changes and provide them with the resources to do it. By the time they leave, many of those same students discover they've been transformed. No longer do they feel like the sheikh's eldest son. Now they feel more like they've inherited new knowledge that makes them a wise one. They know not only that can they live their lives differently than they did in the past, but that they themselves can continue to be the real source of healthful changes.

For those of you who have yet to visit Omega, we hope that this book has been a catalyst for you to see new paradigms and perspectives that can help you to optimize your health and well-being. For those of you who have been to Omega, we hope this book is a way for you to reconnect with some of wisdom you may have experienced here.

Never before in the history of humankind has the possibility of living to the magical and mythical age of one hundred been a reality and not an anomaly for so many. Thanks to science and technology and the wisdom of the past we know it is possible. As a result the question we now face is profound—"If I live to a hundred, what will the *quality* of the life I'm living be like?"

One way to answer that question is to remind ourselves of the example set by the Tarahumara Indians, which we discussed in the chapter on exercise and fitness. The entire tribe *believes* that sixty-year-olds are in the prime of their life, and so they *are*. Among the Tarahumaras, those whom we would call elders can outrun adolescents in footraces that last for hours.

Other cultures provide answers too. Russian Georgians, Afghanistani Huzans, and Peruvian Vallacanbabans all live longer than we do. For them seventy is middle age, and they routinely pass the century mark with their physical and mental abilities intact. Some studies attribute their longevity to certain foods. Others conclude their longevity is related to specific beliefs and expectations concerning the stages of life. Ultimately, their long lives are not the result of any one belief or activity, but the payoff for a lifestyle that optimizes vitality and health. In these societies there is no time urgency or time sickness. Time is *not* of the essence. Paying attention to what is going on in their lives by living life in the present, here and *now*, is.

In one of his movies, the late actor Steve McQueen said, "I know a guy who fell from a ten-story building. As he passed each floor on the way down, he said, 'So far, so good.' " Similarly, the mordant comedian Stephen Wright once looked out at an audience and asked if they knew the sensation of the exact moment when a chair, tilted back on two legs, feels like it's going to fall? Heads nodded all over. "That's how I feel all the time," he commented.

Can you relate to those feelings? Do you "suffer" from vague symptoms of depression, anxiety, fatigue, muscle pain, insomnia, and digestive disorders as well as mood swings and recurring bad dreams that make you feel on the edge or like you're going to crash? If so, might you be setting yourself up to move from the vertical state of health we described in Chapter I to a horizontal state of health that can be even more debilitating and life-threatening?

Understandably, sometimes people ignore minor symptoms that can be indicative of the onset of significant *dis*-ease and illness because the mere idea of a serious condition frightens them. But, in reality, when we deny the early warning signs of emotional and/or physical discomfort, we only perpetuate an illusion of wellness. Far better to say "Maybe my health has been good up to now, but I'd better not take it for granted. Better to pay attention and try to understand what my symptoms are telling me."

> Whatever you can do, or dream you can, begin it.
> Boldness has genius, power, and magic in it.
>
> —GOETHE

What might they be saying? Perhaps that it's time to start eating more nutritious meals or to take measures to manage and reduce stress. Or maybe they're broadcasting the message that it's time to start exercising or to exercise more often to help improve your fitness level. They could also be a reminder that maybe it has been a while since you've put yourself first and that it's time to put into practice some of the time-shifting techniques described in Chapter 3.

Instead of living with a "so far so good" attitude like Steve McQueen's fictional friend or on "the edge" like Stephen Wright, why not reflect upon the symptoms you rated in Chapter 2? Then consider making a new commitment or renewing an old one to use the information, tools, and resources throughout this book to help you put into practice the greatest lesson any one of us can learn from the Georgians, the Huzans, and other long-lived people, that when we face aging optimistically, don't resist the present moment, and become proactive about maintaining a state of wellness, the quality as well as the quantity of our life expands and life is good!

Those studying longevity tell us that there are two different ways in which we age. The first is chronologically, which is a measure of our days. The other is biologically, a measure of how functionally capable or healthy we may be at a particular chronological age. We've all met people who don't look or act their age. In some of those cases the reason may be that biologically they *are* twenty years younger. Sometimes we say these people are *ageless,* because their minds seem as young as or even younger than their bodies. As you might expect, a wellness program such as the one described in this book can help you to age well or become ageless too.

The first step on the road to this vigor and vitality is to acknowledge that your health is, to a great extent, under your control. By following good health habits that amplify our genetic constitution and minimize our weaknesses, we unabashedly proclaim that we know what it means to take responsibility for the well-being of our bodies, minds, emotions, and spirits.

Another step is to recognize our biochemical individuality. With respect to that individuality, at the beginning of this book we invited you to undertake a unique journey toward optimal health and well-being. Throughout the book we have endeavored to provide you with the information you need to start your travels. However, we recognize that no matter how determined you are to travel autonomously from point A to point B, there will be times when you can't make this journey alone. Dozens of Omega and other wellness teachers remind us that perhaps the most important part of the journey comes:

+ when we can open our hearts and reach out to ourselves and others with love

+ when we can forgive ourselves for not being perfect and not expect others to be perfect either

+ when we can be a self who values being separate and unique from others on the one hand and in healthy relationships on the other

+ when we can reach out to others with compassion (which means to be or suffer with) and still "take care" of ourselves

+ when we know we need help and ask for it

+ when we surrender to the fact that our story is our story and it's *all* true, and

+ *when no matter what is happening, the present moment is the only moment there is and we accept it*

We know that whatever journey you are on, it is a bold venture that is uniquely yours. Wherever you now stand on that journey, we at Omega hope that it's on a path leading to optimal wellness and that with joy and conviction you will continue to follow the dictum "Choose life!"

Index

on meditation, 125–126

on retreats, 145

on time-shifting, 90

Autoimmune diseases, 40

Autonomic nervous system, 183

Awareness meditation, 111–112

Ayurvedic medicine, 23

B

Bailey, Covert, 223

Balance, 48, 53

Barasch, Marc Ian, 28

Bar/bat mitzvah, 141

Barry, Dave, 162

Barrymore, John, 131

Bartsch, Jürgen, 150

Beerbohm, Max, 158

Being Peace (Thich Nhat Hanh), 109

Benchley, Robert, 162

Ben Shea, Noah, 69

Benson, Herbert, 26, 28, 59

Benson, John, 129, 131

Best Guide to Meditation, The (Davich), 102

Beta-carotene, 233–234, 239

Bhakti yoga, 182

Biofeedback, 8, 29

defined, 23–24

Birch, Beryl Bender, 183

Blaming, 54

Bland, Jeffrey, 226, 228–230, 239

Blood pressure, 24, 160, 187, 205, 217

Bodhisattvas, 109

Body fat, 169

Body/mind connection, 21–30

Bombeck, Erma, 162

Book of the Golden Precepts, The, 98

Books, 32–33

on fitness, 196–197

on meditation, 124–125

on nutrition, 241–242

on play and laughter, 163–164

on retreats, 144–145

on stress, 66–67

on time-shifting, 89

Boorstin, Daniel J., 116

Boron, 239

Borysenko, Joan, 104

Boundaries, setting, 86

Branden, Nathaniel, 51, 54

Bratt, Larry, 95–97

Breathing, 3, 65, 106–109

British Medical Journal, 239

Buchholz, Ester Schaler, 139

Buddha, 38, 97, 99, 107, 115, 123, 128

Burkitt, Dennis, 6

Burt, Bernard, 129

Bush, George, 210

B vitamins, 233, 234–235

Byers, John, 149

Byrd, Richard E., 143–144

C

Cady, Eileen, 132

Cage, John, 128

Calcium, 227, 233, 237–238

Call, The (Spangler), 14

Call of Solitude, The: Alonetime in a World of Attachment (Buchholz), 139

Calories, 173, 193, 194, 216, 218

Campbell, Joseph, 11, 12, 123, 139, 140

Cancer, 6, 40, 173, 174

nutrition and, 200–202, 217, 224–225

spontaneous remission, 27, 117–118

Canola oil, 225, 226

Carlin, George, 99

Case studies, 31–32, 60, 72–73, 117–118, 150

Catecholamines, 159

Centers for Disease Control and Prevention, 190

Challem, Jack, 223–224

Challenge, 57

Chaplin, Charlie, 162

Chatwin, Bruce, 133

Chemotherapy, 174

Chen, William C.C., 181

Chesterfield, Lord, 71

Chesterton, G.K., 150

Chi, 23, 186

Chinese medicine, 23, 185, 186

Choleric humor, 159

Cholesterol level, 6, 173, 205, 225–226

Christianity, 92

Chromium, 233, 239, 240

Chronic fatigue, 40

Chronic physical stressors, 58

Chuang Tzu, 138

Circulation, 172, 183

Clinton, Bill, 121–122

Closeness, 58–59

Cobalamin, 234

Coenzyme Q10, 240

Cohen, Kenneth S., 185

Collinge, William, 26

Colorado State University, 191

Commitment, 58

Complete Guide to Alternative and Conventional Treatments, The, 23

Complex carbohydrates, 201, 213–215

Comprehensibility, 47

Concentration, 113

Confirmation, 141

Conigliaro, Tony, 169

Connolly, Cyril, 103

Constipation, 207, 238

Control, 57

Cooper, David A., 136–138

Coordination, 169, 183

Copper, 233, 239, 240

Cordain, Loren, 191

Cortisol, 160

Cosby, Bill, 160

Cousins, Norman, 157–158, 162

Csikszentmihalyi, Mihaly, 77

D

Dairy products, 213, 227–228

Dass, Ram, 51

Davich, Victor N., 102

Davis, Adelle, 223

Degeneres, Ellen, 178

Delicious! magazine, 214, 230

Depression, 2, 22, 40

Descartes, René, 25–26

Deuteronomy, 245

De Vries, Peter, 237

Dewey, John, 148

Diabetes, 173, 217

Dialogue exercise, 49, 118

Diamond, Harvey, 216

Diaphragmatic breathing, 65

Dickinson, Emily, 130

Diet (*see* Nutrition)

Diet for a Small Planet (Lappé), 215–216

Digitalis, 207

Discovering the Body's Wisdom (Knaster), 183, 186

Dr. Dean Ornish's Program for Reversing Heart Disease (Ornish), 168

"Doing Time—Inside the Mind" (Bratt), 96

Domar, Alice, 24

Donaldson, O. Fred, 150–153, 156

Dong gong, 185

Dopamine, 148

Dossey, Barbara, 43

Free radicals, 235, 240
Freud, Sigmund, 148, 161–162
Fry, William F., Jr., 159–160
Full Catastrophe Living (Kabat-Zinn), 114

G

Gaby, Alan, 235
Gandhi, Mohandas, 128
Gardening, 193
Gaynor, Mitchell, 200
Georgians, 247, 248
Gibran, Kahlil, 166
Ginkgo, 206–208
Godbey, Geoffrey, 75–76, 81
Goethe, Johann Wolfgang von, 248
Goleman, Daniel, 54–56, 100, 113
Gordon, James, 100
Grace, 4
Graham, Martha, 20
Grains, 213
Guided imagery, 7, 8, 114–122
    defined, 24
Gunaratana, Venerable Henepola, 106

H

Hafen, Brent Q., 117
Hall, Nicholas, 117–118
Hatha yoga, 182
HDL ("good") cholesterol, 173, 205, 223, 225
Healing Words: The Practice of Medicine and the Power of Prayer (Dossey), 29
Health-care system, 4–8
Health & Humor Journal, 159, 162
Health magazine, 236, 237
Health maintenance organizations (HMOs), 4
Health spas, 129
Heart attacks, 44

Heart disease, 40, 168, 171, 174, 201–203, 205
Hecht, Ben, 79
Heraclitus, 139
Herbs, 29, 206–208
Hesse, Hermann, 85
Hippocrates, 120
Holocaust survivors, 47
Homeopathy, 29
Homeostasis, 30, 48
Horizontal health, 29
Huang, Chungliang Al, 181, 185, 188
Hubbard, Elston, 192
Humor (*see* Play and laughter)
Huzans, 247, 248
Hypertension, 24, 40
Hypnosis, 29, 114
    defined, 24
Hypothyroidism, 239

I

"If I Had My Life to Live Over," 85
Immune system, 30, 40, 173
Infertility, 24
Initiation rites, 140–141
Institute for Aerobic Research, 174
International Journal of Obesity, 173
In-the-moment state, 52–53, 76–77
Inuit people, 191
Iodine, 233, 239
Iron, 233, 239, 240
Irritable bowel syndrome, 24
Islam, 92
Isolation, 59
Iyengar yoga, 183

W

"Walking" (Thoreau), 179

Walking, spirited, 180

Walking meditation, 3, 103, 106, 109

Water soluble vitamins, 232

Watts, Alan, 91

Weil, Andrew, 172, 203–204, 225–226, 235

Welsh, Joan, 193

Western emergency medicine, 7–8

Wherever You Go, There You Are (Kabat-Zinn), 80–81, 94, 103

White willow bark, 207

Whitman, Walt, 181, 185

Why Zebras Don't Get Ulcers (Sapolsky), 57–58

Wilcox, Ella Wheeler, 157

Willett, Walter, 202, 223

Wit and Its Relation to the Unconscious (Freud), 161–162

Women's Retreat Book, The (Louden), 132–133, 135, 136

Woodman, Marion, 28

World Health Organization, 153, 171–172

Worldview Laws of Life (Templeton), 53

World Wide Web, 35

   on fitness, 198–199

   on meditation, 127

   on nutrition, 242

   on play and laughter, 164

   on retreats, 145

   on stress, 67

Wright, Stephen, 247, 248

Writing for Your Life (Metzger), 132

Y

Yoga, 7, 8, 23, 114, 179–184, 187, 189

   defined, 25

Yoga Laughter exercise, 156

Z

Zeal, 54–55

Zeaxanthin, 233

Zen, 110, 112–113

Zen Mind, Beginner's Mind (Suuzuki-roshi), 114

Zinc, 233, 239, 240

Zone, the, 77, 168, 179